About this book

The Caribbean poses a significant drugs problem for the UK and the US, as the recent phenomenon of yardie gangs in British cities graphically illustrates. But in the islands themselves ganja, crack cocaine and the policies to control them have become, as this book demonstrates, a veritable social disaster. The authors, who are among the leading local researchers and engaged professionals in the region as well as the former regional head of the UN Drugs Control Programme, bring together new research investigations, insightful policy analysis and practical experience of on-the-ground interventions putting demand reduction into practice.

The dimensions of the illicit drugs market in the Caribbean are made clear. The origins of the problem lie in part, it is argued, with the impact of neoliberal economic policies that have opened up the region's borders and gravely undermined its traditional sources of employment and exports, like bananas and sugar. The islands, in part under external US pressure, have adopted a region-wide policy of criminalization This has involved the creation of specialized drug courts and serious human and social consequences as a result of criminalizing traditional cultural practices around ganja consumption.

Fascinating light is thrown on the difficulties facing drug abuse and rehabilitation centres and the dilemmas they throw up. Harm reduction as a fundamentally alternative approach to the drugs problem is also explored. This is the first book to examine the experiences of Caribbean countries since they adopted a coordinated approach to the drugs problem. There are valuable lessons to be learned at both policy and practical levels for other countries, and in particular those like the UK and US with large Caribbean populations.

Critical praise for this book

'Caribbean Drugs provides substance abuse researchers, clinicians, policy makers, and general readers on both sides of the Atlantic with a collection of interesting and provocative essays. Because the Caribbean Basin is an understudied part of the hemisphere, particularly with regard to the "drug problem," this book fills a major gap. I highly recommend it.' – *James A. Inciardi, Professor and Director, Center for Drug and Alcohol Studies, University of Delaware*

'Policy makers in many parts of the world are interested in the role of Caribbean countries in the production and trans-shipment of illicit drugs. However, the self-interest of developed countries has not been matched by an analysis of drug use and drug problems in the Caribbean itself, and about the way in which the Caribbean region is responding to drugs. This welcome book provides a unique insight into smaller countries' attempts to shape their policy response to drugs in the context of national, regional and international imperatives.' – *Professor Gerry Stimson, Centre for Research on Drugs and Health Behaviour, Imperial College, London*

'About a hundred years ago a few colonial countries plus the USA designed a system of prohibiting drugs that now can be considered as a major problem for human rights and state sovereignty. The Caribbean countries act like a transit area between poor producing and rich consuming countries. Klein helps analyse the situation from many angles that may speed up a thorough overhaul of this obsolete system of drug prohibition.' – *Professor Peter Cohen, Centre for Drug Research (CEDRO), University of Amsterdam*

'A refreshing look at the impact that drug policies have had on the "problem" of drug use in the English-speaking countries of the Caribbean. They show how the criminalisation of ganja has driven a wedge between society and the state, and how the prosecution of possession fills up the gaols while the differential application of the law allows traffickers to go free. One unintended consequence of free trade and the stopping of preferential access to the European market for the banana farmers has meant that they turn to cannabis as a cash crop.

This book is realistic in acknowledging the irresistible pressure from North America and Europe to stop the trafficking, but cogently makes the point that this should not drive domestic policy into more and more punitive responses.

There is a contradiction between a philosophy of zero tolerance and the culture and human rights of people of the Caribbean. Harm reduction policies are seen as the way forward, which would lead to less punitive and more supportive policies.' – *Cindy Fazey, Professor of International Relations, University of Liverpool*

'Only rarely do edited volumes, with multiple essays by scholars, exercise any influence on public policy. But if I had to bet on one book that might, it's this one. The islands of the Caribbean have long been trapped between the powerful dynamics of the illicit drug trade and the dictates of US and UN drug warriors. This book offers a way out, grounded both in science and the political interests of the Caribbean.' – *Ethan Nadelmann, Executive Director, Drug Policy Alliance*

Caribbean
Drugs

From Criminalization
to Harm Reduction

Edited by

Axel Klein, Marcus Day and Anthony Harriot

Ian Randle
Publishers
KINGSTON

Zed Books
LONDON & NEW YORK

in association with
DrugScope

Caribbean Drugs
was first published in 2004 by
Zed Books Ltd, 7 Cynthia Street, London N1 9JF, UK and
Room 400, 175 Fifth Avenue, New York, NY 10010, USA
www.zedbooks.co.uk

First published in the Caribbean in 2004 by
Ian Randle Publishers, 11 Cunningham Avenue,
PO Box 686, Kingston 6, Jamaica
www.ianrandlepublishers.com

in association with DrugScope, 32–36 Loman Street,
London SE1 0EE, UK

Cover designed by Andrew Corbett
Designed and set in 10/12 pt Bembo
by Long House, Cumbria, UK
Printed and bound in Malta by Gutenberg Ltd

Distributed in the USA exclusively by Palgrave Macmillan, a division of
St Martin's Press, LLC, 175 Fifth Avenue, New York, NY 10010

A catalogue record for this book
is available from the British Library

US Cataloging-in-Publication Data
is available from the Library of Congress

ISBN   Hb 1 84277 498 0 (Zed Books)
         Pb 1 84277 499 9 (Zed Books)
         Pb 976 637 194 6 (Ian Randle Publishers)

Contents

Tables and Figures

Tables

Figures

Abbreviations

AA	Alcoholics Anonymous
AAO	Addiction Alert Organization
ADAP	Association for the Advancement of People
BPA	Barbados Plan of Action
CAREC	Caribbean Epidemiology Centre
CARIAD	Caribbean Institute on Alcoholism and Other Drug Problems
CARICOM	Caribbean Community and Market
CARIDIN	Caribbean Drug Information Network
CCM	Caribbean Coordination Mechanism
CICAD	Inter-American Drug Abuse Control Commission
CJS	Criminal justice system
CODAC	Community Development Action Committee
CSDP	Centre for Socially Displaced People (Trinidad)
DCPO	Drug Court Program Office (US)
DWI	Driving-while-intoxicated
DAESSP	Drug Abuse Epidemiological and Surveillance System Project
DEA	Drug Enforcement Agency (US)
DOH	Deutscher Orden Hospitalswerke
ECDCO	European Commission Drugs Control Office
ELN	National Liberation Army (Colombia)
EU	European Union
FARC	Colombian Revolutionary Armed Forces
FATF	Financial Action Task Force
FBI	Federal Bureau of Investigation
GAP	Global Assessment Programme
GDP	Gross domestic product
HFLE	Health and Family Life Education
HR	Harm reduction
IADB	Inter-American Development Bank
IDER	Integrated demand reduction strategy
IGO	Inter-governmental organization
INCB	International Narcotics Control Board
JCF	Jamaica Constabulary Force
JDF	Jamaican Defence Force
JLP	Jamaica Labour Party

LUSAVE	St Lucia Save the Children
MDCs	More developed countries
MDMA	Methylenedioxymethamphetamine (ecstasy)
MIS	Management information system
MT	Metric tonnes
NACDER	National Coordinating Council for Drug Education and Rehabilitation (Guyana)
NADAPP	National Alcohol and Drug Abuse Prevention Programme (Trinidad)
NAFTA	North American Free Trade Agreement
NANCOM	National Anti-Narcotic Commission (Guyana)
NCDA	National Council on Drug Abuse (Jamaica)
NCSA	National Council on Substance Abuse (Barbados)
NDACC	National Drug Abuse Council (Belize)
NDC	National drug council
NDC	National Drug Council (Antigua and Barbuda) (Bahamas)
NGO	Non-governmental organizations
NIDA	National Institute on Drug Abuse
NIP	National Indicative Programmes
NTORS	National Treatment Outcome Research Study
OAS	Organization of American States
PAHO	Pan American Health Organization
PNP	People's National Party (Jamaica)
PSOJ	Private Sector Organization of Jamaica
RSS	Regional Security System
SBIP	Street-based intervention programme
TLC	Tender loving care
UK	United Kingdom
UNDCP	United Nations Drug Control Programme
UNDP	United Nations Development Programme
UNGASS	United Nations General Assembly Special Session
UNICEF	United Nations Children's Fund
UNODC	United Nations Office on Drugs and Crime
US	United States
UVI	University of the Virgin Islands
UWI	University of the West Indies
WHO	World Health Organization
WTO	World Trade Organization

Acknowledgements

Many people have played a part in the making of this book, which we hope will make a substantive contribution to drug policy debates in the region and beyond. First and foremost we acknowledge the contributors, who have given their valuable time to outline, write, redraft and edit their chapters. We were determined from the outset to give voice to both academics and drug field professionals, and it is to the latter particularly that I want to extend my thanks for their forbearance in putting up with the sometimes painfully tenacious editorial process.

The support from my fellow editors Marcus Day and Anthony Harriott has been invaluable in every respect. This publication is the culmination of a constructive, energetic, and at all times good-humoured working relationship stretching over three years. Without their guidance, insight and deep understanding of the region, my efforts would have foundered long ago.

Many friends and colleagues have aided the process in different ways. I am grateful for the initiative and support of the CARICOM secretariat, particularly Lieutenant-Colonel Fairbairn Liverpool of the Regional Coordination Mechanism for Drug Control, Ms Jacquelyn Joseph and Dr Heather Johnson. We also gained much from the many discussions and workshops that have been held in the process. I would like to acknowledge the support of Dr Ken Douglas of CAREC, Dr Charles Thesiger, Ikel Tafari, Esther Best, Shaka Bongo, Patrick Prince and Daurius Figueria.

I would also like to thank Keith Shannon and Neale Jagoe of the Drugs and International Crime Department of the UK Foreign and Commonwealth Office for their vision and broadmindedness. Their financial support was indispensable in bringing this book into print.

At DrugScope I have enjoyed the support of many colleagues who assisted in the many tasks from gathering research material to peer-reviewing copy. A particular note of thanks goes to Vanna Derosas for her editorial support.

Finally, while acknowledging the many contributors and supporters of this project, the opinions expressed are those of the authors, and the editors accept full responsibility for the content of the volume.

Axel Klein

About DrugScope

DrugScope is the UK's leading independent centre of expertise on drugs. It provides quality drug information, promotes effective responses to drug taking, undertakes research, advises on policymaking, encourages informed debate and speaks for its 1000 plus member organisations working on the ground. DrugScope's mission is to inspire and inform policy and practice which lead to the reduction of drug related risk, the alleviation of suffering and the achievement of sustainable drug control. It promotes policies that are humane and based on evidence.

The International Unit has been active in the Caribbean since 2000. Activities include policy advice to national governments and regional organizations, needs assessments and service audits, training for drug professionals, project evaluations and assistance with the resettlement of Caribbean drug couriers. All projects are implemented in partnership with regional organizations from the public sector and civil society.

In this complex policy field DrugScope bridges polarized positions. Working with both governments and drug users, DrugScope occupies a key position by providing constructive criticism and recording views from the margins. DrugScope neither condones nor condemns drug use. It provides professional advice on addressing the problems related to drugs and drug policies.

www.drugscope.org.uk

Preface

The problem of drug use and distribution in the Caribbean has generated major concern on the part of governments, regional institutions and international organizations operating in the region, since the Caribbean is not only a consumer of drugs but a major transit point for the penetration of the North American market. Not surprisingly, there is a growing literature on the subject, which has focused on strategies for dealing with the problem both as a health issue with legal and social implications and as a security concern with major ramifications for the future viability of both state and society in the region. The present volume makes an important contribution to that literature by providing innovative insights into the problem that reflect a fundamental departure from conventional analysis on the subject.

A notable feature of the study is that it assesses not only the efficacy of traditional policy but also attitudes and practices aimed at altering drug use and distribution that have received scant attention despite the growing literature. The study not only identifies the measures being pursued by governments and other stakeholders but also provides a constructive critique of these measures in terms of their relevance as a solution to the problem in the specific circumstances of the Caribbean.

More importantly, the study explicitly challenges a number of assumptions that inform the dominant current policy response to the drug problem. The study sees this policy as externally driven, particularly in terms of its focus on the interdiction of supply, with only limited reference to the need to address the demand side of the equation, in which North America, particularly the US, plays a significant role. For this reason, the current approach is seen as a major constraint on the articulation of a genuine regional policy response that could prove much more effective in dealing with the problem from a Caribbean perspective.

In recognition of these shortcomings, the study advances a number of alternative approaches for dealing with the problem. It specifically points to the need for a human-oriented approach to drug use and distribution, as opposed to the punitive model reflected in the existing criminal justice system with its emphasis on incarceration – a response that has resulted in a significant expansion of the prison population in the region but has given little consideration to the rehabilitation of drug offenders. A case is therefore made for a significant expansion of the Caribbean drug control strategy in order to provide for a range of interventions driven by more endogenous concerns.

The study significantly extends current assessment of the threat to the security of the state and public safety. It sees serious challenges arising from the unintended consequences of ill-advised drug control measures as much as from the criminal activities associated with drug trafficking. It provides a number of new and creative insights that are likely to exercise a significant influence on future approaches to the formulation of strategies to deal with the drug problem in the Caribbean. As such it will be of special interest to policy makers and members of the academic community, as well as the public at large.

The editors and contributors to the volume should therefore be commended for their effort to shed light on a subject that has emerged as a major public policy concern in the Caribbean, which will continue to demand the urgent attention of governments and regional institutions and of international agencies concerned with the problem of drug use and distribution in the Caribbean.

Denis M. Benn
Michael Manley Professor of Public Affairs/Public Policy
University of the West Indies, Mona

Contributors

Catherine Chestnut is currently Manager of the Cayman National Drug Council.

Barry Chevannes is currently Dean of the Faculty of Social Sciences on the Mona Campus of the University of the West Indies (UWI). Professor of Social Anthropology, he has published extensively on the Rastafari movement and other native religions in Jamaica, on African-Caribbean masculinity, and on various aspects of culture. His most recent book is *Learning to be a Man* (UWI Press 2001). Well known for his public service, he recently chaired the National Commission on Ganja appointed by the Prime Minister to consider decriminalization (2000–1). He is an Honorary Fellow of the Royal Anthropological Institute.

Marcus Day is coordinator of the Caribbean Harm Reduction Coalition (CHRC), a regional NGO based in Castries, St Lucia. He was the founder of a low-threshold drop-in centre for homeless crack users in urban Castries that opened in January 2001, and recently completed an assessment of primary health needs among street drug users in Castries.

He has managed a two-year regional drug treatment and rehabilitation project funded by the European Commission in seven Caribbean countries. His recent publications include (with W. Singh, M. Trotman, L. Cuffy, V. Abraca, M. Porter and B. Tkachuk) *Prison and Penal Reform Assessment in Antigua and Barbuda* (St Johns: Government of Antigua–Barbuda, 2003) and (with A. Klein, E. Oppenheimer and A. Harriot) *A Drug Demand Reduction Needs Assessment in the Caribbean Community and Market* (London: DrugScope, 2002).

Jennifer Hillebrand is Project Coordinator (Phare Project) within the Reitox and Enlargement team at the European Monitoring Centre for Drugs and Drug Addiction. Over the past two years she has been supervising several national school surveys and focus assessment studies (qualitative research studies) in the Caribbean as the UNODC Regional Epidemiology Adviser. She was also involved in the publication of a qualitative and semi-qualitative study on the link between drug use and HIV/AIDS among young people in Grenada (UNODC, Regional Office Barbados Report,

2003). Her most recent publications are *Drug Involvement among Students and Youth at Risk in the Metropolitan Area of Port-au-Prince, Haiti (2000)* (UNDCP, 2002) and, with Ken-Garfield Douglas, *The Caribbean Epidemiology Network – Complexities of Developing a Regional Perspective* (forthcoming).

Howard Gough is the co-developer and manager of Richmond Fellowship Jamaica Drug Rehab Centre (Patricia House) in Kingston, and Lecturer at the Northern Caribbean University, Kingston Campus. Formerly Caribbean Regional Coordinator for Richmond Fellowship International, he is currently Coordinator of the Jamaican leg of the European Union–DOH Treatment and Rehabilitation Enhancement Project.

Axel Klein is Head of Research at DrugScope and researcher at the Institute for African Alternatives (IFAA) in London. He has carried out research projects in the Horn of Africa, Nigeria and the Caribbean on conflict, society and culture and on the politics of drug control. His recent publications include (with Tobias Debiel) *Fragile Peace: State Failure, Violence and Development in Crisis Regions* (London: Zed Books, 2002); (with Mohamed Suliman) 'Die Inversion der Ethnizität: Von Wahrnehmung zur Konfliktursache. Die Fur- und Nubakonflikte im Westsudan', in *Friedensbericht 1998* (Zurich: Chur, 1998); and 'Between the Death Penalty and Decriminalisation: New Directions for Drug Control in the Commonwealth Caribbean', in *New West India Guide*, 75, 4 (2001): 193–228.

Marlyn J. Jones is an Assistant Professor in the Division of Criminal Justice, California State University, Sacramento, where she teaches in areas such as gender, race and criminal justice. She is currently a visiting lecturer in the Department of Government, University of the West Indies, Mona. Her doctoral dissertation used Jamaica as a case study to analyse the consequences of US drug control policy on Caribbean nations that are considered drug transit areas.

Anthony Harriott is a Senior Lecturer in the Department of Government at the University of the West Indies, Mona Campus. He has written several articles and reports on crime, crime control and policing in the Caribbean, as well as *Police and Crime Control in Jamaica: Problems of Reforming Ex-colonial Constabularies* (Kingston: University of the West Indies Press, 2000). Recently he has edited *Understanding Crime in Jamaica – New Challenges for Public Policy* (Kingston: University of the West Indies Press, 2004).

Philip Nanton taught Applied Social Policy at the Department of Local Government Studies, University of Birmingham. From 1999 to 2000 he was Chair of the Society of Caribbean Studies (UK). He teaches Policy Analysis in the Centre for Management Studies, UWI, Cave Hill, Barbados.

Michael Platzer headed the UN International Drug Control Program for the Caribbean Region from 2000 to 2003. He has since become the Chief of the operations at the UN Centre for International Crime Prevention in Vienna. This department concentrates on combating organized crime, corruption, trafficking of human beings, and terrorism, as well as reforming criminal justice systems and developing international standards.

Wendy Singh has fourteen years' experience in the field of criminal justice and human rights. She has researched and published several articles on the situation of children and women with regard to human rights and criminal justice, with a focus on establishing links between human security and human development policies. Over the past few years, she has headed the penal reform consultancy missions to St Lucia, Grenada, Dominica, Belize, Jamaica and Antigua.

She is also the former head of two regional organizations: the Caribbean Human Rights Network and the Caribbean and Latin America Office of Penal Reform International. She currently works as an independent consultant.

PART 1

Background and Context

Introduction

AXEL KLEIN, MARCUS DAY
AND ANTHONY HARRIOTT

Few issues of public policy fall within the remit of as many different departments of government as drug control. Formulating a policy response involves, therefore, a process of consultation, negotiation and interdepartmental cooperation of bewildering complexity. Gathering the data on problems, causes and impact that comprise the evidence for such policy relies on the efforts of an array of sector-specific specialists and experts. In the English-speaking Caribbean the number of officials, policy makers and professionals working on different aspects of drug policy has increased steadily over the past ten years. The amount of data available from research and policy publications, unpublished reports and the media has grown correspondingly. Up to now analysis has focused upon the impact of drugs and sought to identify associated problems. Missing from the literature is an analysis of the extent to which the responses in policy and practice have themselves altered the underlying situation. There have been few attempts to evaluate the efficacy of discrete activities or overall policy approaches to drug use and drug distribution.

The importance of impact assessment, and of the inferences drawn from a wider analysis of the role played by drug control in society–state relations located in the social and economic development context, derives from the rationale of drug control itself. The prohibition of identified substances is based on a moral judgement about what constitutes acceptable human behaviour, and on a calculus of social efficacy. Governments pursue a chosen drug policy because they believe it is morally right, and they believe it is the best way for society to manage the evils and threats drug abuse visits on their society. Much drug policy is reactive to events, yet in order to safeguard the validity of programme delivery there must be a continuous absorption of new data and new factors into the policy formation equation. Policy makers, particularly, need to be conscious not only of the intended consequences of their drug policy but also, and maybe more far-reachingly, of the unintended consequences in so far as their entire magnitude can be grasped.

Moreover, while the agencies working at national, regional and international level wholeheartedly subscribe to the moral certitudes of prohibition, they must not shy away from vigorously engaging in evaluation, assessments and impact analysis to test the effectiveness and the efficiency of their policy. As the scale of interventions gathers momentum, there has to be a shift to looking at the aggregate impact in terms of crime, health care and social development. The contributions to this volume combine to form a constructive critique that spans the policy spectrum. Drawing on experience of programmes, policy and research, they include, as well as critical appraisals of the overall direction of drug policy in the Caribbean region, the evaluation of successful alternative practices.

The salience of drug control to the wider issue of social policy is brought out by Barry Chevannes. Political stability depends on adherence to the social contract, 'yet the rule of law is never secure unless it is sanctioned by the moral order'. But in Jamaica 'the state agencies classify ganja as a drug when the popular culture does not'. This discrepancy between popular practice and the law acts like a cancer in society–state relations. The sacralization of ganja by the Rastafarian movement has served as a symbol of cultural-political resistance to what the movement regarded as a repressive state. Understanding the failure to suppress ganja is an exercise in the pragmatism of politics and good governance, as 'to harmonize the law with social morality is the better for the rule of law'.

The discrepancy between social morality and the letter of the law has disturbing consequences. Wendy Singh, having identified the tendency of the Commonwealth Caribbean countries to 'arrest and charge those in possession of small quantities of drugs', reports the inevitable consequence that the policy of drug control is 'filling up the prisons'.

The high incarceration rates across the region forms part of a punitive tradition in social control inherited from a colonial past, which until well into the nineteenth century bore little resemblance to justice. Under the current drug control regime, drug offences have imposed an unsustainable burden not merely on prison populations, but also on the entire criminal justice system. Drug control is placing such a strain on the institutional infrastructure, as well as on social relations, that a range of alternative measures are gradually and at times informally being introduced.

One of the key modalities for easing the burden on the prison system while introducing an element of care into a system of punishment is illustrated in the drug court experiment discussed by Anthony Harriott and Marlyn Jones. An effective instrument for directing drug-using offenders to treatment, drug courts have been introduced into Jamaica and to a lesser extent into the Bahamas, while at the time of this writing Trinidad is poised to begin. Drug courts are resource-intensive and do not address some of the key problems surrounding drug offenders. For example, drug courts focus exclusively on drug offenders and neglect that high proportion of the offender population whose crimes are motivated by drug dependency. Drug courts also exclude offenders charged with trafficking or violent crimes; indeed, 'the increase in violent crimes in Jamaica is in part due to drug trafficking and drug dealing, not the prevalence of a drug-using life style'.

Involvement in the underground economy of illicit drugs is a major source of livelihood for many of the Caribbean poor (if not some Caribbean nations). That this does not need to involve violence is shown in Axel Klein's inside look at ganja farming in St Vincent. Eking out a living on marginal land, many ganja growers are former banana farmers displaced by the elimination of preferential entry into the European Union (EU) market. Klein makes an important point in deconstructing the myth that involvement in the drug economy leads to riches.

Philip Nanton shows how marijuana cultivation fits into the cyclical pattern that has characterized Caribbean cash crop economies from colonial times to the present. The region has been dominated by the export of a series of unprocessed agricultural products, each displaced in turn by cheaper producers employing economies of scale in other regions. The Caribbean dependency on prospects in the traditional export markets underlines both the 'importance of the private sphere and the underlying peripheral nature of the state, both at the level of capital and among the poorest in the labour force'.

Both Nanton and Chevannes advocate the renegotiation of drug control policy with major extra-regional partners. Harriott and Jones and Klein also weigh in with arguments for substantial reconfiguration of the policy frame. Pending such macro-level discussions, health workers, educators, drug council administrators and other practitioners are forced to get on with the job.

Human and financial resource constraints, skill gaps, hostility from the public and suspicions among clients all adversely affect the discharge of professional duty. Yet 'unhealthy competition fostered by personalization and attempted monopolization of the field' adds additional challenges to an already complex situation, as Howard Gough reports in his chapter on the treatment and rehabilitation sector in Jamaica. With drug services still in a developmental phase, professionals have to establish working models and competencies while fending off claims by different constituencies, including the recovering addict as treatment specialist.

While residential centres can follow the experiences of regional and international alcohol and drug treatment services, the pioneers of Caribbean outreach work are pretty much left to their own devices. Marcus Day's evocative account of the establishment of a low-threshold drop-in centre in

St Lucia brings out the complexities of working on the fringes of both existing services and established theories of intervention. Yet engagement with these marginal groups generates fascinating information about the drug–crime nexus. The evidence discussed by Day makes it clear that much of the public nuisance surrounding problematic drug use and accompanying home-lessness can be addressed and alleviated with the infusion of modest resources.

The crucial factor is the knowledge base, knowing when to deliver what intervention to which target group. But, as Jennifer Hillebrand argues in relation to new epidemiological data collection mechanisms, this generation of information entails new challenges that need to be addressed. 'Despite these research activities, drug councils operate without any formal ethical oversight or research protocol that would define some of the core ethical principles that one needs to follow when collecting personal information about illegal behaviours'. She goes on to discuss the need to define ethical principles in determining the role of both researchers and councils, and their relationships with research participants.

Uncertainty about the participant group harbours the danger for the council of badly pitched and misdirected communication. There is a tendency to engage with school-based young people, not merely because of risk factors but because they are readily manageable within the school setting, making them an accessible audience. As long as intervention activities go unevaluated, they can be continued year after year, because it seems the right thing to do.

Yet there are opportunities to direct activity at the wider population by redefining respectively the remit of the drug council, the list of substances, and the definition of risk. Catherine Chestnut demonstrates how, even in the rigidly non-tolerant environment of the Cayman Islands, harm reduction strategies can be introduced in practice and earn much acclaim. 'Public acceptance of the project was therefore seen as further proof of the progress made in terms of changing attitudes towards drug use and abuse. All indications so far suggest greater understanding and support for policies and programmes that aim to reduce harm, even in the absence of a clear mandate for abstinence.'

Alleviating the damage inflicted by drugs at the individual, local and community level has to remain a policy priority. It should involve government and civil society and concentrate on containing the damage and assisting those in need. But the illicit drug trade poses a range of threats that can only be dealt with at a societal level.

In their chapter, the UNODC authors review the trafficking trends in an attempt to assess the meaning of drugs to Caribbean economies. At the end of a difficult exercise, drawing out meaning from unreliable statistics, they can safely conclude that the biggest threat to the region stems from the distortion of the incentives and opportunity structure. 'The most important consequence of illicit drug trade in the Caribbean comes from the disincentive to business entrepreneurship. Facing high returns on investment in the drug trade, the opportunity costs of legal entrepreneurship with more limited long-term returns are disadvantaged.'

Debate on the direction, impact and effectiveness of the current drug policy is likely to intensify over the next few years. Solutions will be urgently needed, and the chapters making up this book may be read as a contribution to that discussion. Evidence-based research focusing on the interpretation of existing drug control legislation, the efficacy of non-custodial sentencing for drug offenders, the need for alternative livelihoods, and the allocation of resources for reducing the problems facing vulnerable groups of drug users provide the materials needed to chart a drug control strategy that is contextually and culturally appropriate.

There is, however, a need to integrate these multiple programmes under an overarching set of principles. At present there is some tension between the agreed principle of abstinence from controlled substances and the growing number of open breaches. In terms of drug control policy it is becoming clear that one size does not fit all. Moreover, the principle of incarcerating drug (read marijuana) users is not endorsed by a significant section of the population across the region. To avoid a conflict of values, on the one hand, and on the other to develop a policy that is realistic and achievable, the region has to look at alternative policy frameworks.

Currently Caribbean drug control policy rests on two pillars. On one side is the emphasis on supply reduction activities. Partially funded by the consumer countries of the north, the goal of supply reduction is to interdict illicit drugs before they reach the borders of the donor countries. Her Majesty's Navy and US Coast Guard vessels regularly patrol the waters of the Caribbean on interdiction exercises that are enhanced by the cooperation and participation of Caribbean marine police and coast guard services. The Caribbean vessels are decommissioned US Coast Guard vessels presented to the governments of the Caribbean by the US with operational costs (training, fuel, vessel maintenance, and salary subventions) also partially underwritten by them. The other pillar is a strong demand reduction programme focusing on both primary prevention strategies (directed at keeping young people from experimenting with drugs) and abstinence-based residential treatment in high-threshold centres. Much of this work is abstinence-oriented. There is little, as yet, in the way of service delivery for that percentage of the population that is engaged in drug-using behaviours. This begs the inclusion of a third pillar, the adoption of a harm reduction philosophy.

Harm reduction is a consequentialist approach based on acceptance that there will be a certain level of drug use in society regardless of what penalties are prescribed. It recognizes that there are limits to the capacity of societies to control the inflow of and the demand for drugs, and therefore aims to minimize the harm done to the drug users, their families, the community and society as a whole.

Harm reduction principles can usefully guide specific interventions by non-governmental organizations (NGOs) and law enforcement, health and education services in their respective areas of work, setting goals that will lead to a coherent and coordinated drug strategy. Law enforcement agencies, for instance, would be better served by adopting a policing strategy that focuses on reducing the overall level of criminality in a neighbourhood, rather than on the repression of particular activities.

It has been argued that the coordination of policies requires an over-arching and organizing objective.[1] This is often interpreted as the re-allocation of resources from punitive to therapeutic, preventive and educative interventions. Given the Caribbean realities, there has to be an ongoing focus on interdiction activities aimed at curtailing the throughflow and the export of drugs, but there is ample room for manoeuvring the actual exercise and implementation of domestic drug control so as to embrace elements of the harm reduction philosophy that is culturally appropriate to the Caribbean.

One of the outcomes of this project has been to identify a number of gaps in the knowledge base that will need to be addressed if future policy formation is to be effective. There is not enough information on the confluence of drugs and other forms of criminality. The sparse evidence available suggests that the distribution circuits as well as the markets for crack cocaine and ganja are quite discrete.

Also urgently needed is an evaluation of the efficacy of the punitive model embraced by so many Caribbean jurisdictions in deterring both crime and drug use. There are disturbing suggestions that, contrary to intention, it is generating a body of crime.

Moreover, there are evident requirements for early intervention, particularly in the development of alternatives to custodial punishment, and in the expansion of treatment and after-care facilities. This volume thus makes a case for a significant expansion in Caribbean drug control strategy, one that embraces the broad spectrum of interventions and provides a set of recommendations for a programme of activities.

NOTE

1 Marcus Roberts, 2003, *Drugs and Crime: from warfare to welfare*, London: NACRO.

CHAPTER 1

The Search for a New Drug Policy Framework

From the Barbados Plan of Action
to the Ganja Commission

AXEL KLEIN

Over the past two decades drug control has become an issue of great concern throughout the English-speaking Caribbean. Most governments have established national drug councils as coordinating bodies and drafted a policy document or strategy. Each country files regular reports on drug trends to the International Narcotics Control Board and participates in the mutual evaluation exercises and training organized by the Inter-American Drug Abuse Control Commission (CICAD).[1] There are regional coordinating mechanisms such as the Inter-Governmental Taskforce on Drugs and Crime to discuss and plan action on drugs. The Caribbean Community and Market (CARICOM) has a section dedicated to drug control with full-time staff, while policy makers and professionals meet regularly for information exchange, planning or training purposes.

Official activism is matched by widespread social concern. In almost every Caribbean country stories about drug use and associated criminality are providing a lurid mainstay for regional newspapers and broadcasting services. Drugs impinge on international relations, as in the case of Jamaican drug mules heading for the United Kingdom in 2002, and they fire the imaginations of the young. For many of the young people in the poor urban areas of Kingston, Port of Spain or Castries the drug don has become a role model.

Drugs, it can be safely asserted, loom large in the collective imaginary and figure high on the list of political priorities. Yet in few other areas of public policy is there such a hiatus between the vigour of rhetoric and available professional expertise. There is much posturing around drug control, but the information base is only slowly consolidating. This is all the more daunting, perhaps, because drugs are a complex policy issue, straddling a multitude of sectors and academic disciplines. Perhaps limited understanding of the phenomenon is part of the explanation for the very shrill note struck in the alarmist official pronouncements of the late 1980s and early 1990s.

Best known, possibly, is the grave prophecy of the West India Commission:

> Nothing poses greater threats to civil society in CARICOM countries than the drug problem; and nothing exemplifies the powerlessness of regional governments more. That is the magnitude of the danger drug abuse and drug trafficking hold for our community. It is a many-layered danger. At base is the human destruction implicit in drug addiction; but implicit also is the corruption of individuals and systems by the sheer enormity of the inducements of the illegal drug trade in poor countries. On top of this lie the implications for governance itself – at the hands of both external agencies engaged in international interdiction, and the drug barons themselves – the dons of the modern Caribbean – who threaten governance from within. (West India Commission 1992)

The Commission identified the disparity between the capability of the small Caribbean states, and the powers of drug trafficking cartels as a present threat.

A decade on there is no sign that the threat has in any way abated. Indeed, by all accounts drugs have penetrated Caribbean society pervasively, with substances like crack cocaine, heroin and MDMA more readily available, cheaper and popular than they ever have been.[2] The political situation in Latin America, meanwhile, has deteriorated further, as Colombia is plagued by seemingly irresolvable civil war, and Venezuela is sliding into crises, opening new wide spaces for organized criminal groups.

Notwithstanding the spectacular success of individual operations, the combined regional and international efforts at turning off the supply flow, or at dissuading people from indulging in drugs, have been manifestly unsuccessful. Yet there is a distinct shift in tone in the policy discussions on the issue. The ominous warnings of impending loss of liberty and stability have given way to preoccupations of a much more operational nature. Law enforcement agencies are adjusting threat scenarios emanating from drug trafficking to the radically different security concerns of their international partner countries. After 9/11, terrorism has upstaged and effectively decentred drugs as the primary security challenge. There are no doubts about the links between drugs and terrorism, particularly with reference to the Colombian rebel movements FARC and ELN, but drugs are now treated as a means to more dangerous ends: as a source of finance for terror, not as the principal danger itself.[3]

One of the reasons why the threat posed by drug dealers and traffickers is viewed more sanguinely now than a decade ago is that the security agenda of the English-speaking Caribbean is co-authored by analysts in the US and, to a lesser degree, in Europe (Bagley and Walker 1994; Griffith 1993; 1996; 2000). Drug trafficking became a major concern in the wake of the collapse of the Soviet threat in 1990, when the security agenda was broadened, to embrace *inter alia* drugs, migration and infectious diseases.[4] The Organization of American States, founded initially to contain the communist threat, turned its attention to a number of shared hemispheric concerns, the foremost of which was how to curb the trade in drugs (Lowenthal 1992: 309). With the emergent challenge of terrorism, the focus has narrowed once again, and drugs are now regarded as a secondary issue.

By interweaving external concerns with Caribbean interests, analysts have approached drugs largely from a trafficking perspective. Caribbean countries are mainly seen as hapless pawns in the wider scheme of Latin American organized crime groups targeting the North American market. The idiom is one of dual victimization, in which ruthless criminals and complacent or even colluding governments issue two distinct security challenges. First, an external military and economic threat arises from the structural vulnerability of mini- and micro-states within asymmetric power relationships: what Griffith describes as a 'subordinate state system' interacting with the 'United States, other important hemispheric actors such as Brazil, Cuba and Venezuela and other states such as Britain' as well as 'international financial institutions such as the International Monetary Fund' (Griffith 1993: 4). Regional security concerns, as well as the register of possible policy responses, are clearly stated as contingent upon the wider security framework determined by the US.[5]

Throughout the Cold War, the main challengers to regional security were conceived as state actors, or insurgents sponsored by state actors. In the Caribbean region, however, the drug trade has raised to a new level the danger posed by 'privatized violence'. According to former Jamaican Prime Minister Michael Manley, the region is 'dealing with a level of international criminal organization that is probably without precedent'.[6] The capabilities of these criminals derive from their alleged level of organization, the amounts of money involved (see Chapter 10) and the quasi-military capacity and ruthlessness of the trafficking organizations. There is an argument, then, that in the wider region, as indeed across the globe, this new phenomenon of privatized violence has 'contributed substantially to the protracted consolidation of the structures of violence' (Debiel 2002: 25). These organizations pose a violent external security challenge, and undermine the viability of the state by corrupting the institutions. This second threat scenario is not only more difficult to assess, but also a topic on which regional and North American scholars part company. According to Maingot, 'none of the important politician writers of the Caribbean in the 1960s, 1970s and even early 1980s have even intimated that the threat to Caribbean security would come largely from corruption, internal to their societies and external to the Caribbean as a whole' (Maingot 1994: 474).

The difficulty in discussing corruption within an international relations context is that too often it rests upon the silent presumption of a corruption-free institutional functioning in North America and Western Europe. This leads to an equivalence of the 'ideal type' with a given historic mani-festation, which in turn compromises the objectivity of the proposition. What begins as an engagement with a local set of problems morphs into a spiky critique based on the irrefutable premise that 'our system is better than yours'. Alert to the danger of reaching this intellectual cul de sac, Maingot quotes Lipmann's insight that it is not corruption but only the exposure of corruption that can be the subject of historical analysis.[7] We are reminded of Galbraith's (1955) observation that fraudulent practice is rife in any market economy, but only becomes exposed in times of crises, when the auditors come in.

Malfunction and corrupt practice, we therefore argue, are par for the course until they become systemic and slide into crises. Once public confidence in the capacity of institutions to deliver is lost, the stability of the state is in jeopardy. An ongoing discussion since independence has questioned whether Caribbean states, given the constraints of the resource base and the asymmetrical relationship with regional neighbours, are viable on their own: hence the involved discussions about a Caribbean Union. The impact of the drug trade, with its lavish emoluments for impropriety and malpractice, has severely tested that viability. It has tarnished the reputation of some Caribbean institutions and sections of its elite, but we would argue that so far — in most administrations at least — the overall integrity of the political system remains. This is no recommendation for complacency, however. In a sense the measures taken in response to the variegated drug threats contain the seeds for social discord and destabili-zation if not addressed in the very near future. We return, therefore, to the framing of the drug problem in both national strategies and the academic discourse.

There is a tendency in the security discourse to recommend conformity with US policy, as this 'can soften US disapproval of a small country's internal policy' (Khan-Melnyk 1994: 499). A simple realpolitik(al) acknow-ledgement that 'American dominance cannot be wished away' (Griffith 1993: 283), when taken to its conclusion, only serves to compromise Caribbean agency and autonomy of response. Regional actors are often presented as go-betweens or pawns, their activity contingent on the success of Latin American criminal groups in corrupting and co-opting state structures when transiting the region en route to North America and Europe. It is in their best interest to organize regional security by upgrading their security facilities (Griffith 1993), thereby implementing the resolutions of the international conventions to counter the drug trade (Maingot 1994: 476).

The commentaries on the Caribbean are less critical than what has been written on Latin America. US academics concede that drug control has been used to promote US hegemony in the hemisphere (Bagley 1994), and that the policy of interdiction and destruction at source is 'predicated upon the belief that drug problems were primarily foreign in origin' (Walker 1994: 12). With regard to the Caribbean, the US actions are treated as factors – the market for drugs which is triggering the traffic, the convicts forcibly returned to their Caribbean countries of origin, the trade policy pushing for a removal of protection for Caribbean bananas while maintaining protection for US sugar producers – but lie outside the realm of policy discussion. The only suggestion found in the publications from the inter-governmental organizations (IGOs) dealing with drugs in the region and among the interventionist scholars is for greater US and European material assistance to Caribbean drug control.

A reminder is needed that drug control policies exported by bilateral partners and promoted by the IGOs are mired in controversy. The effectiveness of treatment modalities, the impact of educational messages, and the link between drugs and crime are all subjects of intensive debate (MacCoun and Reuter 2001). The security discourse tends to gloss over the ideological character of the prohibitionist policy espoused by the US government, albeit with the support of key allies and international organizations. Instead, ideology, where analyzed as a factor, is presented as a phenomenon encountered in the Caribbean, be it in the guise of Cuban-inspired communism or Rastafarianism or militant Islam (Griffith 1993). The ideal of a drug-free world, with its ideological roots in the temperance movement, revivalist Christianity and the search for an identifiable adversary for the state apparatus, does not get a mention.

For the purpose of objective analysis we seek to move beyond the mere admission of 'hyper-puissance' and seek to understand the tenor and objectives of the hegemony in order to carve out a niche for self-determination. The policy framework provided by the 'war on drugs' is therefore open to challenge, particularly within the context of a developing country transit zone with a history of culturally validated substance use. The genuine danger posed by corruption has to be contrasted with a different challenge, with similar distorting consequences: the control of institutions by special interest groups. With reference to the Caribbean justice sector, this danger has been described by the Inter-American Development Bank: 'Government agencies that are so captured lack the autonomy to formulate and execute policies that benefit the general population and instead serve the narrow interests of the small groups of elites that control them' (IADB 2000: 11). The room for change may not be foreclosed by national agencies alone, but also by the activities of external partners, be these bilateral or multilateral. There is always the danger in the asymmetric relationships between agencies in resource-rich and resource-poor countries of pursuing programmes against the evidence of local needs. The paucity of success in drugs interdiction would, in other areas of politics, call for a radical review. A number of circumstances conspire to preclude this: the rhetorical requirement of US (and European) policy makers to be 'tough on drugs' (MacCoun and Reuter 2001); the convenience of 'exporting' the resolution of US (and European) drug problems to producer and transit countries (Walker 1994), and the incentive of government departments working in drug control to preserve as much of their budgets as possible (Mabry 1994: 55). Small amounts of money buy considerable leverage for agencies like the US Drug Enforcement Agency (DEA), the Bureau for International Narcotic and Law Enforcement Affairs, the US Customs Service, and the Department of Defense. With so many Washington agencies involved, 'reallocating or reducing the size of the pie is probably impossible' (Mabry 1994: 55).

There is a danger, then, of national and regional agencies becoming locked into a drug strategy that is based upon a false and ideologically driven analysis of the drug problem, and motivated by particular interests. Indeed, such observations could be made about any part of public policy, all of which is subject to the push and pull of public pressure, changing paradigms and new needs. The difficulty with drugs is that it is such a cross-cutting issue, with tentacles reaching into every aspect of government. This involves, by necessity, a limitless cast of players and interest groups at national, regional and global levels. Moreover, drug policy is the locus of an epic clash between social forces, moral censure and political will. The search for objectivity in the critical analysis of issues, policies or impacts is not always easy. We hope to contribute to an opening of the discussion by raising forbidden topics.

Few issues demonstrate the need for drug policy to become integrated into the wider needs-driven policy framework of the region better than the allocation of technology spending. St Lucia, the Cayman Islands and Trinidad are all countries where scarce resources have been used to acquire drug-testing kits. They are used, for instance, to test prisoners already convicted of an offence to establish if they are drug-free. The social value of this procedure is uncertain. Meanwhile, none of these jurisdictions employ breathalysers, even though drink driving provides the most serious drug-related hazard. But since alcohol is legal, and enjoyed by some of the law makers themselves, no resources are provided to enhance road safety. This is an instance of the spirit of the crusade getting the better of rational policy making. It is in the public interest to assert the primacy of politics and to critically evaluate the policies and models of drug control in the Caribbean region.

While this body of work has been valuable in contributing to the pressure on governments to take the drug issue seriously, it has also impinged on the autonomy of the region in formulating an appropriate response. At a conceptual level, the framing of drugs as a trafficking/ organized crime issue orchestrated by external actors has marginalized the body of local experience with drug use, drug control, the relationship between state and society, the consequences of interdiction, and the economic reality. The dominant paradigm for explaining the spread of crack cocaine is the spillover, defining local consumption patterns as a by-product of trafficking ventures. While proponents of the model recognize the causal significance of the US market, many concur implicitly with the validity of the US-defined, interdiction-centred response. Research over the past five years, instead of seeking to understand the complexities and linkages of drugs and other social issues, has concentrated on surveys and rapid assessments. The main data that these generate is that there is a sizeable community of drug users, without further qualification or analysis. Where programmes have been initiated by external partners, such as the Caribbean Drug Control Coordination Mechanism that grew out of the Barbados Plan of Action and is located at the United Nations Drug Control Programme (UNDCP) office in Barbados, the accompanying literature tends to focus on criminal justice and security matters.[8] Having to cater for both regional and extra-regional stakeholders, programme managers have tended to interpret their requirements in terms of supply-side interventions.

If security concerns and international relations issues dominated the discourse on drugs in the 1990s, the parameters were closely defined and referred mainly to trafficking and organized crime groups. Caribbean involvement has largely been reduced to a lamentable epiphenomenon of metropolitan trends, that was to be countered most effectively by merging supply-side interventions with international control apparatuses. This analysis has largely neglected the impact of drug control measures on domestic security within Caribbean countries. As the impact of policies introduced since the late 1980s has fallen outside the framework, we propose a new research agenda that assesses the impact of the criminalization of different categories of drug offenders on their criminal careers and on neighbourhood security and community relations, thus monitoring the relationship between the people and their institutions.

This volume is an attempt to contribute to the drug policy discussion by approaching critically some of the key issues within the policy spectrum. Drawing on professional experience, the authors provide new insights substantiated by fresh data and rooted in the academic literature. This contribution to the available evidence is part of an urgent and ongoing concern. Given the persistent prevalence rates in many countries, plus the challenge laid down by the troublesome population of problem users, the multiple links between drugs, deprivation and criminality, and the financial and social costs of drug control regimes, there is a pressing need for information and discussion on a range of issues. This information needs to be kept up to date as the situation changes constantly. In few policy areas is this as difficult to achieve as in the drugs field, where moral judgement, the dicta of international treaties, the illegality of the phenomena in question, and institutional self-interest come together to delimit open debate.

All too often discussion is foreclosed by ideology, allowing for a polarizing chasm to divide the protagonists into distinct camps. Constructive argument is overtaken by posturing and polemics, with prohibitionists sparring against the advocates of legalization, while most professionals, and indeed many policy makers in private, hold views somewhere along the continuum. The contributors to this volume hope that their research and argument will help to raise the quality of debate around several critical issues, including:

- What constitutes a drug offence and how should drug offenders be dealt with?

- What do we know about the relationship between drugs, the informal economy and crime?

- Who are the problem drug users and how are they to be reached and treated?

- What should be the framework for a twenty-first century drug policy?

While there is now a large body of literature on each of these topics, there are only sporadic publications relating to the Caribbean experience. At a recent workshop for drug professionals in Trinidad, James Thesiger, the head of the Jamaican drug council, lamented the lack of opportunities for Caribbean drug professionals to publish and share their work.[9] While there is a critical mass of researchers and professionals working in the field, most publications are scattered in academic journals overseas or confined to the shelves of local institutes and drug councils. The absence of dissemination opportunities is an impediment to Caribbean experts bringing their experience to bear on national and international drug policy decisions.

The current volume brings together a range of researchers and professionals with direct experience of working in the region. Recruited from a range of institutions, including the University of the West Indies, UN agencies, national drug councils and NGOs, each author draws on personal experience of working in the drugs field in the region. This book thus presents an attempt to trace the various shifts in drug policy, and to assess the situation in the region after a decade of comprehensive drug control policies. On the basis of these insights, we make suggestions towards a new framework for drug control in the region. Given the recent interest in demand reduction, and the recognition by heads of government that drug control is as much a public health as a criminal justice issue, there is also a need for a new set of overarching principles. These should be constructed from the bottom up, in response to existing needs, and staked within the parameters of the achievable. It should be effective and result-oriented. And it should aim to address the problems caused by and associated with drugs for the user, families and communities. We suggest that the systematic minimization of risk and harm provides the right guidance for a people-centred drug policy in the twenty-first century. Moreover, as drugs play an important role in income generation in the informal sector, drug policy needs to be situated within a development context.

The origins of drug control and the symbolic association of drug use and disorder

Some Caribbean countries have a long history of drug policy – notably Jamaica, where the first legislative measures were introduced in 1913. The evidence base for the controls was formed by anecdotes and casual observation of the impact of cannabis on the 'native population'. One of the council members had 'personal knowledge of the harmful effects of ganjah smoking, for he had coolies under him and often had to threaten them for the habit'.[10] Facile though they may seem to contemporary readers, the racially construed and politically motivated charge of 'native' idleness and a predilection for intoxication runs as a theme through the colonial literature. It relates to a self-conscious association of the European with civilization and the work ethic, set in contrast to the indolent barbarism of the native.[11] In the old plantation economies positing the need for coerced labour on the stereotypes of 'scientific racism' serves to occlude the morally indefensible practices of the former slave societies. The laziness inherent in the native, magnified by alcohol and drugs, justifies rough measures (see Chapter 5).

These mixed motivators, paternalist concern and high prejudice, are also found in European colonial governance in Africa. At the 1889–90 Brussels African conference the colonial powers agreed to prohibit alcohol imports to large parts of Africa. Ironically, distilled spirits had for centuries been a major trade item, and liquor duties were the main source of income of the incipient Lagos colony. Rum was also one trade item that the Americas exchanged directly with Africa (Heap 1999).

With colonial expansion reaching its zenith in the late nineteenth century, imperial apologists could modulate their observation of native conduct to a variety of purposes. Paternalist welfarism, concerned for the medical and spiritual health of the colonial subject incapable of self-rule, runs seamlessly into ruthless mercantilism seeking to preserve the thirst of Britannia's subjects for the product of her distilleries, and on to a brutal assertion of the regime at all costs. The question of drugs is so salient in the Western discourse on colonial governance because the powerful association of alcohol and adulthood is a symbolic proxy for the claim to self-government and the assumption of custodial guardianship. This systematic disenfranchisement by infantilization, so transparent in the customary reference to African men as boys, or the prevailing term for servants' quarters as boys' quarters, is also transposed to the regulation of alcohol use. In different African colonies, then, we find that 'natives' may purchase different forms of beer, but distilled liquor is reserved for whites only – it is deemed unsuitable for the 'excitable' (that is childish) African temper (Heap 1999; Ambler 1990).[12]

In the West Indies, the oldest arena of European expansion, late colonial paternalism is superimposed upon older layers of colonial government. For centuries the taming of the wild did not halt at the colour bar. The old pirate prisons that can still be found in St Vincent, Barbados or Trinidad bear witness to the different shades of 'savagery'. Until the consolidation of the colonial state in the late eighteenth century, the prodigal community of freebooters, pirates, and fortune hunters was not merely a challenge to the claims of imperial authority. They were an offence against the very principles of Western civilization that lent a shred of token legitimacy to the colonial enterprise.

If the success of the imperial project was simply a question of time, given the distribution of resources and the impossibility of collective organization among the region's malcontents, the triumph of morality long remained in the balance. The standards were set by the metropolitan centres in Europe, rather than by the regional elite, among whom self-interest vested in the *status quo* prevailed. This tended to block social progress at every turn. Discussing the process of cultural refinement, one author uses the regional cuisine as a metaphor. 'Refinement began with imitation more than with innovation from the top. The role of slave cooks in creating a fine cuisine was as important in the Caribbean as in Brazil and in the US South. The planters' main contribution was their appetite' (Mintz 1985: 137). The excessive alcohol consumption, as well as coarse and sometimes savage behaviour, was also regularly remarked upon by metropolitan travellers to the islands. The prevailing social system of chattel slavery was the only factor that contributed to the material progress of this class. Only the family histories of the few remaining Barbadian redlegs[13] give a hint of how alcohol could play a role in the economic ruin of white settlers.

In one analysis of drinking practices in the Bahamas, the differences are culturally explained: 'Africans brought with them drinking practices that were ceremonial and ritualistic', while European drinking 'was predominantly utilitarian but with hedonistic and ceremonial dimensions' (Dean-Patterson 1987: 147). If these observations can be applied to the region as a whole, so can the subsequent fusion of practices. In independent Jamaica, then, 'hard drinking by the well off is fairly common, and much boisterous and abusive behaviour tolerated' (Rubin and Comitas 1975: 61). This is perhaps one more instance of the coalescence of attitudes and interests of the new elite and the old.

During the colonial era, then, the alcohol regime in the West Indies differed significantly from those in the later colonial acquisitions in Africa. Rum had long been available, and was seen as a two-edged sword. Cast in a drunken torpor, the wayward subject may brawl, but will not riot. Frustrations are dissipated, energies diverted, as the dissatisfied opt for escapism over rebellion. But in situations of heated confrontation, a good dose of rum may bring the temperature to boiling point.[14] The policy debate surrounding access to and the status of mind-altering substances is therefore rooted historically in wider concerns with the distribution of rights and privileges in the polity. Arguably all items of consumption serve as metaphors for social status, and their legal status is an instrument of social control (Appadurai 1986; Baudrillard 1981). Psychoactive substances, however, are imbued with a power that is missing from other objects of consumption such as clothing, long regulated by sumptuary laws. They can effect a transformation beyond the control of either the subject or the wider society, which is captured by the use of the term 'spirit' for distilled alcohol and the application of epidemiological models to explain diffusion.

The link between outlaw behaviour and one of the Caribbean's most potent exports is epitomized in the remnants of the pirate ditty 'yo-ho-ho and a bottle of rum'. In the course of the twentieth century these fears of social disorder and eruptions of drug-fuelled violence are transposed from alcohol to other substances. Drugs and certain forms of learnt drug use behaviour may no longer be deemed appropriate in a society emphasizing restraint (Goodman et al. 1995). Be that as it may, the controls imposed by the post-independence governments in the Caribbean found support among bilateral partners and IGOs.

The challenging possibility raised by contributors to this volume is that if these policies are not carefully evaluated, calibrated and targeted they may fail to achieve many of their stated objectives. At the same time the unforeseen impact of some drug control interventions will pour fuel on the flames of social discontent. One such scenario, found in the study of other regions, is a gradual increase in both the crime rate and the chronic disaffection among marginal groups, without any tangible reduction of prevalence or availability (Tullis 1995). In order to understand where drug control in the region stands today and entertain alternative future scenarios, we need to trace how the current drug control regime has been derived.

Revisiting the ganja complex

The substance that set the wheels of criminal justice churning and opened political debate is ganja. Spotted in the first instance by the Council of Evangelical Churches in Jamaica, self-appointed custodians of native welfare, it was quickly taken up by the legislature as a subject for control. An opportunity for imposing sanctions arose in 1913 when the Legislative Council added several clauses relating to ganja to the text of the International Opium Convention it had been asked to ratify. Subsequently developed into the 1924 Dangerous Drugs Law, it has been successively amended (1941, 1947, 1954, 1961, 1972). As Chevannes argues in Chapter 2, the tightening of legal restrictions on ganja has in each instance been politically motivated. Other authors have claimed that 'Both the 1941 and the 1961 amendments, which carried increasingly severe penalties, came at points in Jamaican history when there was either political or economic unrest, and when there was fear of [political agitation by] lower class elements' (Rubin and Comitas 1975: 27).[15]

Fear of an uprising by the lower orders is a pervasive and compelling theme in the history of all the former slave societies of the Caribbean, and continues to haunt the imagination of the elite. In 1950 the 'affinity' between ganja and a wide range of property crime was chronicled in the annual report of 1950 Police Commissioner Calver. The rising political class assimilated these anxieties over both social disorder and ganja's subversive power. Shortly after independence, a string of prohibitionist measures was introduced, including mandatory sentencing.

Norman Manley, leader of the opposition, arguing against the motion, pointed out that the government, when presenting the case, had not produced any data relating to Jamaica. This was a continuation of an established trend, as for over half a century drug control in the Caribbean had been based entirely upon anecdotal evidence and opinions received from the US and the UK.

Yet around the same time researchers across the region were beginning to lay the foundations for a scientific evidence base. Statistical information on drug and alcohol prevalence among school children was becoming available for Trinidad and Jamaica (Grizzle and Rose 1976 and Pantin 1971, both cited in Douglas 1997: 7). More ambitious still was the collaboration between a multidisciplinary Jamaican and US team of researchers into the

Jamaican 'ganja complex'. The two-pronged exercise combined anthropological methods, including extensive fieldwork in multiple sites, with clinical, hospital-based work. The US partners were in part motivated by a growing curiosity about cannabis in the US.[16] The results put many long-held assumptions about ganja into question: there was no clear link between ganja and crime; there was no causal relationship between ganja use and psychiatric disorders; and, with reference to the Amotivational Syndrome, it was found 'that heavy ganja use does not diminish work drive or the work ethic' (Rubin and Comitas 1975: 166). The study concluded that the cultivation, distribution and consumption of ganja were so deeply rooted in the culture of rural Jamaica that they referred to these multiple processes as the 'ganja complex'.

Epidemiological research has since attested to an extremely high level of ganja use. In one study in 1990, 47 per cent of respondents in the metropolitan areas reported lifetime use (Stone 1990), while a school survey in 1997 reported that 8 per cent of pupils in grades 9–13 had smoked ganja in the preceding 30 days (Douglas 1997). In Jamaica, at least, ganja use is part of regular 'cultural practice' (see Chapter 2).

For the subsequent growth of addiction studies the research exercise into the 'ganja complex' proved invaluable, with many of the key experts in the region today – including Michael Beaubrun, Barry Chevannes, Melanie Dreher, Charles Thesiger and Marigold Thorburn – participating in some form. The study was commissioned at a particular moment in the history of US drug policy, when the dramatic increase in recreational drug use over the previous decade had generated much interest in mind-altering substances. A regular pastime among the young, drug use was tolerated in 12 states, where consumption had been virtually depenalized.[17] At the same time, however, the US government was stepping up efforts abroad to stop the inflow of drugs.[18]

Jamaica, and later Belize and Guyana, had been identified as major sources of marijuana in the 1970s. The US pressurized national governments to step up the eradication of cannabis fields, and began providing financial, logistical and operational support. Under the Michael Manley government, Jamaican law enforcement began collaborating with the US DEA. By the 1980s cannabis eradication exercises such as Operation Buccaneer had evolved into regular training opportunities for US armed forces (Griffith 1993). An array of law enforcement agencies, including the DEA and the Customs service, were now targeting the organized groups shipping ganja from Caribbean production centres into the US. Over the next twenty years US law enforcement and military teams would become more and more involved in the region. As crack took hold in the 1980s, the tolerance towards drugs that had marked US policy in the 1970s was rolled back sharply. Under the successive Reagan and Bush administrations, US drug policy took on a martial hue, and began making aggressive demands of so-called producer and transit countries. Severe penalties were imposed for non-compliance. Airlines, shipping lines, cargo firms and other carriers were fined heavily if drugs were found on a passenger or in cargo.

State-owned Air Jamaica accumulated fines of US$37 million in 1989–91 for illegal drugs found on its planes in the United States. In 1992 Guyana's Airways Corporation was fined over US$1 million for a seventeen-pound cocaine seizure found in a mailbag without address (Griffith 2000: 22). At national level new pressures have been added but the process of certification, following an amendment to the Foreign Assistance Act, requires the US President to certify countries as to their cooperation in combating drug production and trafficking. Countries deemed non-compliant lose their trading privileges with the US, US aid grants, and access to funds from the international financial institutions.

It is important to remember the variations between the histories of substance use in different Caribbean countries. In the Eastern Caribbean the ganja tradition is fairly recent, going back to the 1960s and 1970s. In Trinidad ganja use had remained confined to the East Indian[19] community for the better part of the nineteenth and twentieth centuries. While East Indians continue to produce the bulk of harvested ganja in Trinidad, both communities now use it. Impulses from American and UK youth culture diffused by returning migrants were instrumental in popularizing cannabis among Afro-Trinobagians in the 1960s and reviving indigenous production (Hamid 1991). Changes in the socio-economic structure, and particularly the neighbourhood culture, had prepared the ground. Economic development, rapid industrialization and incorporation into the world economy were destroying large sections of the neighbourhood-based informal economy. Mainly through the institution of the 'lime' or 'hanging out', young men had previously found gainful local employment in a range of low–medium-skilled, quasi-artisanal tasks that changed with the seasons. As the economy became more differentiated, and imports replaced local production, these opportunities dwindled, thereby changing the character of the lime. What had once been a community forum became a gathering of unemployed and disorientated young men (Hamid 1990).

Marijuana distribution moved gently into this occupational vacuum in the 1960s and 1970s. Local production, initially supplemented by imports from Jamaica and Colombia, was expanded to remote areas of the island. Pushers became organized into 'blocs' and 'gates', and could abandon petty crime for informal trading activity. This new-found status was matched by the growing influence of Rastafarianism, 'an ideology of self-sufficiency and "African self reliance"' (Hamid 1990: 45). According to this analysis, ganja provided an income opportunity and a unifying principle for community organizations.

Moreover, the organizations selling ganja in the neighbourhoods of Port of Spain or Kingston were building links with immigrant groups in the US and the UK. This provided a source of foreign exchange to island communities, and a mainstay for the economy of the immigrant groups. According to one positive reading of these events, 'perhaps the most signal achievement of Rastafari was to "Caribbeanize" completely a sizeable corner of the New York marijuana market' (Hamid 1991: 622). Throughout the 1970s, the association of ganja, reggae and Jamaica developed into a trademark popularized most spectacularly by Bob Marley. The quintessential cool, it came to evoke an alternative lifestyle and a value system that had a global resonance, and is proving impervious to ever more extravagant interdiction efforts.

The work by the interdisciplinary research team in Jamaica had focused on cannabis. Yet even while the researchers were going to press, a new and altogether more potent drug was gaining popularity – cocaine. By 1976 members of the upper class and bridge groups, including hotel employees, hustlers and prostitutes, were switching to cocaine, often in combination with ganja (Chevannes 1988: 31). This trend was being repeated across the region, but it was in the Bahamas that a further change would be reported first.

From cocaine powder to crack

Historically the Bahamas have been a transhipment point for contraband destined for the US. The islands were used as a base by rum smugglers during the 'noble experiment' of alcohol prohibition in the 1920s and early 1930s, and by Confederate mariners during the American Civil War. In view of their economic dependence on the US, one scholar has observed, 'geography has always been the Bahamas' main commodity' (Maingot 1988: 171). In the 1970s the proximity of the US coastline (Florida is 220 miles away) was being exploited by the increasingly powerful Colombian cocaine cartels. Carlos Lehder, one of the trafficking kingpins, set up a base on Norman's Cay in 1977 to tranship large quantities of cocaine into the US. Until his eviction in 1984 this operation displayed the vulnerability of Caribbean states and society. Enormous quantities of drug money were used to buy the acquiescence of officials and politicians and turn the island into a fief of the cartels.[20]

Large quantities of drug money and illicit merchandise were pumped into Bahamian society. According to one witness, 'there was so much cocaine in the Bahamas at the time that people were bored with it'

(Streatfield 2002: 293). One way of re-igniting the interest was a dramatic switch in the mode of transmission, possibly pioneered in the islands. Cocaine was cooked with baking soda and then smoked with a komoke, a pipe made out of glass and tinfoil, for a more immediate, far more intense, and very short-lived high. Known initially as 'freebase' or 'rock' it eventually became notorious as 'crack'. Selling at a considerable discount to cocaine powder, which soon vanished altogether from the market, it attracted a new, hitherto untapped clientele (Allen 1987). One of the first notifications of the incipient epidemic came from the Sandilands Rehabilitation Centre, where the first client admitted for cocaine psychosis as a result of cocaine smoking was admitted in 1979. Over the next few years the number of cases soared, reaching 224 in 1984 (Jekel and Allen 1986).

Other Caribbean countries also reported crack cases, though with a slight time lag. In Trinidad cocaine was 'before 1984 not a significant feature in hospital admissions' (Beaubrun 1987). According to the deputy head of the organized crime unit, powder cocaine was a whim of the rich that filtered down. Insignificant amounts were sold in straws for 25 Trinidad dollars, but the trade really began to mushroom in 1987 when rocks of crack were being sold for five or ten Trinidad dollars.

In Jamaica, however, the arrival of crack cocaine only served to further accelerate the downward spiral of lawlessness and disintegration in the inner cities. Crack impacted adversely at two levels – criminal organizations were veering out of control as they gained economic independence through cocaine trafficking, and internal security was compromised by the burgeoning population of crack users, estimated at 22,000 in the late 1980s (Stone 1990).

There are two widely diverse accounts explaining the spread of cocaine across the Caribbean. One emphasizes the importance of external criminal groups such as the Colombian Cali cartel, represented by Carlos Lehder, or the Medellin cartel, whose most notorious figure was Pablo Escobar. These groups are responsible for organizing the transportation of cocaine through Caribbean waters to North America and/or Europe. Methods vary: at times consignments are dropped by air and picked up by boats for immediate onward shipment; alternatively they are broken up and distributed along the islands. Local operatives involved in the island-hopping or warehousing operations were first introduced to crack cocaine, then paid for their services in kind. Adopting this win–win strategy, the cartels conserve their dollars while opening up new markets.

Most commentators account for Caribbean use as resulting directly from the trafficking 'spillover'. This explanation fits in with the medical metaphor of the epidemic, which explains the spread of drug use as a function of the agent (crack cocaine) and the vector (dealer) rather than as the result of a positive decision by the host (user). While the epidemiological model is problematic in explaining the spread of drug use – though it provides good tools for measuring it – it ties in with the idea of regional victimization, and can be adapted to suit political purposes.

Until the arrival of crack, cocaine was viewed as primarily a North American or European problem, and Caribbean leaders downplayed both the extent of involvement and responsibility of regional traffickers. Demands for closer cooperation by US security forces, especially regarding their entry into territorial waters, or the introduction and enforcement of drug control legislation, were resisted as an infringement on the territorial integrity of nation states. In a rejoinder to President Reagan, the Prime Minister of Antigua-Barbuda, Vere Bird, had protested about the 'attempts to extend domestic United States authority into the neighbouring countries of the region without regard to the sovereignty and independent legal systems of those countries'.[21] With the sharp jump in problem users reporting to the under-resourced and overextended treatment facilities of the region, Caribbean policy makers realized that the drug problem had landed, and needed a considered response. In the first instance the spillover model, with emphasis on Colombian culpability and Caribbean victimization, had its advantages. It diffused Caribbean responsibility for the inflow of drugs into the 'consumer countries'. And it sent a call for assistance to the large bilateral partners at a time when attention was focusing on other parts of the world.

While Colombian operators like Lehder did work across the Caribbean, there are indications that the relationship between Colombian and Caribbean traffickers was much more dynamic. An alternative model of cocaine diffusion allocates a far more active role to regional criminals. It stipulates that some of the players involved in the ganja trade had built up organizational capacity in the 1970s, and were ready to branch out into different activities. Operating in London, New York, and across the US, they could utilize the large West Indian communities in metropolitan centres for camouflage. Most importantly, traffickers could plug into the organizations and structures previously created by the ganja trade. According to one account of importing and distribution operations in Brooklyn, New York, it was Rastafarian entrepreneurs who pioneered the trade in the 1970s (Hamid 1990).

While this seems unlikely, given Rastafarian proscription of any psycho-active substance other than ganja, the corollary ethos of restraint and self-discipline did allow for the accumulation of capital.[22] Profits reinvested in the community helped to build up solidarity, and triggered the 'social bonding' between drug business and a community that would provide cover from law enforcement (Curtis and Wendel 2000). Yet upon entering the cocaine trade, numerous distributors became victims of their own success.

While many 'were delighted by the energy and peachiness' of powder cocaine, the switch to crack resulted in excess and an uncontrolled binge culture. 'Within months, distributors had completely depleted marijuana fortunes that had accumulated over a period of 15 years' (Hamid 1990: 55). Moreover, nothing was ploughed back into the community. 'To this day, the crack traffick has not supported a single vegetarian cook shop in the local community' (Hamid 1991).

It has been alleged that in the small, tight-knit island communities no activities could take place without collusion by high-ranking officials. Even the ganja trade enjoyed its patrons, as Michael Manley alleged in the House of Representatives: 'the people behind the racket were not from the ghettos of Jamaica, but from the best residential areas ... in cahoots with organized crime in North America' (Rubin and Comitas 1975: 35). The implication of the economic elite in the drug trade was matched in other jurisdictions by the entanglement of political leaders. A Bahamian commission of inquiry into drug-related corruption in the Bahamas in 1984 led to the resignation of five government ministers, while the Chief Minister of the Turks and Caicos Islands, one of the remaining UK Overseas Territories, was arrested in Miami in 1985 on drug charges. Yet, by and large, the political elites of most Commonwealth Caribbean states have withstood the threat of cooption. There has never been a scandal in Barbados, St Lucia, or Grenada, and so far only lower-level officials have been implicated in Jamaica

Equally disturbing has been a further development apparent in the garrison towns, where politicians were losing control. Instead of being able to direct and raise their supporters, they were being dragged down, as the tail began wagging the dog. The reasons were strictly economic. When, previously, politicians of the two leading parties had entered into an unholy alliance with urban gangs in downtown Kingston, the politicians returned political support – votes, neighbourhood mobilization, intimidation of rival parties – with favours. Benefits included 'material rewards, down to the dispensation of food, money, jobs, public housing, leases on government land, public contracts, social and welfare services' (Small 1995: 41) and protection from the law. The control that the political overlords could exert over their footsoldiers depended on their ability to provide patronage. With the contracting fortunes of the national economy during recession and structural adjustment, the opportunities for largesse were constricted. At the same time neighbourhood groups, now reformed into posses, were discovering new fortunes and with it independence in the drug trade. There was a shift in local power in some inner-city communities in favour of the dons. Control of local drug markets remained one important source of income and political influence for the dons. But the big money came from organizing shipment to North American and European markets.

Distinctions between crack and ganja

All Caribbean states are widely exposed to the political pressures, economic vagaries, and social impulses emanating from the US. The dilemma in the drugs field is that these messages are so mixed. There is a burgeoning market, and high profits to be realized, while the penalties are severe and the pursuit ruthless. During the 1970s cocaine powder was considered a benign drug among wide sections of the US society.[23] The dramatic change in public attitudes that occurred during the 1980s was in part a consequence of the shift from cocaine powder to crack, which was quick to establish a notoriety unheard of since the days of reefer madness (Streatfield 2002; Musto 1992).[24] In the US, the 'emergence of crack was a key catalyst that fuelled the latest "War on Drugs"' (Belenko 1993: 1). Some critics have argued that the increasingly punitive US approach to drugs is linked to the changing profile of the drug user – from white, cannabis-using college kid to urban, crack-smoking Afro-American man (Lusane and Desmond 1991; Tonry 1995).

Indeed, in both the US and the UK there is a strong perception that crack users are predominantly of Afro-Caribbean extraction.[25] Interestingly, this disavowal of crack is paralleled in the Caribbean. Far from being considered an intrinsic part of the culture, crack is widely regarded as an exotic import, the introduction of which is widely attributed to tourists. Explanations vary, and include a fair number of conspiracy theories. In several islands of the Eastern Caribbean informants have reported that the introduction was preceded by a ganja drought. Dealers and their foreign backers, it is alleged, were opening up the market (Klein 2001). Others report that crack dealers have been targeting ethnic rivals in countries with mixed populations (Figueira 1997). These narratives need to be explained.

A study of perceptions of drug-related harm by crack and ganja respectively among residents in Montego Bay, Jamaica, delivered illuminating results. Respondents not only treated the two substances differently but used them 'to elaborate a series of oppositions: natural versus unnatural, mental stimulation versus mental distraction, Jamaican versus foreign, Black versus White' (Broad and Feinberg 1995: 262). Cocaine was widely seen as 'unnatural', and associated with white people. People explained use as 'escapist', while ganja is an aid for spiritual enlightenment, helping the user to 'meditate'.

Once again substances attain an important symbolic value. Cannabis, celebrated as part of Jamaica's non-European heritage, was instrumentalized – not only by Rastafarians – during the independence struggle as a repudiation of white supremacy. In the hands of dreadlocked black men ganja becomes a proxy call for political independence and cultural autonomy. To the authorities, the smoking spliff presented a barely veiled political challenge, with the possibility of violence. Their response was articulated in the idiom of crime control, and pre-emptive. This attitude was shared by sections of the political leadership after independence had been attained.

Often the debate around ganja brings to a head the distinctive value systems found in the islands, also known as the pursuit of respect or reputation (Littlewood 1988). Yet, while seen as a 'badge of honour of the militant youth of the whole Caribbean, it is also imbibed by the middle and upper classes' (Pilgrims 2000). The consultations held by the Jamaican Ganja Commission (Chevannes *et al.* 2001) found an overwhelming majority in favour of a laxer penal regime for ganja. There are grassroots movements in most of the islands of the Eastern Caribbean calling for the legalization of ganja, with support from elite members. While this may in part be due to the growing experience of ganja use by members of the middle classes, it also indicates how the complex of fears associated with drug use has shifted from ganja and is now projected onto crack.

There is a widespread association of crack and crime at all three levels identified by Goldstein (1985): pharmacologically induced crime (as people become 'mad'), economically motivated crime (acquisition crime to fund crack purchase) and systemic crime (between rival groups). The intensity of popular antipathy stretches right across the social spectrum. According to one recovering addict at the Patricia House treatment centre in Jamaica, 'you can get your head cut off if you are a crack head in this society'. The stigma is acute and lasting. Crack users are known disparagingly as 'paros', because of the paranoid behaviour displayed by some when addiction has become acute.

Sharp distinctions obtain at the drug retail level. In Jamaica, yards where ganja is openly sold and smoked will only rarely allow dealing in crack. There is fear of the police demanding higher bribes that would eat into the profits, as well as of the users themselves. Even in Barbados, according to one informant, 'some guys will sell both but the hard-core Rastas don't sell crack'. In Guyana and the Bahamas, police report that Rastas even inform on crack dealers.

The material from St Lucia, collected by Day (Chapter 7) shows that few long-term crack users can live up to this image of seething violence. Indeed, most of the street addicts, who are often the most noticeable crack users, employ violence-free income generation strategies such as begging, doing odd jobs, and sex work. The data do not allow us to draw conclusions beyond that, but we can infer that the crime rate may vary at different stages of the drug-using career of the crack smoker.

In summary, then, we note that the reputation of ganja is shifting, and that it is increasingly seen as at worst a harmless pastime and at best a cultural icon. Many regard it as a peaceful and mellow aid for spiritual exercises like meditation. Even when stripped of positive imagery, marijuana is not considered a main priority, because according to the head of the Trinidad national drug council 'a guy will not attack you when he is smoking marijuana'. Crack cocaine, by contrast, evokes fear, disgust and contempt. There has been a seamless transition in the rhetoric of substance misuse control from cannabis to crack. The referent is different, the idiom the same.

Regional responses

During the 1980s, then, Caribbean countries were facing multiple drug-related threats: the fallout in medical terms from a rising 'epidemic' of ever cheaper crack cocaine; the security threat posed by organized crime and traffickers; and sharp reprisals for failing to take action by the biggest trade partner.

In an attempt to meet these challenges, governments began to institutionalize their responses on a national basis. National drug councils (NDCs) were pioneered in Jamaica by the National Council on Drug Abuse (NCDA) in 1983, followed by the National Drug Council in the Bahamas (1984) and the National Drug Abuse Council in Belize (1988). These councils initiated a number of different activities, including drug education, awareness raising, and the collection of information on use and prevalence. The main effort however, related to attempts to reduce the flow of drugs. The already mentioned eradication exercises in Jamaica, Guyana and Belize, in cooperation with US forces, were complemented by a tougher enforcement regime on drug use. At the same time the UN drug agencies were becoming proactive in the region as the United Nations Fund for Drug Abuse Control opened an office in Barbados.[26]

Drug control was becoming a cause around which politicians would mobilize. During the 1995 election campaign in Trinidad, candidate Panday's slogan 'Take the country back from the criminals' appealed to a sense of breakdown in public order as a result of drug-related criminality. Yet national resources were regarded as insufficient to meet the challenges. The regional dimension of the trade was first articulated at the 1988 meeting of CARICOM's Council of Ministers. Resource constraints, in terms of financial capacity and expertise, prompted the heads of state to request international assistance. Donors in European governments, the European Comission, the US and Canada proved amenable. Broad regional strategies were hammered out in 1996 in Bridgetown, where regional leaders adopted 69 recommendations on drug control under the Barbados Plan of Action (BPA); the 1996 Hemispheric Plan of Action agreed by the Organization of American States; the 1997 Partnership for Prosperity and Security, also concluded in Barbados between the US and fifteen Caribbean states on a range of economic and security issues including drug control; and the December 1998 Santo Domingo Declaration to further the implementation of the Barbados Plan of Action.

International commitment was accompanied by a considerable transfer of resources. The European Commission emerged as the main donor, with €25 million from its Budget Line and an additional €10 million designated for drug demand reduction programmes from the existing National Indicative Programmes (NIP). The scale of the funds provided a hefty subsidy for regional institutions such as the Caribbean Drug Control Coordinating Mechanism attached to the Barbados UNDCP office, the Caribbean Epidemiology Centre, and the University of the West Indies. It also generated a series of studies, training workshops, and projects. These efforts aided the graduation of a critical mass of informed professionals now working on different aspects of the drug issue. The hysterical tone struck in the early 1990s has given way to a far more considered response. It will be helpful to establish the present status of drug control policy structures and instruments in the Caribbean.

Taking stock – drug control in the Caribbean in 2003

International agreements and policy level

The conferences of the 1990s prompted the accession of all Caribbean countries to the UN and hemispheric drug control treaties. Indeed, this has become a condition for assistance from the EU and the US (Boekhout van Solinge 2002). With the appointment of Lancelot Selman as chair of CICAD, the region has become more involved in hemispheric activities, particularly training operations. The countries of the region also participate actively in the Mutual Evaluation Mechanism, developed as an alternative to the unilateral US certification process. There has been some pressure on particular jurisdictions over money laundering, but with assistance from international partners these concerns have been met, and most countries are now deemed to be cooperating.

At national level, drug control activities are coordinated by the national drug councils, operating in some shape or form in each English-speaking Caribbean country. The efficacy and endowment of these bodies varies, but in most countries they play a crucial role in reporting on trends and activities, initiating demand reduction activities, coordinating interventions, and raising awareness. Drug education usually comes into the NDC purview, run either as a one-off activity or as part of a regular programme. This often requires inter-agency partnership, placing the NDCs at the heart of coalitions of government departments and local or international agencies. Many of the

Table 1.1 Demand reduction in the Caribbean: agencies, strategies and programmes

Country	Executing agency for demand reduction, year of foundation	Annual council budget, $US	Master plan/ Integrated demand reduction strategy	Programmes
Antigua and Barbuda	1. National Drug Council (NDC), 1989 2. National Drug Information Centre, 1992	1. 2. 91,570	No master plan completed, no IDER	HFLE[a]
Bahamas	National Drug Council (NDC), 1985	100,000	Master plan is being formulated IDER in 7 communities	HFLE MIST[b] EAP[c]
Barbados	National Council on Substance Abuse (NCSA), 1995	500,000	National Strategic Plan for Drugs in 1996. Master plan is being formulated IDER in 6 communities	HFLE EAP
Belize	National Drug Abuse Council (NDACC), 1988	200,000 (2000)	National Anti-Drugs Strategy 1999–2004. Approved in 2000 IDER in 6 districts	HFLE
Guyana	National Anti-Narcotic Commission (NANCOM), 1997 National Coordinating Council for Drug Education and Rehabilitation (NACDER), 1992		Master plan 1997 – 2000 New one is being formulated IDER in 3 communities, coming to an end	
Jamaica	National Council on Drug Abuse (NCDA), 1983	675,000	National master plan, 1997 IDER and Community Drug Abuse Action Committees (CODACs) in 30 communities	HFLE
St Vincent	National Drugs Council, Formed 1998 – dormant			
Trinidad and Tobago	National Alcohol and Drug Abuse Prevention Programme (NADAPP), 1988	recurrent: 290,000 project: 5,000	Master plan 2001–4 formulated with help from CICAD IDER in 5 communities, coming to an end	HFLE DARE[d] MIST

Source: CARICOM Drug Demand Reduction Needs Assessment, 2002.
[a] Health and Family Life Education; [b] Military Information Support Teams; [c] Employee Assistance Programme; [d] Drug Abuse Resistance Education

prevention and education programmes (PRIDE, DARE, Youth–Parent Encounters) need to be adapted. A regional programme, developed at the University of the West Indies, has developed a life skills module called Health and Family Life Education (HFLE), which incorporates drugs education.

Regional structures

People working in the field now meet regularly to exchange information, devise policies and formulate responses on drug issues. The Inter-Governmental Task Force on Drugs and Crime is one regular event. A wide range of training events and strategy workshops has aimed to raise the skill base of professionals and practitioners.

Information

Over the past few years the Caribbean Drug Information Network (CARIDIN) has conducted school surveys in most countries. This provides a steady flow of data on drug use prevalence in some of the critical age groups. In addition there have been rapid assessments in most countries – establishing, principally, that there are vibrant local drug scenes.

Law enforcement

A series of training programmes since the early 1990s has considerably enhanced the capacity of law enforcement agencies to intercept trafficking shipments. The good working relationship between Caribbean and US law enforcement agencies highlighted by the Jamaican politician and academic Trevor Munroe (Munroe 2000) continues. The latest report by the US State Department Bureau for International Narcotics and Law Enforcement Affairs (2003) underlines this by stating that 'US law enforcement agencies note that cooperation with the [Government of Jamaica] is generally good and has improved over the past year.... US law enforcement agencies enjoy excellent cooperation from Government of Trinidad & Tobago law enforcement agencies.' It further notes that Dominica and Grenada have been 'extremely responsive to Mutual Legal Assistance Treaty requests'.

With this array of institutions in place and the flurry of ongoing activities, the region is far more confident in handling drug problems today than it was 20 years ago. But, far from being dispelled, the problems have only reconfigured into more complex professional and policy challenges. The body of knowledge that the work has generated, and the impact of the interventions, have set a new agenda for research and policy reform. One of the most pressing realizations in the late 1990s was that the emphasis on supply-side interventions, aimed particularly at deterring the throughflow of drugs, had done little to prevent the steady increase of drug use within

Caribbean countries. At the annual meeting of CCM in Barbados in 2000, Caribbean delegations pressed for the reallocation of resources to strengthen demand reduction. In the following year the Council on Human and Social Development listed drug demand reduction as a strategic priority in order to protect social capital, and submitted a number of key recommendations. At the next Heads of Government meeting in 2002, Caribbean leaders declared that drug control was a public health issue, thereby opening the drug control field for the first time to a large cast of stakeholders. Attempts at defining a regional strategy are being hampered by the lack of clarity over a number of issues. Most urgent, however, is the need for an overarching strategy beyond the elusive goal of a drug-free Caribbean.

What constitutes a drug offence and how should drug offenders be dealt with?

We discussed above how in the early 1990s drugs and drug trafficking were seen as a threat to the very viability of Caribbean states (Sanders 1990). The raft of measures listed above, including the legal provisions, the strengthening of law enforcement capability, the drug councils, prevention campaigns and treatment centres were defensive responses. They have been successful in the sense that alarm has given way to a sense of control over the situation. While the throughflow of drugs has not been curtailed, the states have asserted their single monopoly of force. This primary definitive characteristic of the state had come under challenge from two distinct directions. First, from beyond the region in the form of superior armed force, and, second, from within through the corrosion of institutions, law and order.

During the 1980s it was becoming apparent that Latin American drug trafficking groups[27] involved in transshipping cocaine through the Caribbean could outgun local law enforcement agencies, and buy off judges, thus posing a clear danger to the security capabilities of Caribbean mini and micro states. The terror campaign launched by traffickers known as the extraditables against the Colombian government provided a chilling example of how organized crime groups could match national security forces and bring the state to the brink of collapse. In the event, this first threat receded. In Jamaica and Trinidad the national defence forces, and in the Eastern Caribbean the Regional Security System were all reinforced throughout the 1990s. Foreign partners continue to provide material support and training, and to extend a security umbrella. British and Dutch naval vessels are stationed in the region, and the US Navy has access to Caribbean territorial waters since the signing of the so-called 'ship rider agreements'.

The second identified threat scenario was a potentially deteriorating internal situation of rising crime fuelled by a combination of fund-raising addicts, crazed users, and rival dealers fighting over turf. In countries as economically dependent on tourism and the hospitality business as the Eastern Caribbean, any intensification of street crime poses a real threat. Moreover, when gangs get too powerful for law enforcement agencies, military interventions are required. In Kingston the Jamaican Defence Force (JDF) has been called in regularly to quell uprisings in the inner cities since Operation Ardent in 1992. The JDF has not only successfully asserted the authority of the state, but also retained a high level of public confidence (Harriott 2000: note 7). But countries without such capacity are in the end dependent on international assistance. In St Kitts, the activities of local drug traffickers spiralled out of control in 1994. The local kingpin, Charles 'Little Nut' Miller, plagued the country with a wave of violence, culminating in a prison breakout and urban riot that could only be put down with the assistance of the Regional Security Service (Klein 2001).

Notwithstanding these severe challenges to the state and public safety, it is fair to say that the states of the Commonwealth Caribbean are withstanding the tide of drug-related criminality, and that the criminals remain under control. This analysis is not to be mistaken for complacency, but as a simple observation that drug-related criminal activities, while of concern, do not pose a monocausal threat. Indeed, there is no equivalence between security threats and drug trafficking, though drugs and the various forms of associated criminality are a contributory factor. The reductionist proposition that security issues could be resolved by more effective drug control is not merely illusory, however, but also counter-productive. While this seems at first glance to run counter to the argument proposed so far – that the alarm over drug-related security threats in the 1980s and early 1990s has abated – we believe that some of the defensive measures taken harbour the seeds of serious social unrest in the future. As with so many attempts at imposing rigorous control regimes on the use and distribution of drugs, the robust policy adopted in the Commonwealth Caribbean may ultimately jeopardize the very public safety that it was intended to safeguard.

At the heart of drug control lies a balance between individual rights and the demands of society. Laws arise from social custom to regulate the intercourse of individuals and groups. In the course of imperialism, however, the laws and customs of ruling groups were imposed upon conquered populations. In the most successful instances of imperial management, imperial rulers would adapt the pre-existing laws of the conquered people. The history of the people of the Caribbean, however, does not allow for a return to a pre-colonial situation. It is a hallmark of Creole culture that its values, mores, attributes and essential characteristics have emerged from mixing the different immigrant ingredients thrown into the melting pot. At independence, Commonwealth Caribbean countries therefore adopted the legal framework inherited from the colonial powers, including the international treaties to which Great Britain was a signatory.

Yet well into the nineteenth century, the societies of the Caribbean were marked by a rigid internal division, cultural heterogeneity and, most important perhaps, the absence of a social contract. This meant that the norms and values of the ruling class were not necessarily those of the vast mass of the population, and that the laws and rules established to protect social order were not internalized by that same majority, were furthermore irreconcilable with any notion of natural justice or absolute rights, and were therefore seriously short on legitimacy. While remarkable progress has been made, particularly in the latter part of the twentieth century, when most Commonwealth Caribbean countries came to form an arch of democracy in a hemisphere plagued by military coups and civil war, an undercurrent of opposition to the state and all official forms of authority remains just below the surface. Just as the plantocracy was haunted by fears of social uprising, the contemporary elite retains a sense of vulnerability. The rejection of Babylon, the disengagement with the state and the denial of its legitimacy by the large number of socially excluded remains a continuing challenge.

At this point governmental attitudes to drugs come to play a prominent role. There are several points of tension around drug control, all of which challenge the notion of legitimacy.

1   The issue of equality before the law: there are hundreds of drug offenders in Caribbean prisons, yet data from our fieldwork observations, as well as the prevalence statistics (Gayle *et al.* 2002; UNODC 2003; Stone 1990) suggest that this is a mere fraction of the actual offenders. This discrepancy between the volume of offences committed, and the response by the criminal justice system raises serious issues about the selective application of the law. As it is clear that the law is not applied with equal vigour, those individuals (and their families) who are caught in the clutches of the criminal justice system develop a sense of victimization.

2   The success of Pentecostal Christianity touched upon by Nanton (Chapter 5) allows us to explore a different dimension of the question of selectivity and equality before the law. The Pentecostal rejection of all drugs (habit forming, mind- and mood-altering substances) puts into question why cannabis and cocaine have been singled out, when the biggest killers, alcohol and tobacco, are officially endorsed and celebrated in advertisements. This argument is also used by supporters of cannabis legalization in pointing out the hypocrisy of the law.

3 The argument developed by Chevannes (Chapter 2) with regard to cultural practice takes up a quintessentially Jamaican position, where the prohibition of a popular practice, a source of pleasure that also has perceived medical, social and economic benefits, throws up questions about the purpose of the law, and questions of justice. Once again, this pits the state against the people and dangerously undermines the legitimacy of the government.

These arguments are not unique to Commonwealth Caribbean countries, but the substance of drug control debates the world over. Nor do illicit drugs form a discrete field. Indeed, the vigorous attempts at discouraging tobacco use gathering momentum in Western countries are partly informed by drug control campaigns. And the close relationship between alcohol prohibition and drug control has its roots in the nineteenth-century temperance movement (Jay 2000).

They are pertinent to the Commonwealth Caribbean because of intense popular demands for cannabis legalization, the particular response by governments to drug crime, and the implications for long-term security. It is important to remain aware of distinctions between different countries, and the widespread social acceptance of cannabis in Jamaica needs to be contrasted with a much lower level of tolerance in Barbados. Suffice to say that Rastafarianism has attracted a region-wide following, and that a wide spectrum of support for cannabis legalization can be found in most countries. One of the reasons surely lies in the heightened awareness and intense public discussion of drug issues, and distinctions between ganja and crack cocaine. By and large ganja use is not associated with crime, domestic violence, financial ruin, sex work and all the other social pathologies for which crack and alcohol are notorious. There is also the symbolic importance of ganja, marking an important aspect of Caribbean identity. In the main, however, the drug control measures that have been introduced since the 1980s were protective measures, to safeguard the integrity of the state and the well-being of the young. Yet, perversely, many of the interventions made in the process seem to jeopardize one as well as the other.

Before developing the argument on the unintended consequences of harsh drug law enforcement, we need to revisit the issue of organized crime groups. We have already discussed the role of Caribbean and particularly Rastafarian organizations in importing cannabis and cocaine to the US and distributing them within parts of the same country. We also referred to the breakdown of law and order in St Kitts as a result of the activities of Little Nut. But the vigorous responses in the region, the war on drugs in the US, and the government offensive in Colombia have dismantled the large cartels, albeit without diminishing the traffic. Instead smaller groups have stepped in, dealing in smaller quantities, or running shipments on the back of legitimate business. For risk takers willing to employ violence, becoming involved in the drug trade is not that difficult. The threat of violence can be met by building up a force, often recruited around neighbourhoods, political groupings, or other criminal activities. The lack of capital is once again partly neutralized by the enormous drop in purchasing price the closer one gets to the source. Trinidad and the islands in the Eastern Caribbean are particularly exposed.

According to a senior police source, cocaine trafficking is run by an army of freelancers operating out of the Orinoco delta, who can pick up cocaine at a few hundred dollars per kilo in Colombia to sell for up to US$5,000 in the islands. The risk is considerable. Without organizational backup there are no guarantees that contracts will be honoured. Indeed, the late Dole Chadee, Trinidad's most infamous trafficker, allegedly began his drug-running operation by killing the Venezuelan suppliers for their drugs. But the rewards are substantial, and with an easy supply, insatiable demand, and a scarcity of economic alternatives there is a surfeit of young men willing to jump at the chance.

Equally, in Trinidad, a large number of individuals and small organizations are happy to take the cocaine and pass it on. This seems to be the main function of Eastern Caribbean groups in the US at this point. They no longer have a significant role in US distribution, and mainly manage the transshipment of cocaine consignments. These structural changes now inform a different perception of the threat presented by the successors to the cartels. According to a senior police officer, 'drug trafficking is not organized, it is the most disorganized entrepreneurial endeavour you could imagine'.[28]

As always, it is difficult to generalize across the Caribbean region. Jamaican gangs have established notoriety for both the importing and the distribution of cocaine in the UK. The large number of drug couriers arrested at UK airports from flights coming in from Jamaica has prompted several measures, including the introduction of ionscan machines at Kingston and Montego Bay airports in June 2002.[29] In the UK press, attention has focused on the high number of Jamaican cocaine couriers, the involvement of yardies in crack cocaine distribution, and the high profile of associated crime. It is important that both charges be brought into perspective. First, the volume of the traffic may be high in terms of operatives, many of them women. Yet there are serious limits to what any individuals, known in customs parlance as stuffers and swallowers, can conceal in their bodily orifices. The total volume of each courier is measured at best in hundreds of grams, which needs to be compared to the tens and even hundreds of kilograms that are regularly being trucked in from Spain and Holland by the main trafficking groups.

According to press and police, competition over the distribution of crack cocaine has caused a string of killings across the UK. There is serious concern among the public at large and the Afro-Caribbean community in particular over the ready use of extreme violence and the availability of firearms. The presence of professional yardie criminals who often arrive from Jamaica bearing false passports seems to have lowered the threshold of violence. Yet these two circumstance seem to confirm the theory advanced in an earlier analysis of the Brixton drug markets – that the ready recourse to violence and the high profile of outsiders points to a marginal activity rather than a pivotal role in the drug trade. Professional criminals seek to avoid police attention, which any shooting with fatalities is guaranteed to attract (Zaitch 2002; Ruggiero 1993; Ruggiero and South 1995).

While the evidence base remains insubstantial, we work on the hypothesis that the proliferation of crack-related violence is a symptom of marginality rather than of significance in the trade. In spite of efforts to open up new markets, Afro-Caribbean cocaine dealers in the diaspora are largely confined to their communities. This means that involvement in the illegal drug trade, far from offering an economic quick fix for a disadvantaged community, is simply an extra burden. For new immigrants and disadvantaged minorities, the criminal economy may provide ease of entry, but structural obstacles not so dissimilar to those found in the mainstream, formal and licit economy hamper expansion and upward movement.

These developments in the Caribbean trafficking scene are corroborated by the new understanding of the structure of organized crime in Europe. The image of hierarchical, tightly managed mafia-type organizations akin to *bona fide* businesses is giving way to the idea of loose networks of criminal specialists coming together for particular operations. This explains why policing interventions have no impact on the drug market except in the short term, as small-scale operators are readily replaced. Thus the key professionals and big operators – with connections into the corrupt end of law enforcement, politics and the judiciary – are only one element in the ready reproduction and multiplication of criminals. The most important element is the criminal scene, a ready pool of men and women willing to be employed in a criminal enterprise. Drug policy in the Commonwealth Caribbean, far from combating and containing this milieu, is designed to fertilize and encourage it. We would argue that no policy seems as ideally designed for the long-term generation of crime and the embedding of criminal lifestyles as the criminalization of drug use and petty drug production and distribution.

Criminalization of petty drug users and long-term security

The first issue for consideration lies in the sense of equality before the law. Even law enforcement agents are struck by such glaring discrepancies as those reported by the UK Drug Liaison Officer at the 2000 meeting on drugs and crime in Antigua: a St Lucia trafficker with 20 kg of cocaine was fined EC$20,000 and an Antiguan trafficker with 6 kg was sentenced to 21 days of hard labour, while ordinary citizens smoking a spliff regularly get locked up for three months.

Such latitude in the application of the law can deliver short-term benefits, of course, as in the case of one cocaine bust reported by a senior police officer from one of the UK Overseas Territories:

> We got the boat with several kilos of cocaine, arrested the crew and confiscated the vessels. They posted US$6 million bail and we informed the DEA who took the drugs. Next day the Colombians had gone, and the bail money was forfeited. Everybody was happy, the government kept the money, the Americans had the drugs and we kept the boats.[30]

Happy too are the traffickers, who, having made a getaway, can write off their losses and try again.

In some respects, then, drug money in the form of bail bonds and fines does provide cash injections into the exchequer. But the price, in terms of social unrest and a perception of injustice, is incalculable. Part of the problem lies in the application of model laws developed by the UN agencies. In Guyana one minister admitted that the legislation adopted wholesale from Vienna in the 1980s, including mandatory sentencing for cannabis consumption, was too draconian, allowing corrupt police officers to shelter behind narcotics legislation and frame innocent people. Once the allegation was made, the accused was denied bail and incarcerated on remand for up to two years before the case could even come up.[31] Under combined pressure from the Guyana Bar Association, the Prison Service and former president Janet Jagan, this law has since been amended and lighter penalties introduced.

There is a body of opinion that holds this dual system to be part of a wider social policy. A respected Rastafarian scholar in Barbados describes the use of marijuana as a safety valve for the Caribbean poor, as the 'herb is an orgasmic alternative'. But it is deliberately kept illegal, so the 'shadow of crime is kept over drugs by the politicians so that they can control the poor'.[32] According to this analysis, the punitive model employed in drug policy is motivated by a hidden agenda of social control, rather than the laudable objectives of public health. Since this proposition cannot be tested, we should focus instead on the efficacy of the punitive model in deterring crime and upholding public safety.

A recent study of Caribbean justice systems by the Inter-American Development Bank raises some of these concerns. The purpose of the criminal justice system is introduced and evaluated:

> First it deters wrongful conduct by providing safety and protection against crimes for persons or their wealth. Increasingly it is no longer true that 'crime does not

pay'. A growing minority of individuals perceives that the risk of getting caught and punished for some illegal activities is smaller than the economic gains to be had. Thus, institutions and organizations that previously served to deter crime are no longer able to do so. An increase in applications of the same types of policing activity, methods of adjudication and punishment may not directly counteract the rise of the newly profitable crimes but instead only serve to apprehend and imprison more of the relatively petty criminals.[33]

In terms of drug policy this means that an intensification of anti-drug efforts ensures that particular forms of conduct are punished with increasing severity, without either achieving a significant reduction in that conduct, or addressing the underlying reasons for it.

The punitive model: instrument of drug control or manufacture of criminality?

The majority of drug offenders who come into contact with the criminal justice system (CJS) have committed minor marijuana offences. This raises the second important issue: how criminalization turns wayward drug users into criminals. The large-scale incarceration of ganja users is in itself already a major departure from the original road map. When the savants of the West India Commission or statesmen like Michael Manley uttered their prophetic warnings in the late 1980s and early 1990s, their concern was over the might of high-powered cocaine-trafficking organizations with tentacles across the globe. But now time and resources of the police, courts and the prison system are taken up by local boys caught on street corners with a spliff.

The net outcome of extending the region's severe 'punitive model' (see Chapter 4; Platzer and Mirella 2002) to drug control has been to set the prison population on an upward spiral. But according to the IADB study, 'the Caribbean Justice sector is not structured to rehabilitate the imprisoned to a more productive post-jail life in society'.[34] Caribbean officers elaborate on the origin of some of these problems. In Trinidad

> we have problems concerning the prison system achieving its objectives – which is to reduce crime. The judiciary is ill informed about what the prison services are doing, as magistrates and judges rarely visit the prison. The other sectors of the CJS, like the police, have a high profile and receive the resource allocations – but if the penal system fails, the CJS fails.

Other problems include the inconsistency of sentencing and the lack of treatment facilities. 'If you're sentencing people for drug offences you need treatment programmes.'[35]

These views are echoed by a colleague in Guyana, 'Prison is not the right place for drug offenders; we need rehab and probation service.' Moreover, the prisons are being filled with alleged drug offenders who are often people arrested for loitering and charged with drug offences. Instead of being delayed for a year until the case comes up, they plead guilty.[36]

The UK experience suggests that, unless treatment is provided, 'problem drug users will on release simply resume both their drug using and their criminal careers where they left off' (Hough 1996). Even more disturbing is some of the evidence regarding drug use in prison. The supply in Guyana's prisons is provided by a variety of sources, including prison officers and the practice of 'vaulting' by prisoners returning from labour or leave. Most dramatic perhaps are the regular supplies thrown over the prison wall, varying from tennis balls to a large sack with 6 kg of cannabis.

Prison, then, is not an effective way of weaning problem users from their drug habit. What does it do, however, for their attitudes towards crime? The report goes on to argue that, with the average age of prisoners being 25, there is a large number of juveniles and young men moving through the system. No special provisions are made for them. Young offenders, minor offenders and preventive prisoners are kept together with serious repeat offenders. It points out that 'such mixing fosters a more hardened criminal out of the youth and minor offenders' (IDB 2000: 91).

Many young men do get caught up in the CJS after becoming involved with the drug economy, largely because of the lack of alternative opportunities. Once sentenced they enter prison as users and petty dealers, only to emerge as hardened criminals – alienated from society, embittered and dehumanized by the experience, with a new set of practical skills and attitudes learnt from their fellow inmates. Most importantly, perhaps, they emerge with a network of criminal contacts. While the information base on the prison culture needs to be built up, there are suggestions that prison provides a place of recruitment into gangs and acts as a place where debts are built up that need to be paid off upon release, often in the form of participating in criminal activities.

Mainstream society, by contrast, points towards the criminal record and turns its back on the jailbird. Given the tight job market in all Caribbean countries a spell in prison as good as ends a young man's hopes of finding licit employment. According to the proponents of labelling theory, the stigma of prison alienates the individual from conventional society and promotes contacts with deviant referent groups (Braithwaite 1989). Few islands have systems in place to give ritual expression to the need for forgiveness and reintegration. Only in the Caymans have prison staff reported that inmates are welcomed back by their families with large parties held to celebrate their return.[37]

The end result, then, is that men (and increasingly women) on the margin of society who engage in drugs as a leisure pastime or an economic coping strategy are penalized by a criminal justice system ostensibly operating for the protection of society. The offenders enter the system on drug charges and emerge as criminals, who are likely and willing to engage in all manner of other crime. In a sense then, the punitive approach to drug control manufactures criminality. What is disturbing is that in the public perception the re-offender is characterized as a drug-addicted criminal. The criminal behaviour is exemplified by the drug use, which in turn goes to explain the criminal behaviour. The argument has not only become circular, but also provides a ready diversion from the underlying issue of wealth creation, income opportunities and social equity. Crime is not analysed as a consequence of social injustice, but as a pharmacologically induced aberration. The secret of a safer society then lies in more effective supply reduction, not social reform.

Wendy Singh in Chapter 4 gives us a sense of the magnitude of this trend. In most jurisdictions the drug offenders make up the largest single cohort of prisoners: Belize 58 per cent (1998), Grenada 21.6 per cent (1995), Guyana 23.6 per cent (1997) and Trinidad & Tobago 31 per cent (1998). The figures are already dated, but as the trend has been constant, we assume that the current situation is even starker. In the main they are picked up for marijuana-related offences, usually possession or petty dealing. As marijuana use is becoming normal behaviour among large sections of the population, there has been a sharp rise in arrests, trials and convictions, with the result that the courts are clogged up and the prison system over-populated – excluding Suriname, prisons across the region are over-populated by an average of 200 per cent of their official capacity.

The US experience provides a salutary reminder as to where this trend can lead. According to statistics from the US Bureau of Justice, 57.6 per cent of the 130,000 prisoners in federal gaols are drug offenders, of whom 46 per cent are first-time offenders (US Bureau of Justice). The figure for the 1,206,400 prisoners held in state prisons is 21 per cent. This population is constantly being replenished by an arrest rate – by the FBI alone – of 1,579,566. Of these, 41 per cent are arrested for marijuana possession. Given that 66 per cent of drug offenders are rearrested within 3 years – but only 41 per cent on another drug charge (according to the FBI) – the gulag fuels its own growth. The most frightening calculations refer to the future. 'Thanks to the world's toughest incarceration policy, 11.3 per cent of boys born in 2001 will go to jail in their lifetime. For black men it will be one in three' (*The Economist* 2003).

If we then consider the impact of imprisonment on the individual offender – the crime manufacturing process of the prison experience – in the context of the sharp rise in incarcerations, we realize that the drug control policy that evolved during the 1990s contains a time bomb. There are also reservations about the inequity of meting out harsh punishments to petty offenders 'while large-scale traffickers walk away scot-free'.

However pressing the fiscal needs of the state, and however worthy the programmes and policies engendered by government, the signal set by a two-tier justice system is utterly corrosive of the social compact holding Caribbean societies together. There is already widespread opposition to the prohibition of marijuana in all the islands. The fear of crime and the middle-class values of respectability, sobriety and order provide the main pillar of support at present. It is unlikely that the argument can hold out indefinitely against the evident hypocrisy of serving hard justice on the poor, while allowing the rich impunity.

The call for the legalization of marijuana, made with different degrees of vociferousness in Jamaica, Antigua, and St Vincent, is already part of a wider social protest movement. Marijuana is in the process of becoming a contested symbol of social protest, cultural identity and the assertion of religious and civil rights. If this claim for indigenous self-determination is merged with an agenda for social justice, fuelled by the obvious mis-carriages discussed above, it will result in the serious polarization of society.

Unfortunately, the current trend is oblivious to the inherent dangers. Drug policies remain repressive, and the criminal justice sector punitive. There is some recognition of the need for a policy shift, but the pace of reform is wanting. Alternatives to custodial punishment, in the words of the head of the Jamaican national drug council, 'are up and crawling'. Introduced in the Bahamas, Jamaica and Trinidad, drug courts provide an alternative to imprisonment for non-violent drug offenders. The idea was born in Florida in 1989, a state that 'excelled' in the punitive model of drug control, and has since been adopted in different countries. Effectively, it is a sentencing to treatment. Decried in some quarters, on the assumption that the voluntary commitment of the client is a prime condition for successful treatment, it is held up by supporters of tough drug policies as a humane alternative to incarceration.

While there is a danger of confusing punishment with treatment, the move away from a purely punitive approach is surely a step in the right direction. But there is an urgent need for clarity over the true purpose of particular interventions, and over the actual social problems that are being tackled. Regarding the drugs/crime nexus, a Trinidadian officer commented: 'Drug abusers do crime to sustain the habit but on a minor scale. As for the crime wave attributed to them, there is no reality in this.' Other social ills are the main causes, including unemployment, disparity in income and poor education. Yet the press always latches on to drugs whenever there is violence in the towns. Hence while drugs may form part of a lifestyle that includes crime and even violence, the actual causal relationship is not clear. A recent case of gang violence, which the press had reported as a fight for turf between rival drug distributors, was in fact fought to control the employment relief programme.[38]

Drugs, then, provide a ready scapegoat for all manner of social pathologies, at the risk of diverting the attention of policy makers and academics. As the eminent Colombian economist Francisco Thoumi has argued, the Colombian crisis is not the result of drug trafficking and production: Colombia faces a crisis of state, civil society and the depletion of social capital. The drug economy is an expression of these weaknesses, and then becomes an aggravating factor – the danger being that, if the underlying causes are allowed to deteriorate, the drugs nexus becomes a powerful and independent set of factors with its own dynamic. Drug control policies follow a similar trajectory, particularly if they emphasize repression without understanding the root causes of the illegal drugs industry.[39]

Drugs as a development issue

The relationship between drugs, the informal economy and crime

The rise of the drug economy in the 1970s and 1980s was interwoven with the economic difficulties of Caribbean economies. Following independence, most Commonwealth Caribbean countries had identified the state as the motor for development in all spheres. Their populations, empowered by democratic systems which have survived in most countries to this day, had placed great expectations of their economic advancement and the provision of welfare services on the governments of the day. When states were unable to match these as the economic slowdown of the 1970s was followed by the structural adjustment process of the 1980s, the result was not only an economic crisis but also a crisis of political legitimacy. Emigration provided one solution for individuals and families, but the economy at large bore the costs arising from the skill gap occasioned by their departure. Openings in the private sector were limited. Moreover, the structural conditions prevailing in most countries constrained the chances of diversification.[40]

The instruments employed to offset these disadvantages proved vulnerable to global political events unfolding during the 1990s. The trend towards trade liberalization championed by the World Trade Organization would lead to the abolition of the 'banana regime' that had allowed Caribbean farmers privileged access to the lucrative European Union market. Without the benefits of high tariff walls to keep out South American bananas, Caribbean producers were uncompetitive and overpriced.

At the same time international development assistance budgets were being reallocated towards former communist countries in transition. For the rest of the world the main principle was poverty eradication.[41] As a middle-income region with staunchly Western credentials,[42] the Commonwealth Caribbean was suddenly losing out on both counts. Even the most resilient sector of the economy, tourism, was beginning to suffer from competing Asian destinations.

In the face of state decline, the inadequacies of the private sector and a hostile external environment, a growing number of economically active people resorted to the informal sector. This in itself is not a surprising development, but in the region, the 'informalization' of labour presented a challenge to the political order. In the newly independent countries of the Commonwealth Caribbean the legitimacy of the state and the stability of the government were tied up with the ability to provide economic and social benefits. Budget cuts and reduction of services were not mere inconveniences but an existential threat to many citizens, and subsequently to the government and even the state itself.

In the Caribbean the illicit drug economy is therefore of both political and economic significance. For rural cannabis growers, transporters, packers and urban distributors it provides a livelihood; for larger players and traffickers it is even a means for the accumulation of capital. Illicit and clandestine, the drug economy carved out a sphere that is not only outside the regulation of the state, but actually challenged the assertion of the state as the principle generator of economic development. The expanding drug economy was seen as a threat to the political order and a disavowal of the claims of the state itself.

It is probably fair to say that across the Commonwealth Caribbean the conception of the state has shifted from the state-centric development model towards a leaner and lighter model in line with the neoliberal prescriptions of the structural adjustment process. This allows it more readily to accommodate an under-regulated informal sector. On the other hand, the already discussed strengthening of the law enforcement agencies in direct response to the drugs threat has left a leaner and meaner state better equipped to tackle any external challenges head on. This model, however, does carry the risk of incurring a legitimacy deficit and resource overstretch if unaccompanied by a comprehensive development strategy focusing on livelihoods. The transformation of state functions from welfare provider to the maintenance of law and order can only be sustained if livelihood alternatives are provided. Where this is not the case, states may become police states, and/or suffer the collapse of authority in some regions, an ominous precursor of future failure. Drug control policy aimed at curbing one of the principal means of informal sector income needs to combine repressive interventions with positive development efforts.

Rural and urban development

The island economies of the Caribbean are pushing against natural resource boundaries, particularly land. The scope for achieving higher profit margins through aggressive cost reduction is limited, particularly because of the distortion of international markets for agricultural products.[43]

The classic response is for farmers to shift to new, higher-value products, such as cannabis. Indeed, when faced by such structural obstacles farmers may find that trespassing the boundary of the law may be the only viable form of continued activity. Indeed, formal prohibition may be a precondition for a flourishing ganja industry in the Caribbean islands. Any changes to its legal status would open the door for economies of scale in rivalling producer countries, and even see Jamaica's domestic crop supplanted by imports.

Be that as it may, there are a number of conditions in the current situation that inhibit the development of legal alternatives, and lock ganja farmers and traders into illegal activities. These include the insecurity of property rights, the weakness of institutions, and the inadequacy of financial systems for capturing agricultural savings. Farmers in developing countries everywhere have to contend with these problems (Ashley and Maxwell 2001), but in the Caribbean, circumstances are exacerbated by drug control policies. Crop eradication and property rights are difficult to reconcile, and money-laundering measures put into place to discourage international cocaine dealers are preventing small-scale ganja farmers from accumulating savings. This not only produces a cash economy, with resultant binge buying and instability, but also prohibits the emergence of an exit option for ganja cultivators.

Aggressive eradication of ganja cultivation alone will not succeed in curtailing production in the long term. Temporary market droughts will only stimulate production elsewhere, and drive existing clusters of ganja farmers further into common land. In ecological terms the 'tragedy of the commons' (Hardin 1968) is plain to see in the destruction of St Vincent's remaining rain forest (see Chapter 11). An imaginative rural development approach needs to be taken to foster both farming and non-farming incomes in such areas as tourism, services and small-scale industry.

The most difficult challenge for a development-oriented drug control policy comes from the urban areas, where involvement in the drug trade provides an income source for a wide range of operators. It is helpful to consider the leading precepts of contemporary development thinking, as summarized by Ellis and Biggs (2001): sustainable livelihoods, good governance, decentralization, critique of participation,[44] sector-wide approaches, social protection and poverty eradication.

Pride of place goes to 'sustainable livelihoods', the idea that development interventions should enable individuals and households to gain a livelihood over time, without depleting the resource base. This is highly pertinent for the drug economy. While the implicit assumption is that the resource in question is a natural resource, it translates well into human and social resources. The impact of drug use itself degrades the human resource, and in the case of crack cocaine with frightening celerity. As consumers become impoverished as a consequence of addiction and incapacitation, incomes can only be sustained through expanding the market. Due to the legal status, this will attract the attention of both law enforcement and rival operators, and runs the risk of violence. Moreover, the condition of the client base, or at least a part of it, becomes a social liability. Communities suffer from the depredations of crack users: the crime committed in its acquisition, and anti-social behaviour. They often organize themselves, or turn to law enforcement agencies to eliminate cocaine distributors.

The same argument cannot be made with regard to ganja. There are no reported incidents of ganja-triggered acquisition crime or sex work. In Jamaica, but also in parts of the Eastern Caribbean, distribution is self-regulated and informally organized. While consumption may still have adverse health and economic consequences, these are contained and no worse than those occasioned by the use of licit substances such as alcohol.

Involvement in both ganja and cocaine, however, runs the risk of arrest, the confiscation of trade goods, forfeiture of assets, and incarceration. It is difficult to speak of sustainability against such conditions, but the region abounds with ganja operators at every level from production to retail who have been in business for a very long time. The key issue is the underlying demand for drugs, which remains dynamic and diverse, thus fulfilling key criteria for sustainability.

The main variable affecting the sustainability of the ganja economy is police activity, which leads the discussion to the next principle of development – good governance. In a way, the entire discussion surrounding the direction of drug control pertains to governance: the choice between a hard line 'war on drugs', or modified responses in accordance with local practice, as argued by Chevannes in Chapter 2. Questions of equality before the law, the integrity of the criminal justice system and discrepancies between legislative intent and enforcement practice, discussed above, all enter the equation. It is merely important to reiterate that good governance, the functioning of institutions, the rule of law, and the alignment of law and social norms are prerequisites for development.

While it is difficult to speak of the drug economy as a sector *per se*, it is important that interventions are assessed and evaluated for their impact. Interdiction efforts in particular tend to concentrate on strictly tactical objectives – the seizure of drug consignments, the arrest of traffickers, the dismantling of criminal organizations – without paying heed to impact and consequences. Too often celebrated operations have little impact on either availability or mid-term prices, as new players simply fill the void. There is no systematic information about the importance of drug incomes for household economies. Anecdotal information suggests that the arrest of a breadwinner or contributor to domestic expenditure often leaves bereft dependents who then have to turn to criminal activities themselves.

Drug control must devise a strategy on income that avoids locking successive generations of urban poor into criminal activity. It must also consider how to target interventions so as reduce the most adverse effects of deprivation on the drug users and petty dealers themselves, as well as on social goods. The development principles of poverty eradication and social protection are well demonstrated by the St Lucia outreach service (see Chapter 7) that provides basic necessities for street people using crack cocaine – food and water. This not only improves their physical well-being, but also reduces vandalism and social disorder as the water they need for washing cars can be obtained from the project standpipe.

Outreach work at the lowest level of the drug economy may have little impact on drug availability or market configuration, but it can significantly enhance the quality of life of the affected individuals and communities. A project worker at a Trinidad drop-in centre generated income opportunities by plugging into the subterranean economy of the centre. He began to sell fruit juice and show videos on Saturday nights. The income was then used for micro-credits, with an interest rate of 25 per cent. The scheme was so successful he put the local loan shark (who had been charging 200–500 per cent interest) out of business. But it also reduced the need for begging, petty crime and public nuisance.[45]

Working at community level for the protection of public goods, such as freedom from crime, reduction in vandalism and begging, are approaches that are not resource-intense but promise immediate benefits. The process can be enhanced through the distinction between crack and ganja markets, the deliberate targeting of distribution networks that recruit school children, and of course the policing of the export trade. It is beyond question that the room for manoeuvre Caribbean countries have in their drug policies depends entirely on cooperation with their overseas partners in reducing the out- and throughflow of cocaine, and to a lesser degree of ganja. If these partners perceive a trafficking threat, or even a lack of cooperation from the governments and agency counterparts, retribution can be swift and severe: cuts in assistance transfers, loss of trading privileges, indirect export penalties, withdrawal of loan facilities. A hard line on drug exports remains a non-negotiable development condition. A differentiated approach to the domestic management of drug control is, however, a negotiable *quid pro quo* that should allow for creative thinking at ground level.

The contributors to this book take different positions on how such responses should be calibrated. While Chevannes and Klein suggest an easing of the most aggressive interdiction efforts, UNODC warns of the disincentive effect of the drug economy. Indeed, the rise of the don as a role model in urban Jamaica is a troubling indication of how ingrained the illicit drug trade has become. It is even more disturbing in that the social polarization on the issue poses an egregious threat to social capital in terms of community cohesion, trust, and common norms and values. At the same time drug-related economic activity will be driven by market demands, both within the region and beyond, and it is no good wishing it away. The key issue is identifying what, given the paucity of resources, is achievable and what can and should be prioritized.

Who are the problem drug users and how are they to be reached and treated?

When in 1956 Michael Beaubrun used the Jellinek formula to estimate the Trinidad alcoholics population at 25,000, 'much medical scepticism was expressed' (Beaubrun 1967: 644). Within the same year the first 20-bed treatment facility was opened on the grounds of the mental hospital and 332 clients admitted for treatment. To this day alcohol remains the number one problem substance, causing the greatest amount of suffering in the form of car crashes, domestic violence and a host of medical conditions. But apparently it remains 'so much a part of our way of life in the Caribbean that it would be a mistake to reduce consumption by too drastic a programme of legal measures' (Beaubrun 1983: 223). A further argument for not tinkering with the legal status of alcohol is made later on: the law makers themselves enjoy it. Still, the fact that every Caribbean country now provides alcohol detoxification services and can boast an Alcoholics Anonymous (AA) group is significant. There has been a major shift in the perception of alcohol and a recognition of the associated risks.

The provision of medical and social services for substance-induced problems therefore depends to a large extent on the framing of the problem. The idea that alcoholism was an illness was first introduced in the early nineteenth century, when the habits of alcoholics were likened to 'other mental derangements'. With the birth of the AA in 1935, the disease concept was revived as a therapeutic strategy. Previous attempts to shame the alcoholic by defining the condition as a sin or crime had failed, while the idea of a medical condition raised self-esteem and aided motivation (Beaubrun 1981: 2). This approach has succeeded in allocating responsibility for problem alcohol users to the medical professions. The law enforcement agencies only come in when the alcohol user commits an offence, sparing families the drama of arrest and society the costs of prosecution.

The treatment of cannabis and cocaine users, by contrast, has been defined predominantly as a criminal justice issue. Users are first and foremost criminals, and more likely to encounter a police officer than a doctor. Yet most Commonwealth Caribbean countries are making some effort towards the 'balanced approach' adopted officially by the international community in 1998.[46] This includes a duty of care for the drug user, and the provision of treatment services to enable him or her to break the habit. Indeed, the provision of treatment is crucial to drug control policy in two regards. It proves the underlying compassion of government policy, allowing harsh prohibitionist policies to be presented as tough love. And it establishes the concept of addiction, a crucial argument for the justification of prohibition. For if the substances in question did not cause addiction, it would seriously compromise the rationale of their being controlled in the first place.

Addiction is understood as loss of control over substance use signalled by a predictable change in behaviour pattern (Edwards and Gross 1976; McMurran 1994). Although it is relatively uncontroversial to describe, the explanation of its causes remains riven by controversy.[47] According to some interpretations, the alcoholic suffers from a 'biological or psychological abnormality that was either present in their constitution or triggered by use' (McMurran 1994: 22). In the authoritative reference books, terms like 'sociopathic personality disturbance' (*Statistical Manual for Mental Disorders II*, 1968), or 'disorders of character, behaviour and intelligence' (WHO's *International Classification of Diseases (ICD)*, 8, 1974) show how 'behaviours that may be a threat to society have been pathologized'. Regardless of the claims to scientific objectivity, the classificatory underpinnings of treatment take us to an arena 'where the moral and the disease models meet' (McMurran 1994: 20). The *ICD* (9, 1978) lists three separate disorders under 'neuroses, personality disorders and other non-psychotic mental disorders' – alcohol dependence, drug dependence and non-dependent abuse of drugs. By ruling out non-pathological drug use – be it for recreation, experiment, self-medication or in pursuit of pleasure – the medical profession has left the final decision as to the mental state of drug users in the hands of law makers.

Interestingly, many problem users have welcomed the addiction model. It enables them to explain their anti-social behaviour in terms of a quasi-medical condition. In some cases, the stigma has even been inverted into an achievement and a job qualification, as Gough shows in Chapter 6. The theoretical difficulties with the concept have to be balanced against the therapeutic benefits. As Beaubrun explains, 'There is a world of difference between therapeutic and research orientations in this respect. The therapist knows that the semantic distinction between addiction and disease can make all the difference to his patient's sobriety. It is the distinction between a criminal and a sick person' (Beaubrun 1967: 654).

The difficulties do not end here, as the outcome of residential detoxification and treatment is often disappointing. Many addicts drop out of treatment, and among those who do complete, lapse and relapse rates are high. Treatment professionals are therefore redefining their objectives. Instead of looking for a return to abstinence, they now look for reductions in overall drug use, the use of street drugs, risk behaviour and exposure to infectious diseases and crime. And to this end treatment is highly successful, and far more cost-effective than criminal justice interventions (NTORS).[48] There are other benefits, with workers in low-threshold facilities often arguing that just admitting a client to the centre will improve physical health, emotional stability, and social well being.[49] Some of the programme objectives of the St Lucia drop-in centre were no different to those of other charities working with the destitute: to provide food, shelter, perhaps medical care, with no conditions attached (see Chapter 7). But to succeed in stabilizing the client, and helping him/her on the road to abstinence, motivation is crucial. Here the definition of the issue and the deployment of words and labels play an important role.

In this way society certainly plays a role in making recovery possible – although not without resources upfront and a general shift in orientation. With CARICOM heads of government now committed to a public health approach to drugs, the time is right to adopt the disease model as the foremost definition of drug dependence. Needless to say, the actual provision of treatment service still lags behind the robust efforts made at supply reduction.[50] And even within demand reduction, field treatment, or tertiary demand reduction, has had to compete with primary prevention activities, and particularly 'public awareness raising campaigns', which are far easier to organize.

Patricia House, the first residential drug abuse treatment centre in Jamaica, was founded in 1986 when school and household surveys indicated a significant level of crack use. It now deals almost entirely with crack users. Many countries now have a dedicated establishment, such as Verdun House in Barbados, Crossroads in Antigua, Pitparo and New Life Ministry in Trinidad, and Sandilands in the Bahamas. They provide residential rehabilitation, with detoxification, counselling and preparation for reintegration into society.

Such treatment is costly, and most of the centres are plagued by financial problems. The director of Patricia House reported having to assist his best counsellor in finding alternative employment because he was unable to pay him. Such resource constraints are chronic across the region, with the evaluator of the Trinidadian treatment system reporting that centres are impoverished and staff in need of training (Brathwaite 1998). In response, some organizations have had to be imaginative, obtaining funding from the private sector, as Verdun House did in Barbados, or using the high fees charged to overseas clients to subsidize a number of places for local clients, as Crossroads did in Antigua.

Material problems are relatively straightforward compared to the difficulties in identifying treatment models. Addiction studies and the disease model were developed in the alcohol field and could not be transferred easily because alcohol is not classified as a drug, and cocaine and ganja are illegal. Caribbean professionals often draw on external treatment models and travel to North America and Europe for work experience and training. This has been a fruitful exchange for all parties, and the 14-step model developed by Sandilands in the Bahamas is proof of adaptation to local need. Yet until recently drug treatment in North America and Europe was primarily designed for heroin users, with a very different trajectory of use to crack cocaine.

One of the key problems is binge use. One client in the Bahamas recorded a five-day session, with little food, sleep or hydration. 'After a cocaine binge … the addict experiences a state of anhedonia. The dopamine stored in the pleasure centres of the brain is depleted … causing the receptors of nerve cells to become supersensitive, producing a craving' (Allen 1987; David 1987). Crack sessions can degenerate into potlatch-like spectacles of wealth destruction, as users light rock after fleeting, pleasure-inducing rock to 'chase after the first high'. Opiate injectors face no such problem. Heroin, morphine and opium are central nervous system depressants that send the user to sleep. Overdoses arise from adulterants, faulty administration and unintentionally high dosages. They are due to failures of information about purity and personal tolerance, rather than pursuit of continuous intoxication.

The addiction complex and its correlative treatment profile are distinct. Crack cocaine exerts a psychological hold over the user, but presents no physical addiction in the sense of withdrawal symptoms. There is no physical discomfort as reported for both opiate and alcohol treatment. Consequently, there is no substitute drug like methadone to ease the discomfort and restore a sense of well-being. For opiate dependants in recovery, the substitute can provide an object for a new fixation, allowing for the addiction to be transferred to a less harmful substance and a controlled process. While it does not lead to overcoming the addiction, far less to abstinence, it does enable the recovering addict to become stable and begin the process of reintegration.

It is becoming evident that recovering crack cocaine addicts need to be engaged in meaningful activities to build up a life outside the drug scene, and to enjoy pleasures other than intoxication. Relapse avoidance is not always easy, as small suggestive experiences, often at subconscious or subliminal level, can trigger a relapse. Treatment centres are therefore increasingly concerned to maintain contact with their clients after the residential episode has been completed. This may even be seen as the first stage in the recovery process. Working with the community to ensure the integration of recovering addicts and a corresponding reduction in relapse risks has moved treatment from the medical to the social field. It has also fused primary, secondary and tertiary preventions, as community activities aimed at reducing the space and the opportunity for drug use within the communities affect experimental and dependent users alike.

Such approaches have been pioneered in Jamaica with the formation of neighbourhood-based Community Development Action Committees in the 1980s. The strategy was based on the assumption that drug problems were the symptom of deeper underlying social problems that need to be identified and addressed in the community (UNDCP 2001). Realizing that drugs become a problem where institutions are weak, social structure eroded, and services poor, they tried to galvanize communities into self-help. The model has since been rolled out to the Bahamas, Barbados, and Trinidad & Tobago, among others. The idea of community action has also been adopted by organizations working with vulnerable young people like Addiction Alert in Jamaica, which is training and supporting young people in setting up youth projects within local areas of Kingston.

The holistic analysis that makes community approaches so promising is also their greatest operational weakness. Empowering communities, encouraging participation and mobilizing endogenous resources, building local institutions and promoting social capital is the stuff of social development proper. Drug councils and the other agents of drug policy have neither the remit nor the resources to carry this through effectively. Project coverage is therefore bound to be patchy, leaving some of the risk groups to fall through the net.

But the community development approach also provides the analytical basis for targeted medical interventions. Given that problematic drug use is a symptom of wider social malaise, the most vulnerable clients are most likely to be involved in a range of anti-social behaviours and to congregate in deprived and marginal neighbourhoods. Instead of waiting for these clients to approach the services, the services have to go after them. This is the classical definition of outreach work, based on the assumption that drug users form 'hidden populations' and that contacting such 'hard-to-reach' users is a productive starting point (EMCDDA 1999).

The Commonwealth Caribbean country with the most extensive experience of working with such hard-to-reach clients is Trinidad. It is the only country, for example, to provide a residential treatment service dedicated exclusively to women problem users (Serenity Place). There are several treatment centres providing different services, including a Daytop model at Pitparo, and a therapeutic community at Chagaramus.[51] There are high-threshold residential centres and casual drop-in facilities, plus outreach services with street workers. This comprehensive service has developed in response to the challenges of a vibrant street culture. A network of shelters has been set up, including the Court Shamrock Centre, and the Centre for Socially Displaced People (CSDP). The latter is a monument to both the spirit of innovation and the magnitude of the problems encountered. Established in a disused multi-storey car park, the centre provides shelter to a maximum of 200 homeless people. New arrivals start at the lower levels and work their way up to the top. Permanent staff provide security and basic assessment, and regular visits by doctors and nursing staff lay on some medical care. The purpose of the project is to get people back into society, and here the centre is facing two distinct problems, which are characteristic for low-threshold services. There are the success stories: men who get themselves onto their feet, keep a tidy bunk on the less densely populated sixth floor, and go out to work. Some have stayed for years and are either unwilling or unable to move on – while in order to maintain a throughput, and retain the upgrade options for other clients, their spaces are needed. Yet the clients remain vulnerable and, if turned out, may well fall back on their old ways. Ultimately, it seems, the centre cannot effect the rehabilitation of street people without the support of family, community and social services.

While most street people welcome the medical services provided, many resent the rules imposed on their behaviour by the staff. They are allowed neither drugs nor weapons, have to control their language and tempers, and are subjected to myriad senseless-seeming rules, such as a prohibition on spitting. Finding the garage too formal an environment for their liking, a core of 20–30 people have made their home on the doorstep of the concrete structure, creating a margin on the margin they refer to as 'Baghdad'. Here, within view of centre staff but beyond their control, a lively market in drugs and all manner of goods has opened up, catering mainly for the residents. It is illustrative of the problem created once a population of socially displaced people has reached critical mass.

Drugs are an important, but not the sole, factor in their predicament, and one that needs to be addressed for rehabilitation to succeed. Moreover, helping these clients to get a grip over the drug habit is also a key for reducing criminality and the associated social nuisance, including vandalism and begging. The objective of workers for organizations like St Vincent and Paul, which provides a regular service in Tamarind Square, the social centre for the displaced (and only a stone's throw from the CSDP car park), is to bring these people into contact with services. Jo speaks of the great loneliness on the street, as some have no remaining human contact and only speak to their dealers. Working over time, towards incremental achievement of improved medical welfare and social functioning, street workers have brought people into treatment and off the streets.

These activities are one of the keys to addressing drug-related problems across the Caribbean region. Facilities that are easy to access, and where staff are willing to assist with basic survival, social and health worker skills. The difficulty in allocating treatment funds is that upon first contact few clients will be willing to even contemplate kicking their drug habit. After all, for those on the street, the pharmacological fix is one of very few positive experiences. It needs to be understood, however, that working at this level is important if the spread of infectious diseases, and especially HIV/AIDS, given the ready resort to sex work, is to be prevented. A regional strategy for low-threshold centres and outreach programmes has to become an urgent agenda item for drug demand reduction policy in the coming years.

Where next in Caribbean drug control?

Much has changed since the colonial powers first began to legislate on the use of drugs. Drug control comes into the purview of different government departments, including those responsible for security, health and education, with each engendering activities and interventions in pursuit of the preventive aims. And much more emphasis is now placed on establishing a scientific basis for such activity. It is important that governments not only prove their understanding of an issue, but are also prepared scrupulously to assess and evaluate the benefit of their work. Where in 1913 the status of cannabis in Jamaica was determined on the basis of casual observations, in 2001 it was subject to a rigorous analytical examination by a multidisciplinary team known as the Ganja Commission. For nine months they consulted literally hundreds of witnesses across Jamaica. Moreover, they drew on a body of literature spanning epidemiology, cultural studies and jurisprudence. Barely 80 years after the first definitive piece of drug-related legislation, drug studies have grown into a complex and involved field of scientific inquiry. Caribbean researchers and authors have made valuable contributions to this global discourse.

Yet there are constants. Drug control policy in the Commonwealth Caribbean is still being developed in response to external stimulus. The introduction of cocaine from Latin America, driven by demand in North

America and Europe, has introduced a powerful psychoactive substance and a criminal economy. Demands by the partner governments have had to be met by legal and institutional changes. Working with international organizations, techniques, instruments, frameworks and models have been adapted. There is an organizational infrastructure and a cadre of skilled professionals to deliver interventions across a range of fields.

This collection of essays is a contribution to finding an orientation for a regional drugs policy by reviewing the impact on crime control, development and demand reduction. We have found that the policy has succeeded in averting identified threats, but at the price of future problems that need to be addressed now. We argue that changes in the configuration of trafficking organizations have defused the threat to national security. To maintain the aggressive, punitive system in place will only marginalize further a significant and volatile section of the population.

This is notwithstanding the fact that external concerns have to be integrated into overall strategies. It is recognized that the trafficking function of many Commonwealth Caribbean states poses a threat to its major partners. Their demands for robust measures to meet this threat are non-negotiable. It is in the national interest to comply with such requirements, and this has already been achieved in most administrations.

There is also a responsibility to national populations, whose security is thereby affected. Police officers inspecting outgoing containers in Kingston harbour cannot patrol the streets in Trench Town. Such a deliberate allocation of scarce resources to assist a partner country at the expense of domestic benefits is a legitimate trade-off that is entirely rational within an overall evaluation of the national interest. Yet local demands, in a democracy, cannot be avoided forever – particularly when the alignment of policies has had unintended consequences of magnitude. The criminalization of ganja-using youth will have severe consequences for public safety and the level of crime in the near future. It is becoming clear that a particular set of measures has had a profound and unforeseen impact that needs to be assessed and addressed. Would such a revision jeopardize the constructive engagement with partner countries? Not necessarily. There is no reason why the harsh line on the export of cocaine cannot be matched with a shift from warfare to welfare on drug use internally and the replacement of incarceration with treatment.

Among professionals there is much support for the principles of treatment, community prevention, and distinction between substances and users. Initiatives are being taken in most countries to involve individuals, families and communities to mobilize on preventing the conditions that attract pathological behaviour. Yet often states do not respond with the alacrity that the situation requires. It has taken from 2001 to 2003 for the

CARICOM-led demand reduction needs assessment to deliver the first input. The difficulty in accelerating this process lies mainly with finding a shared policy objective. What is the ultimate purpose of both demand reduction strategy and drug control in general? The policy of suppression, in keeping drugs out and crime down, has not produced the hoped-for result. The region follows a global trend of drugs becoming cheaper and more readily available, their use more prevalent, and drug-related crime more frequent. The need for action is urgent, and professionals are looking for strategic direction. We propose the adoption by the Commonwealth Caribbean of a policy of harm reduction, within the room for manoeuvre allowed by the United Nations Conventions on drug regulation and outlined by the Ganja Commission.[52] There is antipathy from some partner countries, and even the United Nations Office on Drugs and Crime (UNODC) avoids the term. Yet its former Secretary, Pinot Arlacchi, has clarified the position by agreeing with the principles of harm reduction, provided 'it was not a Trojan horse for legalization' (*DrugLink* 2001).

But harm reduction provides a set of overarching principles with which a comprehensive, multisectoral drug policy can be framed. Given the discrepancy between Caribbean mini-states and the partners, a regional forum provides the appropriate platform for negotiations with partners. The interpenetration of Caribbean countries adds a further recommendation: a regional policy on reducing harm by drugs in the areas of crime, development, health, social welfare, youth and international relations, carried out within each territory and supported by a network of regional bodies – policy that shifts from being tough on drugs to being tough on crime, from crime detection to crime prevention, and that moves from dealing with the psychoactive symptoms to ameliorating the risk-generating conditions.

NOTES

1 The Inter-American Drug Abuse Control Commission, established under the auspices of the Organization of the American States in 1986, is a forum in which Caribbean states felt marginalized throughout the 1990s. With the appointment of Lancelot Selman (Trinidad & Tobago) as chair in 2001, and the organization of a Caribbean work programme, the Commission has gained new significance in the region.

2 The surveys that have been conducted in recent years with technical assistance from the United Nations Office on Drugs and Crime (UNODC) have established the widespread use of cannabis (Barbados 75 per cent, Bahamas 25 per cent) and a core of cocaine users (Barbados 6 per cent).

3 As Assistant Drug Enforcement Administrator Casteel told the Senate Judiciary Committee, there are close links between terrorism and drug trafficking. But while terror groups do rely on drugs trafficking for substantial portions of their funding, drug trafficking as a phenomenon seems indifferent to the involvement of these politically motivated players.

4 However, President Reagan's National Security Decision Directive No. 221 of 8 April 1986 declared drug production and trafficking a threat to the security of the Americas.

5 Indeed, there has been a position within the US policy foreign community that has equated US and world security and has been aggressively pushing for 'the necessary investment in technological transformations' (Kagan 2003: 92).

6 Michael Manley, Speech to the UN, Jamaica Office of the Prime Minister, Kingston, 9 June 1989.

7 Lippmann's observation that in the US corruption was endemic could apply to any country.

8 See the CARICOM publications on Caribbean Drug Trends.

9 Caribbean Evaluation Training Workshop, Port of Spain 10–14 February 2003.

10 *Daily Chronicle* report, quoted in Rubin and Comitas. The penalties stipulated a fine of up to £100 or up to six months imprisonment for a first offence of cultivation, possession, sale or smoking of ganja. See also Chevanne, Chapter 2.

11 Nanton points out how the constant struggle to establish Caribbean civilization, initially a European project, against the countervailing forces of 'native' savagery, has since been adopted by post-independence nation builders.

12 In Trinidad popular opinion long held that East Indians could not handle alcohol.

13 Name given to the white settlers of low socio-economic status.

14 The deliberate distribution of drugs, mandrax and crack cocaine by security forces with a racist agenda to undermine and destabilize black communities has been reported in apartheid South Africa (Truth and Reconciliation Commission Final Report, Part 4, sections 20–24) and the US (Gary Webb, 1998).

15 In Trinidad & Tobago cannabis was banned in 1925, and in Guyana even later.

16 The intense interest in marijuana during the 1970s is illustrated by the number of newspaper articles on the subject. Interest fades in the 1980s and 1990s (MacCoun and Reuter 2001).

17 Oregon (1973), Alaska, Colorado, Ohio (1975), California, Maine, Minnesota (1976), Mississippi, New York, North Carolina, South Dakota (1977), Nebraska (1978).

18 This tension between latitude towards domestic drug users, coupled with a stepped-up crackdown in producer and transit countries, has arisen once again as a thorny issue in the wake of European drug policy reform of the 1990s.

19 The term refers to the descendants of the indentured labourers from the Indian sub-continent who migrated to the region from the 1850s onwards to make up for the drop in the labour supply after the abolition of slavery.

20 The other inhabitants were 'encouraged' to leave, and visitors, including the leader of the Bahamian opposition, were muscled off by Lehder's thugs (Streatfield 2002: 276).

21 Quoted in Griffith 1993: 98.

22 According to Hamid, a passage in Revelation (2: verses 17–29) about a white stone with which the chosen will be rewarded was invoked to provide a minimal justification for a troubled conscience.

23 In 1981 *Time Magazine* ran a cover story featuring cocaine as the 'All American Drug'. In 1982 the National Institute on Drug Abuse found that approximately 29 million Americans had tried cocaine (Abelson and Miller 1985).

24 An anti-cannabis propaganda film widely shown in the US during the 1960s. It made extravagant claims about the deleterious effects of cannabis and was almost instantly discredited by experts and users.

25 In 2001 arrest referral workers working in UK police stations with offenders suspected of drug use made 6,619 assessments; nearly 50 per cent reporting crack (and not heroin) use were black (GLA 2003).

26 United Nations headquarters of the International Narcotics Control Board (INCB) and the former United Nations Drug Control Programme (UNDCP), now UN Office on Drugs and Crime (UNODC).

27 Known as cartels in common parlance, even though they display few cartel characteristics.

28 Personal communication, 9 July 2000.
29 According to Gilbert Scott, deputy chief of the Ministry for National Security, arrest rates have shot up sharply: *Miami Herald*, 10 August 2003.
30 Personal communication with a senior police officer, Tortola, 2002.
31 Interview, Georgetown, Ministry of Home Affairs, 12 July 2000.
32 Interview with Ikel Tafari, Barbados, May 2000.
33 Challenges of Capacity Development. Towards Sustainable Reforms of Caribbean Justice sectors, Vol. 1: Policy Document, Inter-American Development Bank, 2000.
34 Limited rehabilitation programmes are provided in the Bahamas, Barbados, Belize, Guyana, Jamaica and Trinidad & Tobago criminal justice systems.
35 Interview with John Rogier, Assistant Commissioner for Prison Services, Port of Spain, 9 July 2000.
36 Interview with Dale Erskine, Director of Prisons, Georgetown, 13 July 2000.
37 Interview with prison training officer Dave Jobling, Grand Cayman, 22 May 2003.
38 Interview with Superintendent Raymond Craig, Port of Spain, 9 July 2000.
39 Thoumi 2002a.
40 For a discussion of the constraints suffered by textile manufactures and the informatics sector respectively, see Freeman 2000.
41 The primary development objective of the 7th European Development Fund and the UK Department for International Development.
42 With such exceptions as the Grenadian New Jewel Movement.
43 Thus, for example, US sugar markets are closed to Caribbean sugar cane exporters. And while Caribbean hucksters pay fuel taxes when trucking their produce to market, North American and European airfreight is exempt from fuel tax.
44 Critique of the particular technique of Participatory Rural Appraisal developed in the 1990s.
45 Interview with Joe, Port of Spain, 10 February 2003. Craft production and credit unions have also been set up at the Shamrock shelter for the socially displaced.
46 At the United Nations General Assembly Special Session (UNGASS) on drugs in New York.
47 (1) Narrowing of the drinking repertoire: drinking to the same extent regardless of occasion; (2) Salience of drink-seeking behaviour; (3) Increased tolerance to alcohol; (4) repeated withdrawal symptoms; (5) relief of symptoms by further drinking; (6) subjective awareness of compulsion to drink; (7) reinstatement after abstinence: once drinking starts it will rapidly return to previous levels of consumption.
48 The National Treatment Outcome Research Study (NTORS) is the first prospective national study of treatment outcome among drug misusers in the United Kingdom. It used a longitudinal, prospective cohort design, collecting data by structured interviews at intake to treatment, one year, two years and at four and five years. The sample comprised 418 patients from 54 agencies and four treatment modalities.
49 Interview with L. Richards, Programme Manager for Rebirth House, Port of Spain, 9 February 2003.
50 Figures for Caribbean jurisdictions need to be collated; external donors have historically emphasized supply reduction intervention, with capital-intensive equipment provision and extensive training programmes. The UK's Department for International Development has now begun allocating 10 per cent of funds to demand reduction. For a discussion of EU and UNDCP allocations in the late 1990s, see Klein 2001 and the response by Platzer and Mirella 2002.
51 'Therapeutic communities' are centres where a number of addicts live together. Their therapeutic power is believed to lie in rehabilitation through work and their 'scientific justification' is to be found in behaviorist theories.
52 See the paper by the UNDCP Legal Section, 'Flexibility of Treaty Provisions as Regards Harm Reduction Approaches', E/WCB/2002/W13. See also Jamieson (2001).

REFERENCES AND SELECT BIBLIOGRAPHY

Abelson, H. and J. D. Miller (1985). A Decade of Trends in Cocaine Use in the Household Population', in National Institute on Drug Abuse (NIDA), 1985, *Cocaine Use in America: Epidemiologic and Clinical Perspectives*. Rockville, Maryland: NIDA.

Allen, D. F. (1987) 'Modes of Use, Precursors and Indicators of Cocaine Abuse', in D. F Allen (ed.), *The Cocaine Crises*, New York: Plenum.

Ambler, C. (1990) 'Alcohol, Racial Segregation and Popular Politics in Northern Rhodesia', *Journal of African History*, 295–313.

Appadurai, A. (ed.) (1986) *The Social Life of Things: Commodities in Cultural Perspective*. Cambridge: Cambridge University Press.

Ashley, C. and S. Maxwell (2001) 'Rethinking Rural Development', *Development Policy Review*, 19, 4.

Bagley, B. M. and W. O. Walker (eds.) (1994) *Drug Trafficking in the Americas*, New Brunswick: Transaction Publishers; Coral Gables: University of Miami.

Baudrillard, J. (1981) *For a Critique of the Political Economy of the Sign*, St Louis: Telos Press.

Beaubrun, M. (1967) 'Treatment of Alcoholism in Trinidad & Tobago', *British Journal of Psychiatry*, 113: 643–58.

—— (1981) 'The Nature of Alcohol Dependence and its Recognition', in *Medicine Digest*, 8, 1.

—— (1982) 'Conversation with Michael Beaubrun', *British Journal of Addiction*, 77: 229–34.

—— (1987) 'Cocaine update', in D. Allen (ed.), *The Cocaine Crisis*, New York: Plenum Press.

Belenko, S. (1993) *Crack and the Evolution of Anti-Drug Policy*, Westport: Greenwod Press.

Boekhout van Solinge, T. (2002) 'Drugs and Decision Making in the European Union', <http://www.cedro-uva.org/lib>.

Braithwaite, J. (1989) *Crime, Shame, and Reintegration*, Cambridge: Cambridge University Press.

Brathwaite, B. A. (1998) *Evaluation of Substance Abuse Treatment and Rehabilitation Centres in Trinidad & Tobago*, Port of Spain: Office of the Prime Minister, NADAPP/DRUGTEL.

Broad, K. and B. Feinberg (1995) 'Perceptions of Ganja and Cocaine in Urban Jamaica', *Journal of Psychoactive Drugs*, 27, 3 (July–September): 261–76.

Chevannes, B. (1988) 'Background to Drug Use in Jamaica', Working Paper No. 34, Institute of Social and Economic Research, University of the West Indies, Jamaica.

——, Webster Edwards, Anthony Freckleton, Norma Linton, DiMario McDowell, Aileen Standard-Goldson and Barbara Smith (N.D.), *A Report of the National Commission on Ganja to Rt. Hon. P. J. Patterson, Q.C., MP, Prime Minister of Jamaica*. Kingston, Jamaica.

Clarke, N. A. (1987) 'Drug Abuse 1975–1985: Clinical Perspectives of the Bahamian Experience of Illegal Substances' , in D. F. Allen (ed.), *The Cocaine Crises*, New York: Plenum.

Comitas, L. (1975) 'The Social Nexus of Ganja in Jamaica', in Vera Rubin (ed.), *Cannabis and Culture*, The Hague: Mouton, pp. 119–32.

Cope, J. (1998) 'A United States View of Strategic Balance in the Americas', in Joseph S. Tulchin and Francisco Rojas Aravena (eds.), *Regional Perspectives on Strategic Balance and Confidence Building Measures in the Americas*, Stanford: Woodrow Wilson Center, pp. 60–75.

Curtis, R. and T. Wendel (2000) 'Towards the Development of a Typology of Illegal Drug Markets', in Natarajan M. and Hough, M. (2000) *Illegal Drug Markets: From Research to Prevention Policy*. Crime Prevention Studies, Vol. II, New York: Criminal Justice Press.

Dean-Patterson, S. (1987) 'Cocaine and the Bahamian Woman: Treatment Issues', in D. F. Allen (ed.), *The Cocaine Crises*, New York: Plenum.

Debiel, T. (2002) 'Do Crisis Regions Have a Chance of Lasting Peace? The Difficult Transformation from Structures of Violence', in T. Debiel and A. Klein (eds.), *Fragile Peace*, London: Zed Books.

Douglas D. G. (1997) *Situational Analysis Needs Assessment and Proposed Model for Treatment and*

Rehabilitation of Drug Abusers, Kingston, Jamaica: National Council on Drug Abuse.

—— (1998) *Patterns of Substance Use and Abuse Among Post-Primary Students in Jamaica: Prevalence and Long-Term Trends*, Kingston, Jamaica: University of the West Indies.

Dorn, N. (1992) *Traffickers: Drug Markets and Law Enforcement in the Single Market of the European Communities*, La Rotta della Droga. Genova: Costa and Nolan, pp. 68–82.

DrugLink (2001) 16, 2: 5.

Economist, The (2003) 368, 8338.

Edwards, G. and M. M. Gross, 1976. 'Alcohol Dependence: Provisional Description of a Clinial Syndrome', *British Medical Journal*, 1, 1058–61.

Ellis, F. and S. Biggs (2001) 'Evolving Themes in Rural Development', *Development Policy Review*, 19, 4: 437–48.

EMCDDA (1999) *Outreach Work among Drug Users in Europe: Concepts, Practice and Terminology*, Lisbon: European Monitoring Centre on Drugs and Drug Addiction.

Figueira, D. (1997) *Cocaine and the Economy of Crime in Trinidad & Tobago*, Trinidad and Tobago: Darius Figueira.

Fineman, M. 'Economy Hooked on Marijuana', *San Jose Mercury News*, 6 February 1999.

Freeman, C. (2001) *High Tech and High Heels in the Global Economy: Women, Work, and Pink Collar Identities in the Caribbean*, Durham: Duke University Press.

Galbraith, J. K. (1955) *The Great Crash*, Boston: Houghton Mifflin.

Gayle, Carol, Debra Wedderburn, Maxine Wedderburn and Pansy Goldstein, P. J. (1989) 'The Drugs/Crime Nexus. A Tripartite Conceptual Framework', *Journal of Drug Issues*, 14: 493–506.

Godfrey C, G. Eaton, C. McDougall and A. Culyer (2002) *The Economic and Social Costs of Class A Drug Use in England and Wales, 2000*, Home Office Research Study No. 249, London: Home Office.

Goldstein, P. J. (1985) 'The Drugs/Crime Nexus. A Tripartite Conceptual Framework', *Journal of Drug Issues*, 14: 493–506.

Goodman, J., E. Paul Lovejoy and A. Sherrat (eds.) (1995) *Consuming Habits: Drugs in History and Anthropology*, London: Routledge.

Gossop, M., J. Marsden, D. Stewart (2001) *National Treatment Outcome Research Study (NTORS) After Five Years: Changes in Substance Use, Health and Criminal Behaviour During Five Years After Intake*. London: National Addiction Centre.

Griffith, I. L. (1993) *The Quest for Security in the Caribbean: Problems and Promises in Subordinate States*, New York: M. E. Sharpe.

—— (1996) 'Caribbean Security on the Eve of the 21st Century', McNair Paper 54, Institute for National Strategic Studies, National Defense University, Washington, DC.

—— (2000) 'Drugs and Political Economy in a Global Village', in I. L. Griffith (ed.), *The Political Economy of Drugs in the Caribbean*, Basingstoke: Macmillan, pp. 11–28.

Griffith, I. L. and T. Munroe (1995) 'Drugs and Democracy in the Caribbean', *Journal of Commonwealth and Comparative Politics*, 33: 358–75.

Hamid, A. (1990) 'The Political Economy of Crack-related Violence', in *Contemporary Drug Problems*, 17, 1: 31–78.

—— (1991) 'From Ganja to Crack: Caribbean Participation in the Underground Economy of Brooklyn, 1976–1986. Part 1. Establishment of the Marijuana Economy', *International Journal of Addiction*, 26, 6: 615–28; 'Part 2. Establishment of the Cocaine (and Crack) Economy', *International Journal of Addiction*, 26, 7: 729–38.

Hardin, G. (1968) 'The Tragedy of the Commons', *Science*, 162: 1243–8.

Harriott, A. (2000) *Police and Crime Control in Jamaica: Problems of Reforming Ex-colonial Constabularies*, Kingston: The University of West Indies Press.

Heap, S. (1999) 'The Quality of Liquor in Nigeria during the Colonial Era', *Itinerario*, 23, 2: 29–47.

Holder, P. (2001) 'DrugUse and Crime among Young Males in La Horquetta', unpublished

MSc thesis, Imperial College, University of London.

Hough, M. (1996) 'Drug Misuse and the Criminal Justice System: Review of the Literature', Drugs Prevention Initiative Paper 15, London: Home Office.

IDB (2000) *Challenges of Capacity Development: Towards Sustainable Reforms of Caribbean Justice Sectors*, Barbados: Inter-American Development Bank.

US State Department Bureau for International Narcotics and Law Enforcement Affairs (2003) International Narcotics Control Survey Report , Washington: US State Department.

Jamieson, A. (2001) 'International Drug Conventions, National Compliance and UN Commentaries: the Shaming Mechanism', in N. Dorn and A. Jamieson (eds.), *European Drug Laws: Room for Manoeuvre*, London: DrugScope, pp. 219–54.

Jay, M. (2000) *Emperors of Dreams. Drugs in the Nineteenth Century*, London: Dedalus.

Jekel, J. F., H. Podlewski, S. Dean-Patterson, D. F. Allen, N. Clarke, P. Cartwright (1986) 'Epidemic Freebase Cocaine Abuse: a Case Study from the Bahamas', *The Lancet*, 1 March.

Kagan, R. (2003) *Paradise and Power: America and Europe in the New World Order*, London: Atlantic Books.

Khan-Melnyk, A. (1994) 'Politics and US–Jamaican Drug Trade in the 1980s' in B. M. Bagley and W. O. Walker (eds.), *Drug Trafficking in the Americas*, New Brunswick: Transaction Publishers; Coral Gables: University of Miami, pp. 481–509.

Klein, A. (2001) 'Between the Death Penalty and Decriminalization: New Directions for Drug Control in the Commonwealth Caribbean', *New West India Guide*, 75, 4.

Legget, T. (2003) *Rainbow Vice: the Drugs and Sex Industries in the New South Africa*, London: Zed Books.

Littlewood, R. 1988. 'Vice to Madness: The Semantics of Naturalistic and Personalistic Understanding in Trinidadian Local Medicine', *So. Sci. Med.*, 27, 2.

Lowenthal A. F. (1992) 'The Organisation of American States and Control of Dangerous Drugs', in P. H. Smith (ed.), *DrugPolicy in the Americas*, Oxford: Westview Press, 1992, p. 305.

Lupton, R., A. Wilson, M. Tiggey, H. Warburton and P. J. Turnbull (2002) *A Rock and a Hard Place: Drug Markets in Deprived Neighbourhoods*, Home Office Research Study No. 240, London: Home Office.

Lusane, C. and D. Desmond (1991) *Pipe Dream Blues: Racism and the War on Drugs*, Boston: South End Press.

Mabry, D. (1994) 'The US Military and the War on Drugs', in B. M. Bagley and W. O. Walker (eds.), *Drug Trafficking in the Americas*, New Brunswick: Transaction Publishers; Coral Gables: University of Miami.

MacCoun, R. and P. Reuter (2001) *Drug War Heresies*, Cambridge: Cambridge University Press.

McMurran, M. (1994) *The Psychology of Addiction*, London: Taylor and Francis.

Maingot, A. P. (1988) 'Laundering the Gains of the Drug Trade: Miami and Caribbean Tax Havens', *Journal of Interamerican Studies and World Affairs*, 30, 23: 167–87.

—— (1994) 'The Drug Trade in the Caribbean: Policy Options', in B. M. Bagley and W. O. Walker (eds.), *Drug Trafficking in the Americas*, New Brunswick: Transaction Publishers; Coral Gables: University of Miami.

Miers, S. and I. Kopytoff (eds.) (1977) *Slavery in Africa: Historical and Anthropological Perspectives*, New York: Madison.

Mintz, S. W. (1985) 'From Plantations to Peasantries in the Caribbean', in S. W. Mintz and S. Price (eds), *Caribbean Contours*, Baltimore: John Hopkins University Press, pp. 127–54.

Munroe, T. (2000) 'Cooperation and Conflict in the US–Caribbean Connection', in I. L. Griffith (ed.), *The Political Economy of Drugs in the Caribbean*, Basingstoke: Macmillan, pp. 183–200.

Musto, D. F. (1992) 'America's First Cocaine Epidemic: What Did We Learn?' in T. R. Kosten and H. D. Kleber, *Clinician's Guide to Cocaine Addiction: Theory, Research, and Treatment*, New York: Guilford Press.

NCIS (2002) *UK Threat Assessment 2002: the Threat from Serious and Organised Crime*, London: National Criminal Intelligence Services.

Platzer, M. and F. Mirella (2002) 'United Nations Inernational Drug Control Programme Responds', *New West Indian Guide*, 76, 1 and 2: 89–93.

Rubin V. and L. Comitas (1975) *Ganja in Jamaica: a Medical Anthropological Study of Chronic Marihuana Use*, The Hague: Mouton.

—— (1996) *Effects of Chronic Smoking of Cannabis in Jamaica*, New York: Research Institute for the Study of Man.

Ruggiero, V. (1993) 'Brixton, London: a Drug Culture without a Drug Economy?', *International Journal of Drug Policy*, 4, 2: 83–90.

Ruggiero, V. and N. South (1995) *Eurodrugs: Drug Use, Markets and Trafficking in Europe*, London: UCL Press.

Sanders, R. (1990) 'Narcotics, Corruption and Development: the Problem in the Smaller Islands', *Caribbean Affairs*, 3, 1: 79–92.

Small, G. (1995) *Ruthless; The Global Rise of the Yardies*, London: Warner Books.

Stone, C. (1990) 'Extracts and Summary of the National Survey on Use of Drugs in Jamaica', *Jamaican Nurse*, 29, 1: 54–7.

Streatfield, D. (2002) *Cocaine*, London: Virgin.

Taylor, J. S. (2001). 'Dollars Are a Girl's Best Friend? Female Tourists' Sexual Behaviour in the Caribbean', *Sociology*, 35, 3: 749–64.

Thoumi, F. (1995) *Political Economy and Illegal Drugs in Colombia*, Boulder: Lynne Rienner.

Thoumi, F. (2002a) 'Characteristics of the State and Society That Make Colombia Prone to Produce Illegal Drugs and the Implications for Drug Control', paper at Second European Conference on Drug Trafficking, Paris.

Thoumi, F. (2002b) 'Illegal Drugs in Colombia: from Illegal Economic Boom to Social Crises', *Annals of the American Academy of Political and Social Science*, June.

Tonry, M. (1995) *Malign Neglect*, New York: Oxford University Press.

Tullis, L. (1995) *Unintended Consequences: Illegal Drugs and Drug Policies in Nine Countries*, London: Lynne Rienner .

UNDCP (1998) *The Community Fights Back: the Implementation of Integrated Demand Reduction Programme in the Caribbean*. Barbados: United Nations Drug Control Programme.

UNDCP (2001) 'The Community Fights Back', Unpublished report, Barbados: United Nations Drug Control Programme.

UNODC (2002) *Global Illicit Drug Trends 2002*, New York: United Nations Office for Drug Control and Crime Prevention.

US State Department Bureau for International Narcotics and Law Enforcement Affairs (2003) *International Narcotics Control Strategy Report 2002: the Caribbean*, Washington, DC: United States State Department.

Walker, W. (1994) 'The Bush Administration's Andean Drug Strategy in Historical Perspective', in B. M. Bagley and W. O. Walker (eds.), *Drug Trafficking in the Americas*, New Brunswick: Transaction Publishers; Coral Gables: University of Miami.

Webb, Gary (1998) *Dark Alliance: The CIA, the CONTRAS, and the Crack Cocaine Explosion*. New York: Seven Stories Press.

West India Commission (1992) *Time for Action: Report of the West India Commission*, Bridgetown, Barbados: Black Rock.

World Health Organisation (1974) *Glossary of Mental Disorders and Guide to their Classification in Conjunction with the International Classification of Diseases*, 8th revision, Geneva: WHO.

World Health Organisation (1978) *Mental Disorders: Glossary and Guide to their Classification in Accordance with the Ninth Revision of the International Classificartion of Diseases*. Geneva: WHO.

Zaitch, D. (2002) *Trafficking Cocaine: Colombian Drug Entrepreneurs in the Netherlands*, London: Kluwers.

PART 2

Policy Responses

**Adapting the Legal Framework
to Meet the Needs of the Region**

CHAPTER 2

Criminalizing Cultural Practice
The Case of Ganja in Jamaica

BARRY CHEVANNES

I

A National Commission on Ganja set up by the Prime Minister of Jamaica in 2000 recommended the decriminalization of the private use of the substance and possession of small quantities towards that end. This chapter tracks the historical background leading to the enculturation of ganja, its subsequent criminalization, and the failure of the state to suppress it; reviews the work of the Commission; and explains the recommended line of approach to decriminalization without violating the United Nations Conventions on drug regulation (1961, 1971, 1988: see index).

The fact that in Jamaica *cannabis sativa* is known by its Hindi name is proof enough of its place of origin – India. We assume that it was taken there by Indian indentured workers, who were recruited to work on the sugar plantations vacated by the Africans following the end of slavery throughout the British Empire in 1838. As there is no written or oral historical record to suggest that it was known in the island prior to that, and as the large-scale influx of Indians into Jamaica began only in the early 1850s, it is safe to conclude that the use of ganja in that country is no more than 150 years old. During that time, however, the cultural contact between the two ethnic groups on the plantations and adjacent communities led to its assimilation and ownership by the African population, over what period of time we can only guess. According to an old informant, long since deceased, ganja was regularly sent by ship to 'Colon' for the black Jamaican workers who migrated there to work in building the Panama Canal, an indication that by the turn of the century it was no longer identified exclusively with the Indian population. The same could not be said of the African populations of Guyana and Trinidad, countries that received the largest proportions of Indian indentured workers. And the explanation for this difference is to be found in the fact that the larger numbers taken into those two British colonies made cultural contact with the Africans less of a necessity, whereas in Jamaica – due to their relatively smaller numbers[1] – close cultural exchange was inevitable.[2] The result is that in Jamaica ganja use became a part of the folk practices within a relatively short period of time; and not only was it used but it also gained a place in the folk pharmacopoeia, alongside other herbs, roots, barks and plants. When therefore the law was first passed in 1925 making its cultivation, possession, peddling and use a crime, the government's aim was the suppression of a practice that had already become part of the culture of the people. Seven decades later, it has to be said, this battle is as good as lost.

The suppression of ganja in Jamaica has undergone three phases: (1) 1913 to the 1950s; (2) the 1950s to 1972; (3) 1972 to the present. The first phase might be characterized as a period of gathering storm clouds. It began with Jamaica ratifying the International Opium Convention by adding *cannabis sativa*. There were no compelling reasons for the addition. Members of the Legislative Council were apparently satisfied that ganja produced a 'demoralizing, criminogenic influence on coolie (East Indian) labourers' and the native population (Rubin and Comitas 1975: 21), though their real reason was more probably the fear of the black population, for '[l]ocal legislatures, dominated by the plantocracy, attempted to deal with social problems mainly by repressive control' (Rubin and Comitas 1975: 23). In 1924 a Dangerous Drugs Law was passed, which increased the penalties for possession, cultivation, sale and smoking.

In the United States, ganja was already being widely smoked by African- and Mexican-Americans, who as they migrated from the southern to the northern states, took the practice with them, hence the name that has achieved the greatest currency in that country, marijuana or marihuana. Outside of these minority ethnic groups, however, it was virtually unknown as a psychotropic substance, until the Bureau of Narcotics campaign against it and passage of the Marihuana Tax Act in 1937. At the time the main concern had been with alcohol, the imposition and ultimate failure of prohibition against it, and repeal of the prohibition laws. The story of the campaign against this relatively unknown substance, against a background in which hemp had been in use for industrial purposes by many states of the Union, has been interpreted by some, not without plausibility, as a conspiracy motivated by economic interests that saw hemp as a competitive alternative to pulp, and used racial hysteria to mobilize public opinion. There was certainly little scientific evidence of any credibility to support the allegations proffered in support of anti-marijuana legislation that marijuana was the source of criminal behaviour, indolence and other social pathologies. But immediately following the passage of the Act, Mayor La Guardia of New York set up a commission of experts drawn from the New York Academy of Science to study the effects of the substance.[3] After six years of painstaking work, the commission found no evidence that warranted the passage of a law to suppress its use. The Mayor La Guardia Commission became the second major Commission to have studied and exonerated cannabis; the first being the Indian Hemp Commission of 1894.[4] However, the media campaign on the evils of this substance had already produced its desired effect on the general public.

It also gave a fillip to colonial authorities in Jamaica, who intensified their attempt at suppression by amending the Dangerous Drugs Act in 1941 to include mandatory sanctions for possession with intent to traffic. During the next twenty years, the Act would undergo three amendments – in 1947, 1954 and 1961 – making the penalties stiffer. The police force also tried its own version of the United States Bureau of Narcotics campaign in trying, but without much success, to link ganja smoking with the rise of crime, including rape. But it was the growing link to the Rastafari that proved decisive in marshalling public opinion for the steeper measures of 1961.

For most of this period, despite passage of the Dangerous Drugs Act, ganja remained easily available. An old informant, in explaining his ability to cope with the economic hardships of life in Kingston in the late 1930s, cited his turn to peddling ganja for a living, for it was readily available from 'higglers' – food and commodity vendors – in the market. Yet the fact that one of the early preachers of Rastafari, Robert Hinds, instructed his members to refrain from using ganja within the confines of his King of Kings Mission so as not to give police any pretext to invade the premises would suggest that notwithstanding the easy availability of ganja in this period the law remained a tool that could be used conveniently by the police.[5] It was so used by the police character in Roger Mais's novel *Brother Man*, but by then the period of stepped-up police prosecution had begun.

Thus by the middle of the 1950s the storm clouds began to deliver. A period of intense repression set in, lasting for nearly two decades. It was met with equally intense resistance, ending not surprisingly with a change of government in 1972. Apart from the international pressure to wipe out ganja use, developments internal to Jamaica served to polarize the society, and to pit the police against a popular democratic movement for change. The first of these developments was the aggressive stance adopted by the Rastafari movement, which came under the influence of religious radicals who sought to create distance between the movement and the wider society. They did so by a number of means, one of which, namely the cultivation of uncombed locks, had the desired effect of making them outcasts. Another was the identification with and sacralization of ganja. Adopting ganja as a sacrament, the Rastafari invited the persecution of the state, and thereby sharpened its own critique of the society. For, so went their justification, if ganja was a known folk remedy, the prosecution of it represented a prosecution of the people themselves. Further, by tracing its mythic origin to the grave of King Solomon, the Rastafari skilfully exploited Christian tradition, thereby increasing the contradiction posed for the state.

However, to the state there was no contradiction, for the Rastafari represented a marginal group to begin with. Its marginal position was exacerbated by the Claudius Henry affair in 1960. Henry, the head of a Rastafari group, was accused and found guilty of treason felony, for having in his possession a cache of arms and a letter allegedly inviting Fidel Castro to take over Jamaica. And to compound his situation his son Ronald was exposed as the leader of a guerrilla band that engaged the armed forces, killing two soldiers in the exchange. The hysteria that swept the country as a result interpreted Rastafari marginal status as having hostile intent towards the society, and so set the stage for the police to target them, with and without the pretext of prosecuting ganja. The hysteria began to abate only with the publication of the findings by the group of three scholars assigned by the University of the West Indies to make a study of the movement, and not before passage of the 1961 amendment, which increased the mandatory imprisonment to up to five years for growing and trafficking.

Two years later the Coral Gardens incident provided yet another pretext for widespread assault on the Rastafari. A dreadlocked man of unsound mind chopped to death two gas station employees at Coral Gardens, a suburb of Montego Bay, before he too was killed. Many innocent members of the Rastafari movement were rounded up, beaten, imprisoned and wounded, without cause. This set the stage for yet another amendment. The 1964 amendment made five years at hard labour the mandatory minimum for 'cultivating, or selling or otherwise dealing in ganja' for a first offender, with the possibility of up to seven years. For a second or subsequent conviction, the minimum term of imprisonment was seven years, and the maximum ten. For possession, a first offence attracted a minimum mandatory sentence of eighteen months, with a maximum of three years, and for subsequent offences, a minimum of three years and a maximum of five.

By this time Jamaica had just become independent (August 1962) and was being governed by the centre-right Jamaica Labour Party (JLP), founded and led by Alexander Bustamante, a popular labour leader, who was opposed in the new Parliament by his cousin Norman Manley, one of the leading barristers in the then British Empire, at the head of his social democratic People's National Party (PNP). Under the JLP the years following independence were marked on the one hand by rapid economic growth, but on the other hand by widespread social dislocation and repression. Unemployment doubled, from 13 per cent in 1962 to 26 per cent in 1972, as the migration outlet to Britain was closed and the economy proved unable to absorb labour at adequate rates. On top of that, the government took a hostile, no-

nonsense approach to popular movements, as the Coral Gardens incident showed and the experience of the Black Power movement of the late 1960s was to confirm. It placed a ban on books about revolution and race relations, refused the re-entry of Walter Rodney, a Guyanese national lecturing at the University and leading Black Power advocate, and withdrew the passports of several intellectuals who visited Cuba.

The targeting of the Rastafari by the state had the opposite effect to that which was intended. The movement grew rather than declined. It grew not so much in numbers as in influence. For one thing, its persistent championing of Africa and identification with the African liberation movements gave it legitimacy among important sections of the intelligentsia, so that when an independent Jamaica took its seat in the General Assembly of the United Nations, and began associating with independent nations from Africa, the Rastafari could no longer be seen as a lunatic fringe. The politically timed[6] state visit of Haile Selassie in 1966 found ruling elements of the society courting the Rastafari, thereby enhancing Rastafari credibility among the popular masses. Second, Rastafari idealization of race, particularly in the form of a black God and the promotion of the black self, made it a ready-made part of the black power movement which swept Jamaica in the 1960s and early 1970s, the result of influences from the United States. Third, Rastafari grew when the generation that grew up during the first decade of independence took the movement at its word. It swelled the ranks of those holding and acclaiming the divinity of His Imperial Majesty, but lent the movement its own creative voice, the voice of the reggae artiste. By the end of the 1960s most artistes wore dreadlocks. They became the new missionaries, spreading the message of Rastafari in the far-flung reaches of the world, while at home giving the movement the energy and defiance of youth.

The anti-ganja measures could be, and were, read by many as anti-Rastafari, and therefore anti-populist, in so far as the Rastafari were beginning to enjoy great popularity, especially in the area of popular culture. Not surprisingly, young people played a significant role in changing the government in 1972.[7] They put words to music, joined the campaign bandwagon of the opposing party with their popular songs, and voted, believing 'better must come'.

A powerful symbol of defiance was the cover picture on Bob Marley's second album with Island Records, *Burning*, which depicted him with a large ganja spliff – a popular icon defying the establishment in promoting the use of ganja. But it was left to Peter Tosh to make of himself a living icon of defiance. This rebel, who, in a typical Rastafari play on words turned 'system' into 'shitstem', in reference to its oppressive nature, defied the police by publicly smoking his spliff in the most crowded square of the city, Half-Way-Tree, resisted arrest by fighting, and ended up badly beaten and imprisoned. Such living testimony was not to be lost on the youth, who by then could be seen smoking spliffs on the street corners in their communities, sometimes without any effort at disguising it.

Despite the draconian measures, then, ganja production increased and its use proliferated. Increased production was fuelled not so much by internal demand as by the demand in the United States. The lucre to be realized from exports to that country proved a greater attraction than the fear of the sanctions was to prove a deterrent. And any risk of running foul of the law could be minimized by corrupting critical law enforcement agents.

Thus, unable to crush the popular use of ganja, the state shifted tack. In 1972 it repealed the mandatory minimum sanctions for possession, restored the discretion of the courts and ushered in the third and current phase, the phase of amelioration. The Minister of National Security justified the amendment by reference to the fact that all mandatory sentencing – ganja offences being one of several examples – had had the opposite effect to that intended. Crime had increased, not abated. Opposition member Edwin Allen, in supporting the amendment, revealed that in using mandatory sentencing as a tool to suppress crime, his government, fresh into independence, was sensitive to the need to give the fledgling tourism sector a chance to develop and attract foreign capital. Allen also made another interesting point. His government's thinking, where ganja was concerned, was also influenced by the consideration that by removing discretion from the court they intended to plug the loophole through which people of the higher social classes could escape the full force of the law. Allen's admission was most revealing: the rural and urban masses were not the only ones in violation – the middle and upper middle classes were also engaged in the traffic and/or consumption of the substance.

The amendment was also assisted by the much-publicized study by Vera Rubin and Lambros Comitas. Under a grant from the National Institute of Mental Health, these two scholars from the Research Institute for the Study of Man, in New York City, assembled a team of researchers, many of them based at the University of the West Indies, Mona, to study the effects of long-term habitual use of ganja. Their report was serialized in *The Daily Gleaner* and later published in 1975 under the title *Ganja in Jamaica*. Then, in the first serious attempt at some form of decriminalization, Parliament, on a motion initiated by the Opposition, set up a Select Committee of the House to study the issue and to make recommendations. In 1978 the Committee recommended decriminalization for medical use and a drastic reduction in the sanctions for personal use. However, the report was shelved as the country passed through the most divisive period in its modern political history, with the struggle for political power taking an armed dimension. Nonetheless, both parties stood in favour of the amelioration.

The period has been marked, then, by the introduction of measures to educate the youth and general public, by the continued spread of ganja use and, in its later stage, by the adoption of an approach to drugs that treats it less as a criminal issue and more as a matter of health.

Government's main effort at education rested on the establishment of the National Council on Drug Abuse (NCDA) in 1983. The NCDA implements objectives through the establishment of Community Drug Abuse Action Committees (CODACs), which are clubs of young people operating at community level, educating their peers and others about the harmfulness of drugs. The CODACs have been very successful in increasing awareness among the youth population, but not successful in reducing ganja use. A random sample survey of 5,000 households carried out in 1990 by Carl Stone, recorded a 45 per cent use of ganja, with highest incidence among males in their twenties and thirties. Four years later, Sam Wray (1994) found a use rate of 11.6 per cent, but this study, while national in scope, in the sense of covering every parish, was not based on a national sample selected at random. The third survey, Hope Enterprises (2001), similarly found a lifetime use of 19 per cent and a current use of 11.5 per cent. Its sample, however, could have been compromised by the need to stratify the sample of 2,380 'using the following criteria: NCDA region, urban/rural characteristics, *presence or absence of CODACs*' (Hope Enterprises 2001: 9, emphasis added). Until a survey of the type and quality of Stone's is conducted it is difficult to establish definitively whether or not the use of ganja is contracting or proliferating. Testimony given to the National Commission on Ganja by one of the CODACs, and by members of other CODACs representing themselves, expressed the difficulty in effecting a demand reduction because of the official classification, contrary to popular perception, of ganja as a drug similar to cocaine.

Latterly, since ratification of the 1988 Convention, the ganja offender, as also any other drug offender, appears before a drug court. If found guilty, and if he accepts the offer of the court to undergo rehabilitation, he is released without fine or sentence, and is discharged on receipt by the court of a positive report by the caseworkers. But if he refuses, or if at the end of the period of rehabilitation the court receives a negative report, then he may be fined or sentenced to prison.

The use of ganja, particularly the smoking of it, has not abated. If anecdotal evidence is anything to go by, it has increased among schoolchildren, especially boys. It continues to be used openly at stage shows and on construction sites where workers find it a stimulant. Given the ethos of stage shows, the open use of ganja by artistes and their followers, as well as the general music-loving audience, is not surprising. But the source of the belief in its stimulating qualities is the rural sugar cane workers and small cultivators.

Rubin and Comitas (1975: 75) conclude from their analysis – three thousand minutes of videotapes and over two thousand minutes of audiotapes, films, objective measurements of food intake and energy expenditure, and laboratory studies of energy metabolism – of small cultivators in a rural community, that 'ganja smoking alters the rate and organization of movement and increases the expenditure of energy'. Actual output, however, failed to vary significantly from that of non-smokers.

In summary, for nearly ninety years the state has engaged in suppressing the use of ganja and has failed. It took the first four decades to communicate its resolve and to force ganja use underground, spent the next two in very repressive measures, and, when those failed, resorted to softer measures, including education and rehabilitation. The reason for that failure lies as much in the culturally entrenched nature of ganja and the practices surrounding its use as it does in the mistake of state agencies in classifying it as a drug, where the popular culture does not. So the message that ganja can be harmful encounters an impenetrable mental block.

II

In recent years the lobby for legalization of ganja has steadily grown. The Rastafari are no longer the only section of the society campaigning for the dismantling of the laws against it. A National Committee for the Legalization of Ganja, drawing on a cross-section of people including professionals from the middle classes, has lent respectability to the cause, which they see as including economic considerations as well, since hemp has many industrial uses. As a result of the agitation of this Committee, a motion was passed in the House calling on government to set up a commission to look into the issue of decriminalization. Acting on this, the Prime Minister appointed a commission in September 2000 to consider and recommend whether government should decriminalize ganja for personal use in private. There were two notable points about the terms of reference, one being the distinction between decriminalization and legalization. Legalization of ganja would encompass the repeal of all laws pertaining to the proscription of this substance, its cultivation, possession, trafficking, and use, whereas decriminalization refers to a limited legalization, to wit the use of the substance under prescribed conditions. For example, the so-called 'medical marijuana' is the decriminalization under the prescribed condition of having legal medical authorization to use it.

The second point was that the remit of the Commission included consideration of its use 'for religious purposes'. What was notable here was that the terms did not specify the Rastafari, although most people would have identified the Rastafari as the intended beneficiaries should the recommendation be favourable. The wisdom of leaving the terms general rather than specific is immediately evident if one were to consider what would happen were the Commission to close the door on Rastafari use. The Commission would open itself to the charge of being anti-Rastafari in a way that could not apply were it to close the door on religious use.

The composition of the Commission was also carefully considered. It ensured an island-wide spread in terms of eastern, central and western Jamaica; religious representation; representation of medical expertise; youth representation; legal representation; representation of the academy; and representation from the NCDA – all within the limits of seven persons, a comfortable working group. Immediately on its being announced, the composition of the Commission was attacked by the National Committee for the Legalization of Ganja, which felt that the Commission was loaded with anti-ganja people in order to guarantee a recommendation against decriminalization. The Committee felt that the medical doctor on the team, a member of the University of the West Indies community, who was also a Vice-Chairman of the NCDA, and, curiously, myself would have been biased against decriminalization, and faulted the absence of a representative of the Rastafari movement to provide a counter-balance. They were not the only ones to lament the exclusion of the Rastafari. Rastafari themselves and others sympathetic to decriminalization were of the feeling that for all its sacrificial witness to the benefits of ganja, no Commission could be set up to consider decriminalization of ganja that did not include the Rastafari. Such persons, however, failed to take the full picture into account. Rastafari inclusion could just as easily have elicited the accusation of weighting the Commission in favour of decriminalization, especially because it could not have been assumed that the other members were not in favour. The critics also failed to see that a recommendation in favour, without a Rastafari presence, would serve to strengthen the case for decriminalization, since persons who had no known personal interest in favour of it would have taken the decision. And what if such a Commission were to recommend against decriminalization? There is little doubt, based on the precedent of the 1961 Mission to Africa, that there would have been a majority report and a minority Rastafari report.[8] In short, the membership of the Commission was one of the best possible, well balanced and including persons known for their professionalism and integrity.

Method of work

It took two months after the announcement and meeting with the Prime Minister before we were able to begin our work. Despite being able to obtain a majority should the Commission be deadlocked, we took the decision to work by consensus. However, decisions on issues were a long way off, since our first task was to gather data. This we would do by ensuring the widest coverage of the island and representation of views of all the important sectors and stakeholders of society. We interpreted our mandate not as a polling of opinion, which could be done scientifically and possibly more cost-effectively by random sampling, but rather as an uncovering of and deliberation on the issues involved. Decisions were to be based not on majority opinions but on consideration of all the legal, scientific, ethical, cultural, political and international issues as they were identified.

Hearings were to be of two sorts – *in camera* and in public, a balance which it was felt would allow those who might have felt intimidated or compromised by the presence of others to make their depositions in confidence, while affording as many people as possible the opportunity of being heard. In addition the Commission invited representation from a wide range of private sector and professional organizations, and organizations of civil society, as well as commissioning briefs on the legal and international treaty dimensions. A web page and email address opened up the Commission to views from interested persons overseas. Finally, the Commission took advantage of a business trip by one of its members to gain first-hand information on the controlled decriminalization of cannabis use that has been a feature of the drug policy of the Netherlands.

Not long into the hearings the Commission had to adjust its method, when the staging of the planned public hearings failed to bring forth much response; it decided to take the hearings to the people in targeted communities and urban centres. Thus, the combination of hearings held *in camera* and in town squares and markets characterized our visits to every parish of the island. With these adjustments, it found that people, male and female, of all ages and walks of life, were generally forthcoming and willing to share their views. As most of these were extolling the virtues of ganja, the Commission made a deliberate attempt to seek out sources it thought might be contra. Thus were visits made to one church and two seminaries, and comments invited from the leadership of several Christian denominations.

The issues

What then were the issues identified which formed the substance of the Commission's deliberations? The most salient ones may be summarized. The first in logical priority was whether cannabis was harmful, sufficiently so to warrant the sanctions imposed against it. A review of available medical and scientific evidence established that ganja could produce acute but temporary disorders such as anxiety, paranoia and psychosis, not to mention impairment of certain cognitive functions. This was not surprising. Ganja, after all, is a psychoactive substance. Against these effects the Commission had to place many well-known benefits, some of them already part of Jamaican folklore for generations, and providing important clues for medical scientific investigation. The Commission took note of the rise of 'medical marijuana', which an increasing number of states had begun taking on board. It had to place in its deliberation the fact that virtually all ingested substances, including prescribed medicinal treatments, often produced unwelcome, even harmful, side effects, leaving open the issues of over-use, tolerance and personal psychic disposition to explain differences in effects. One effect that was of concern to the Commission was the 'Amotivational Syndrome', a condition to which adolescents were reported to be especially vulnerable, leading to lower levels of educational achievement and dysfunction.

A second issue was the matter of the perceived inequity in the treatment of substances, such that alcohol and tobacco, which were known causes of incapacitation and death across the world, were legal, but cannabis, far less debilitating and not known in its history of use for causing a single death, was not. To many people, especially those influenced by Rastafarian beliefs, this created a sense of victimization, ultimately serving to undermine the rule of law. Others, however, while conceding the inequity, felt that the decriminalization of cannabis would make an already bad situation worse.

Third was a cosmological argument, which, by distinguishing natural from man-made substances, reasoned that the natural form in which ganja was consumed and banned in Jamaica not only precluded its classification as a 'drug' with other artificial substances like cocaine and alcohol, but placed it in the same category as any other vegetable matter or herb. The sanction against this plant flew in the face of the natural order and was therefore tantamount to hubris. According to the leader of the influential Roman Catholic Church, because sin lay in abuse rather than in use *per se*, the use of ganja was not of itself sinful or immoral, but the abuse of it was.

A fourth issue was the extent to which ganja contributed to the proliferation of a drug culture, whether by association (by virtue of its criminal status) or by inducing the use of harder substances. Although the charge of its being addictive has been dismissed, and its inducement of predisposition to other substances is unproven, there was still the argument that – the criminal drug network being the same for ganja as for cocaine and crack – the passage from ganja to cocaine was made easier. This argument was used by both those for and those against decriminalization. For the former, decriminalization would serve to isolate crack/cocaine and other hard drugs; for the latter, by removing the cover of illegality it would expose more people to the hard substances. Those against also feared that decriminalization would lead to more widespread use of ganja itself, while those for it believed that ganja already being so widely available with impunity, whatever increase in use decriminalization would cause would be minimal and insignificant.

Fifth was the extent to which ganja use and its cultural significance in Jamaica posed problems for law enforcement. The Commission received evidence from a wide cross-section of people, including some law enforcement officers, that the inability of the police to suppress the criminal activity of ganja use was serving to undermine respect for the police and the rule of law. Indeed, there were allegations that some law enforcers were not above using it, which was not surprising, given the evidence of its endemic nature.

Deliberating on these and other issues, taking account of the opinions for and against, the Commission came

> to the unanimous conclusion that ganja should be decriminalized for adult personal private use.
>
> Its criminal status cannot be morally justified, notwithstanding the known ill effects it causes in some people. It contravenes natural justice, seeing that it has been, like other natural substances, a part of the folk culture in Jamaica for decades prior to its criminalization, a part of recognized medical practice for centuries, and a part of herbal lore for millennia in other parts of the world. Nor was its criminal status first recommended by scientific evidence in any way remotely resembling the proliferation of research, some of it of questionable value, now being called on to justify its current status.

In reaching that conclusion, the Commission basically left the *status quo* untouched, except in one singular respect. By *status quo* was meant the stand-off between the existing sanctions and enforcement, on the one hand, and the widespread, uncontrollable use of ganja, on the other. Ganja, though retaining its illegal status, was nonetheless available for use with relative impunity. The exceptional change would be in the great relief decriminalization would give to the five or six thousand Jamaicans of all ages who annually run foul of the law, whose careers were often wrecked as a result.

III

Once the decision had been taken the immediate consideration was how it might be acted upon. The preamble to the terms of reference drew attention to the existence of 'international treaties, conventions and regulations to which Jamaica subscribes that must be respected'. The pertinent international conventions were (1) the 1961 Single Convention on Narcotic Drugs; (2) the 1971 Convention on Psychotropic Substances; and (3) the 1988 Convention Against Illicit Traffic in Narcotic Drugs and Psychotropic Substances. None of these Conventions require the prohibition of the consumption or use of cannabis, but they do require the prohibition of possession. Although the Secretary-General's Commentary and the interpretation given by the International Narcotics Control Board explained that the intent of the 1961 Convention was to criminalize possession for the purpose of trafficking and not for personal use, the 1988 Convention made explicit the requirement to criminalize 'possession, purchase or cultivation ... for personal consumption'.

How then would it be possible to decriminalize personal use but not purchase or possession for personal use? To the legal mind, this is unworkable. And this was the conclusion reached by Professor Stephen Vasciannie in the very detailed brief he prepared for the Commission. The Conventions would require subjecting to criminal law 'all important stages preceding consumption, but not consumption itself'. Thus, the possibility of decriminalizing consumption was but a formal one, 'implausible in practice'.

An important rider limitation to the Conventions is their subjection to the constitutional principles and basic concepts of the legal system of each Party, and this is set out in the pertinent articles. For example Article 3, paragraph 2 of the 1961 Single Convention reads:

> Subject to its constitutional principles and the basic concepts of its legal system, each Party shall adopt such measures as may be necessary to establish as a criminal offence under its domestic law, when committed intentionally, the possession, purchase or cultivation of narcotic drugs or psychotropic substances for personal consumption ....

This limitation, the Commission was of the view, opened the way for Jamaica to decriminalize possession for personal use and use itself, if the Charter of Rights made the right to privacy and to freedom of religious belief and expression inviolate. At the present time a saving clause in Jamaica's constitution allows all laws in force prior to the day when the constitution came into effect (6 August 1962) to supersede the human rights provisions in the constitution, where they conflict. However, both government and opposition have tabled draft amendments to the constitution that would effectively remove the saving clause and allow Jamaica to take advantage of the limitation clause. The intention of both drafts is to make the human rights of the citizens subordinate only to the requirements of public emergencies, public disasters, and not to any other laws. Thus, the Commission's recommendation would first require an amendment to the constitution that entrenched a charter of rights.[9]

But is the decriminalization of use unworkable? The Commission thought of the possibility of allowing the growing of a limited number of the plants in the private space of one's home, but felt that such a concession would be open to abuse. Given the still–flourishing export trade, and the difficulty of policing the tens of thousands of householders who would now become legitimate growers of a small number of plants, what would prevent these private user/growers from selling their crops to the exporters? What would prevent non-users from growing cannabis for this kind of export? Decriminalization is unworkable only in an abstract sense. In the real world of twenty-first century Jamaica it is quite feasible, since as things now stand the overwhelming majority of users evidently do procure the substance with impunity. The Commission's proposal would make procurement still subject to sanction, but, under the constitutionally guaranteed right of privacy, possession of small quantities for use in private not so subject.

IV

Decriminalization represents an initial and necessary step in correcting a grave ill. Clearly, what is called for is the complete legalization of ganja, which is possible only by amending the UN Conventions to remove cannabis from the list of banned substances. But the imposition of the law in the first place and the failure of its prosecution over the years raise an important issue concerning the rule of law, or, more generally, the relationship between the state and society. Does the fact that behaviour is culturally meaningful mean that it cannot be sanctioned? What makes cockfighting illegal but boxing not? What is the meaning of independence if the post-colonial people are still subject to the colonial laws?

From an anthropological point of view, law is the codification of customary manners and behaviour. It works in synchrony with morality, protecting society against deviance. Laws that depend solely on the naked power of the state for their enforcement are repressive, and they succeed only to the extent that the balance is tipped in favour of the state. But as the history of colonialism shows, such victories are only temporary, unless the hegemonic classes succeed also in bringing about moral conformity to the law. The rule of law is never secure unless it is sanctioned by the moral order.

Jamaica's dilemma lies in maintaining a colonial order in a post-colonial state, a task that demands repression and must undermine the moral foundation of the independent state. During the colonial times, Rastafari opposition to the rule of law, particularly where ganja was concerned, sought to undermine the moral authority of the colonial state. This was in effect the thrust of their defiance, for which they were willing to pay the price of marginalization and imprisonment. The failure of the post-colonial state to remedy this contradiction has contributed in no small measure to the rise of open defiance of the law, such that now ganja is smoked openly on the streets and at public gatherings such as football matches and popular music concerts. Indeed, many of those who oppose decriminalization oppose it because of its association with what they see as a breakdown of the moral (read colonial) order, such that people can publicly flout the law at will.

The sooner the state is able to harmonize the law with social morality, the better for the rule of law. The longer it vacillates, the worse. Already in at least one other area, the public use of 'bad words', or Jamaican expletives, enforcement of an obsolete law has led to its defiant violation, so that enforcement depends on the power of the state rather than on repulsion and ostracism by the general public. The lesson from cannabis is that the state may criminalize cultural practice at its peril.

NOTES

1   According to George Roberts (1957, 1979) Jamaica received only 8 per cent of the immigrants over the entire period of indentureship.

2   Ganja use was not the only practice assimilated by the Africans. Indian influences can be seen in the foodways, particularly in the use of curry, and in the Jamaican folk religion, Revival, in the presence of the Indian spirit.

3   Mayor's Committee on Marihuana (1944) *The Marihuana Problem in the City of New York: Sociological, Medical, Psychological and Pharmacological Studies*, Lancaster, Pennsylvania: Jaques Cattell Press.

4   Great Britain, 1969, *India Hemp Drugs Commission, 1893–1894. Marijuana Report*, Silver Springs, Maryland: Thomas Jefferson.

5   See Barry Chevannes, 1994, p. 131. Robert Hinds was one of the four persons credited with spreading the Rastafari movement during the 1930s and early 1940s. The others were Joseph Hibbert, Archibald Dunkley and Leonard Howell, credited with being the very first to preach that Haile Selassie, the Emperor of Ethiopia, was God.

6   A general election was planned to be held in 1967.

7   See Carl Stone, 1974.

8   The government accepted the recommendation of the team of University of the West Indies scholars that studied the Rastafari movement to send a Mission to Africa to investigate the possibilities for migration there. (See M. G. Smith, Roy Augier and Rex Nettleford, 1961.) The nine-man Mission included three members of the Rastafari movement, who submitted their own Minority report. Despite this, however, the Majority report was accepted. A Technical Mission to work out the details was already on the continent when the government lost the elections and so the project had to be aborted.

9   At the time of writing, a charter of rights is still pending Parliamentary debate and passage.

REFERENCES AND SELECT BIBLIOGRAPHY

Chevannes, B. (1994) *Rastafari: Roots and Ideology*, New York: Syracuse University Press.

Hope Enterprises Limited (2001) *National Household Survey of Drug Abuse in Jamaica*, Kingston, Jamaica: National Council on Drug Abuse.

Roberts, G. (1979) [1957] *The Population of Jamaica*, Millwood, New York: Kraus.

Rubin, V. and L. Comitas (1975) *Ganja in Jamaica*, The Hague: Mouton.

M. G. Smith, R. Augier and R. Nettleford (1961) *Report on the Rastafari Movement in Kingston, Jamaica*. Mona: Institute of Social and Economic Research.

Stone, C. (1974) *Electoral Behaviour and Public Opinion in Jamaica*, Mona: Institute of Social and Economic Research, University of the West Indies.

Vasciannie, S. (2001) 'International Law and the Decriminalisation of Marijuana in Jamaica', *West Indies Law Journal*, 26, 1 and 2 (May and October).

CHAPTER 3

Drug Courts in Jamaica

Means to an End
or End in Itself?

ANTHONY HARRIOT AND MARLYN JONES

This chapter reviews the adoption of drug courts in Jamaica and questions whether they are the appropriate response to Jamaica's drug-related problems and will lead to a reduction in arrests for violations of Jamaica's Dangerous Drugs Act. The chapter concludes by questioning the recommendation, in Jamaica's recently concluded Commission for the Decriminalization of Ganja, that decriminalizing the use and possession of marijuana would help to alleviate Jamaica's problems of crime and violence.

Crime is universal and independent of drug use. However, there is a complex relationship between drugs and crime, which falls into three categories: drug-defined crimes, drug-related crimes and crimes associated with a drug-using lifestyle (Walker 1998: 247). Many methodologically rigorous research projects indicate a strong drug–crime nexus that holds in different contexts, including the major drug-producing countries (Andrade 1995), the major drug consumer markets (Sechrest 2001, citing Ostrow 1998) and the transit countries of the Caribbean (Maingot 1989; Griffith 1997). While drug trafficking and dealing tend to be strongly associated with some categories of violent crime, drug use tends to be primarily but not exclusively associated with property crimes. Yet, despite a growing awareness that for most drug offenders treatment is more useful than incarceration, in some Caribbean countries the criminal justice response to drug use has been in the main to increase the number of incarcerations for these offenders.

After almost a century of anti-drug policy making, problems associated with illicit drug dealing and use persist with renewed vigour and greater complexity. Confronted by administrative problems of court overload, overpopulation in the prisons, and, in some instances, public pressure to revise official attitudes to the use of selected drugs (and perhaps even elicit an acknowledgement that incarceration is futile in addressing drug use), reform efforts within and beyond the Caribbean have sought to develop alternatives. One such reform is the implementation of drug courts that have now gained support from numerous categories of stakeholders and a broad segment of the public. Consequently, drug courts are now considered 'one of the major justice reforms of the last part of the twentieth century in the United States' (Goldkamp 2000: 1).

The success of drug courts has led to their proliferation and expansion within the United States and their consequent adoption in many other countries (Cooper 2001; National Drug Court Treatment Survey 1999).[1] Burdon notes that in 1994 there were only 21 drug courts in operation in the US (2001, citing General Accounting Office 1997). By December 2000, however, the US Drug Court Program Office reported that there were approximately 600 drug courts, with an additional 465 in the planning stage all over the United States and its territories.[2] The 2000 *Drug Court Survey Report* identified over 1,200 drug courts – four times the number in existence in 1997. Of these, 434 had been in existence for more than two years, 337 had been implemented recently and 467 were in development (Cooper 2001: 2). By 31 May 2001, during the Third International Association of Drug Court Professionals, six countries (England, Canada, Australia, Ireland, Jamaica and Brazil) had joined the United States in the implementation of drug courts, with several other countries contemplating the same action.[3]

Drug courts are now being established in the Commonwealth Caribbean. In December 1999, Jamaica passed its drug court legislation, The Drug Court (Treatment and Rehabilitation of Offenders) Act. The Jamaican legislation was justified on the basis that the services provided are necessary to change the behaviour of non-violent drug-abusing offenders, and in 2002 the first drug court was established. Jamaica's drug courts were implemented to offer drug abusers the option of treatment and rehabilitation instead of a jail sentence. These were the first such courts to be established in the Commonwealth Caribbean. Since then, the heads of government of the CARICOM countries have signalled an important shift in drug policy within the region by stating that drugs should be treated as a public health issue.[4] On this basis one may reasonably expect new initiatives that are consistent with this policy, including the introduction of drug courts in other jurisdictions in the region.

Although it was the Canadian government that provided Jamaica with practical support in erecting the drug courts, the US provided the model for these courts. Therefore the chapter begins by reviewing the history, main features and effectiveness of drug courts within the United States. The review sets the stage for examining Jamaica's adoption of drug courts and provides a context within which the applicability of alternatives can be considered.

History and main features of drug courts in the United States

Drug courts are special judicial proceedings generally used for non-violent drug offenders. They feature supervised treatment and periodic drug testing. The movement commenced in the United States during the 1980s in response to the deluge of drug-related cases (Burdon 2001; Hoffman 2000; Miller 2001; Shichor and Dale 2001). The US drug court movement was intended to bring drug treatment systematically to the criminal justice population entering the court system. Three basic elements common to many drug court programmes are the goals to reduce recidivism, reduce substance abuse among participants, and rehabilitate participants. Programmes vary, however, in terms of approaches used, participant eligibility and programme requirements, type of treatment provided, sanctions and rewards, and other practices. For instance, some programmes are limited to first-time offenders, while others have wider-scale applicability (DCPO 1998).

The main purpose of drug court programmes is to use the authority of the court to reduce crime by changing defendants' drug-using behaviour (Cooper 2001). In exchange for the possibility of dismissed charges or reduced sentences, defendants are diverted to drug court programmes in various ways and at various stages of the judicial process, depending on the circumstances. The National Association of Drug Court Professional Standards Committee (1997) identified the following ten key components that are essential for drug courts. Drug courts should:

- incorporate drug testing into case processing;
- promote a non-adversarial relationship between defendant and court;
- identify eligible participants early and promptly place them in the drug court programme;
- provide access to a continuum of treatment and rehabilitation services;
- do frequent monitoring and testing for abstinence;
- have a coordinated strategy to govern drug court responses to participants' compliance;
- include ongoing judicial interaction with each drug court participant;
- monitor and evaluate programme goals to assess their effectiveness;
- provide interdisciplinary education to promote effective drug court planning, implementation and operation;
- promote strong partnerships among drug courts, public agencies and community-based organizations that generate local support and enhance drug court effectiveness.

Having described the main features of the drug courts, we may now discuss its effectiveness in the context of the US.

Evaluation of the effectiveness of drug courts

Evaluation is an integral element of policy implementation. It allows one to know if a programme is achieving its intended purpose(s) and may generate information and insights that inform improvements to the programme. With respect to drug courts in the US, 'to date, approximately 60 evaluations of varying methodological sophistication have been completed' (Burdon 2001: 77). Many of these were process evaluations focusing more on drug court design, implementation and operation, and less on post-programme outcomes. Other evaluations focus on and solicit the views of individuals who are involved in drug courts (Goldkamp *et al.* 2002). Nonetheless the range and diversity of programmes, population and judicial structures makes it difficult to evaluate the effectiveness of programmes conclusively (Cooper 2001: 1).

The Drug Court Program Office (DCPO) notes that monitoring and evaluating are critically important functions but acknowledges that 'evaluation of drug courts is a particularly troublesome area'.[5] One of the factors identified as having an impact on evaluation is the infancy of most drug courts. Among the obstacles identified are: difficulty in identifying appropriate comparison groups; constant change in such matters as eligibility criteria; unclear prioritization; and inadequate management information systems (MIS). With regard to the latter, the DCPO recommends that a priority issue for drug court practitioners should be the development of an effective MIS that integrates the following key characteristics:

- ability rapidly to record and transmit a wide range of information about individuals subject to the court's authority;
- effective linkage to secure integration with existing criminal justice, treatment, public health, and social services agency information systems, enabling rapid retrieval and exchange of information between and among courts and other agencies;
- structures that can be programmed easily to yield reports needed for monitoring and evaluation purposes.[6]

For Burdon, while most evaluations have been positive, there is insufficient data to conclude definitively that 'drug court programmes have a significant and long-lasting impact on the reduction of drug use and associated crime' (Burdon 2001: 77). Gebelein also cautions that early evaluation results are not definite because different kinds of drug courts produce varying results. Nonetheless, while drug courts will not solve the drug problem or eliminate crime, when properly implemented they have considerable potential for improving public safety (Gebelein 2000: 5). Despite the limitations, some consistent findings have emerged about drug courts. The most consistent is that drug courts, because of 'their design and stated objectives, are better able to closely supervise drug offenders in the community than other forms of community-based supervision, such as probation' (Burdon 2001: 77). Areas where drug courts appear to be more effective than traditional treatment include: reducing recidivism and drug use (Cooper 2001; Spohn 2001), increasing the employability of graduates (Gebelein 2000: 5), supervising defendants in pre-trial status and convicted offenders, responding promptly to non-compliance, integrating drug treatment with other rehabilitation services, freeing-up criminal justice resources to handle violent and other serious cases, and reuniting families (Drug Court Clearinghouse 1997). These successes, asserts Gebelein (2000: 5) 'appeal to all political philosophies and go far to refute the notion that "nothing works"'.

Overcoming the limitations

Treatment retention has emerged as a critical outcome measure and the best predictor of a client's long-term success (Miller and Shutt 2001; Young and Belenko 2002: 299, citing Gerstein and Harwood 1990; Hubbard *et al.* 1997; Simpson *et al.* 1997). According to Miller and Shutt (2001: 92), high enrolee failure is a primary threat to continued improvements as failure rate has been higher than 90 per cent in some drug courts.[7] Nonetheless, recidivism rates continue to be reduced for both graduates and individuals who enter but do not complete and retention rates remain high (Cooper 2001: 5).

Questioning whether drug courts work, Goldkamp (2001: 31) suggests that the issue should be reformulated in two logically sequential parts. The first issue should address whether a drug court produces better results in dealing with certain categories of criminal cases in comparison with not having a drug court. Second, one should ask: if a drug court works, how does it work? Since there may be unrealistic expectations for crime reduction, the question becomes, for whom and what do drug courts work?

It is acknowledged that some formats of drug courts work. Programmes work for those who stay (Cooper 2001: 5); the challenge then is to reduce the drop-out rate. Miller and Shutt (2001) suggest that screening could be used to maximize retention and increase efficiency in drug court treatment. Screening refers to the practice of choosing applicants most apt to succeed. While acknowledging the potential for 'creaming' or 'cherry picking' being used as a tool for exclusion, Miller and Shutt (2001: 93) suggest that cases can be screened for beneficial background variables, a process in which both clients and services are screened for selection.

Cherry picking has consequences for internal validity, but for the community's sake, it could be used to redirect drug courts to serve segments of the population that are amenable to treatment (Miller and Shutt 2001: 102). Thus an advantage of screening is its potential to 'underscore treatment needs of more risky admittees thereby leading to tailored programmes, innovation and improved retention' (Miller and Shutt 2001: 103). However, variables such as recidivism, crack as the drug of choice, existence of criminality before drug use, prior drug treatment, and social stability are significantly related to the failure of drug courts and should be integrated as vital elements in screening mechanisms (Miller and Shutt 2001: 101).

There are several perils of drug courts. Some researchers have suggested that success should be more realistically defined since results of more sophisticated evaluations may not support the early claims to success, and evaluations that suggest more modest outcomes may result in diminished support for the courts (Gebelein 2000; Hoffman 2000). Moreover, differences in treatment options and the characteristics of participants may affect outcomes (Miller and Shutt 2001: 102). Additionally, success often carries with it the germ of failure and budgetary constraints may prevent an increase in resource allocation despite increased clientele.

Eligibility criteria

An aspect of drug courts that has been subjected to much criticism is the choice of eligibility criteria. Saum et al. (2001: 107) note that although little is known about the effectiveness of drug court programmes for other offenders such as those with lengthy criminal histories, drug courts are slowly expanding their admission criteria from first-time drug offenders. Consequently, some courts now include the participation of more chronic and serious offenders with more extensive criminal histories and more complex cases. The 1997 Drug Court Survey Report found that only 12 per cent of the reporting programme limited participation eligibility to defendants with no criminal charges. However Cooper (2001: 1), reporting changes since the 1997 Survey, observes that programmes appear to target more severely addicted defendants and defendants with more extensive prior contact with the criminal justice system. Consequently, fewer programmes now focus on the first offender.

A problematic element is the extension of programmes to encompass offenders convicted of several felonies and individuals with criminal histories that qualify them with habitual offender status. Most programmes, including the Jamaican programmes, still limit participation to persons with histories of non-violent criminal offences and tend to terminate the participation of clients who commit a violent offence while in drug court programmes (Saum *et al.* 2001: 108).

However, as Saum *et al.* explain, there are problems inherent in the definition of violence and differences across states as to what constitutes violence (2001: 109). For example, what may be considered a non-violent misdemeanour in some jurisdictions may in others be termed a violent felony. Similarly, first-time burglars who steal to support a drug habit may be denied treatment due to their 'violent' past. The practice of excluding violent offenders is motivated by the political mandate to get tough on crime. Yet because most violent criminals will be released from prison at some point, and given the association between drugs, crime and violence, violent offenders could benefit most from substance abuse treatment (Saum *et al.* 2001, citing Goldstein 1995; Inciardi and Saum 1996). If community safety is the primary evaluative focus, then in the long run the savings could be greater if the more problematic offenders were rehabilitated. This outcome led Saum *et al.* to conclude that the drug court model may be the best tool for managing the more serious offenders, who may face the greatest barriers to successful rehabilitation (2001: 108).

Another problem of eligibility stems from the practice of using an offender's current offence as the criterion for admission to drug court treatment programmes when the current offence may not be the best indicator of their criminal history. Thus despite the proliferation of drug courts, only a small proportion of drug-abusing offenders receive treatment while being involved with the criminal justice system (Burdon 2001; Saum *et al.* 2001: 109). Therefore, it appears that it would be more advisable, when selecting candidates for drug court, to look at the extent of offenders' charges and the type and/or seriousness of the substance abuse problem, rather than simply at whether there is any history of violence.

Problems arising from the criteria used for eligibility to participate in drug court programmes include the use of drugs as the criterion of admission rather than assessments of the extent of the drug problem and the type of drug used. The assumption that all offenders who have committed drug crimes are also drug users is incorrect. Similarly, as noted by Saum *et al.* (2001: 109), assuming that all offenders with substance abuse problems will benefit from similar types of treatment also limits the utility of drug courts.

Coercion

Drug courts, by their very nature, are coercive. As described in the National Drug Control Strategy (Budget Summary for fiscal year 2003), drug courts 'provide alternatives to incarceration by using the coercive power of the court to force abstinence and alter behaviour through a combination of escalating sanctions, mandatory drug testing, treatment, and strong aftercare programmes' (ONDCP 2002: 4). As drug courts are behaviourally oriented, based on clear rules and expectations with specific punishments imposed by the judge for non-compliance, they rely heavily on punishment for inappropriate behaviour rather than reinforcing appropriate behaviour (Burdon 2001, citing California Association of Drug Court Professionals 1997; Cooper 1995; Goldkamp 1994; Terry 1999). The literature on drug court evaluation and treatment indicates that:

- the drop-out rate is greatest at the beginning;
- the longer an offender is in treatment, the better the outcome;
- the combination of court and treatment is superior to each on its own;
- participants are less likely to reoffend, commit less serious crimes when they reoffend, and commit fewer crimes.

Coercion may be regarded as a useful lever that is essential to the success of the courts or alternatively as an obstacle to successful rehabilitation. On the other hand, others have urged that the tension between the development of coercion and voluntary treatment must be resolved. The early indications are that the coercive element may be useful. But is the coercive element essential to successful treatment? This is by no means a settled issue. Young and Belenko's evaluation of three mandatory drug treatment models found that the likelihood of staying in treatment for six months or more was nearly three times greater for clients in the most coercive programmes (2002: 314).

However, it may be argued that, instead of coerced treatment, prevention should be emphasized, whereby a drug-dependent individual could get early treatment through voluntary programmes rather than criminal justice intervention after problems have arisen.[8] The caution against the overuse of the criminal justice system as a mandate entry point for treatment has merit because the potential exists that the availability of coerced treatment could relieve the pressure to expand voluntary treatment, and/or could crowd out spaces for voluntary admission in programmes that are already operating at capacity.

The relative success of coerced criminal justice treatment compared with voluntary treatment has implications for budgetary allocations. For example, a concern with the implementation of California's Proposition 36 was that other addiction funding would be reduced. Thus an increase in the number of offenders treated may reduce the available resources per client leading to a deterioration of treatment quality. Although greater success can be achieved by continuing to improve the operations and expanding to large populations, the full potential of drug courts will require 'continued partnership and increased sophistication to develop optimal service delivery, funding mechanisms and information management' (Peyton and Gossweiler 2001: 20).

In an article entitled 'Drug Court Scandal', Hoffman summarizes quite sharply concerns about the proliferation of drug courts despite the inability to conclude that they reduce drug use and associated crime. He notes:

> Despite an enormous reservoir of data, enormous federal financial incentives to prove effectiveness, and an express congressional directive to undertake meaningful effectiveness studies, the evidence on drug court effectiveness remains breathtakingly weak (Hoffman 2000: 1498).

Hoffman (2000: 1500) goes on to say that 'drug courts are being adopted across the country with no meaningful discussion or debate'. Moreover, despite wide-scale acceptance of drug courts, it 'present[s] issues that demand healthy scepticism and continued scrutiny … [because] Drug courts can be abused just as drugs are …'[9] Healthy scepticism is important, with its most valuable expression being ongoing evaluation; yet scepticism is not always viewed favourably. According to Tauber (2001), challenging their existence at a time when the drug courts have evolved into the most important criminal justice reform movement of this generation constitutes an error of political judgement that endangers the advances that the courts represent. Tauber also sees drug legalization initiatives and legislation such as California's Proposition 36[10] as having the potential for eroding the gains of drug courts. The rationalization for this belief is that these propositions set the stage for the next step in the legalization movement's agenda for *de facto* legalization of dangerous drugs (Tauber 2001).

This leads one to question whether drug courts should be viewed as a means to an end or an end in themselves. Are drug courts simply a political tool to be used in a wider engagement for legalization, a political bridge to legalization, or an institutional response to the drug problem that is of value for its effectiveness and the political values that it represents? These perspectives are not mutually exclusive, but attitudes to these courts will differ according to which aspect is emphasized. Related to this is a second issue – can alternative options achieve the same or better results?

Applicability to non-US jurisdiction

Drug court evaluations are moving from questioning whether drug courts work to when and how they work. Acknowledging that what works best in one jurisdiction may not work in another, Scotland decided against the implementation of drug courts. The Scottish feasibility study noted:

[Drug courts] appear to have demonstrated benefits in every jurisdiction where they have been introduced not just for those brought before them but also for society more generally in both social and financial cost terms ... [yet] establishment of full time specialist drug courts in Scotland would not sit easily within the Scottish system and may in any case be impracticable, given other demands on the system.[11]

Similarly, Jamaica should undertake a critical evaluation of the utility of drug courts for addressing its needs. Using the components identified by the National Association of Drug Court Professionals Standards Committee, this section assesses the adoption and evaluates the applicability of drug courts within the Jamaican context. Although there are ten key components, the issues raised here are ongoing judicial interaction; frequent monitoring and testing; continuum of treatment and rehabilitation; and the monitoring and evaluating of the programme and its cost. Two issues of concern with respect to the potential effectiveness of the drug court are the commitment of judicial time and the availability of treatment resources, including facilities for drug testing – factors that are grossly inadequate in Jamaica.

Judicial resources

Involvement of the judiciary is an integral part of drug court programmes. In the drug court, the judge in consultation with treatment professionals directs the treatment programme and holds the defendant or offender personally and publicly accountable for treatment progress. Judges preside over drug court proceedings; monitor the progress of defendants through frequent status hearings; and prescribe sanctions and rewards as appropriate in collaboration with prosecutors, defence attorneys, treatment providers, and others. Importantly, in the case of the Jamaican courts, these others include the members of the family of the drug-dependent person – and their views are carefully considered. Within contemporary society, trial within a reasonable time is a fundamental due process right. The Wolfe Report identified delay in cases being adjudicated to be among the problems being experienced by the Jamaican judicial system. An overburdened justice system was identified as the primary factor causing the delay (Wolfe 1993: 77). The devastating consequences on the justice system led Wolfe to recommend that 'the jurisdiction of the Resident Magistrates Court be seriously reviewed and the Court relieved of the responsibility of adjudication on simple offences which could otherwise be disposed of' (Wolfe 1993: 78).

In the United States, where federal resources for the implementation and continuation of drug courts abound, the popcorn effect has had a deleterious impact on judges both in and out of drug courts (Hoffman 2000: 1504). For example, in Denver, drug court judges typically have on average a high of 140 and a low of 88 defendants on their docket each day, whereas non-drug courts handle an average of eight to 12 defendants per day. Bench warrants have also become problematic for Denver drug court judges. The sheer size of drug courts and a greater likelihood of failure to appear resulted in the number of bench warrants issued. Consequently, the additional burden of bench warrants added to the time judges already spent on massive dockets. This created a backlog of bench warrants that increased each year, thereby adding to the work of each subsequent drug court judge (Hoffman 2000: 1505).

Drug courts have been critiqued for turning judges into super-parole officers, robed therapeutic administrators and policy makers, areas for which judges are not suited. Thus Hoffman (2000: 1524) states that 'no court's "purpose" should be to curtail a perceived social problem, no matter how lofty the curtailers' motives or how scurrilous the perceived problem ... [their] function is to ensure that the rule of law is justly enforced'. Consequently the drug court alliance between the triage of services and the cooperation attendant on such alliance may (usefully) put the adversarial nature of courts at risk. Drug courts, notes Hoffman, are the living embodiment of judge-created policies that impinge on legislative and executive functions and 'waste judicial talents' (2000: 1526–7). Moreover, 'judges, are not social workers or psychiatrists. [They] administer the criminal law because the criminal law is its own social end. It is not, or at least ought not be, a mean to other social ends' (Hoffman 2000: 1478). From a Caribbean perspective, this is quite an arguable point, but he rescues it somewhat by suggesting that it is perhaps difficult to find 'a more dangerous branch (of government) than an unrestrained judiciary full of amateur psychiatrists poised to "do good" rather than to apply the law' (Hoffman 2000: 1479). The following summary is quite pertinent:

> The apparent paradox of more drug defendants going to prison out of courts designed specifically to send fewer drug defendants to prison is not surprising at all. It is a direct and predictable consequence of dismal recidivism results coupled with massive net-widening ... there is no small amount of irony in the fact that one of the most important promises of the drug court movement – to keep treatable defendants out of prison – has turned out ... to be one of its most abject failures ... [because the] paternalistic effort to throw the criminal nets wider and wider in hopes of finding more treatable defendants ... [the] nets are now so wide that there are more untreatable defendants going to prison than there were in the old days, when we did not pretend to be able to distinguish the treatable from the untreatable (Hoffman 2000: 1512–13).

Supervised treatment and periodic testing

Supervised treatment and periodic testing are critical elements of a drug court programme. Essential criteria for the effective operation of drug courts are the capacity to conduct frequent, accurate and random drug testing of participants, and to obtain these test results quickly. Other critical elements of a drug court testing programme include adequate staffing and the ability to maintain the integrity of the process (Robinson and Jones 2000: 7–11).

Drug court programmes initially require a significant outlay of financial resources because drug testing costs are not necessarily fixed price services, the initial cost for procuring equipment may be substantial, and drug testing technology tends to change fairly rapidly (Robinson and Jones 2000). In addition, there are significant costs associated with operating the programme, including staffing, training, facilities, and storage of specimens. Since an array of institutional and financial commitments needs to be assembled before any drug court will work, implementation of a programme without empirical research can mean putting scarce resources into areas without the requisite returns.

Programme evaluation

At the time of writing, there were only two drug courts in operation in Jamaica – one in the capital city of Kingston and the other in Montego Bay, the island's tourism capital. At the time of writing these courts had been in existence for less than one year and there were reportedly less than 40 persons in the programme.[12] Of these, the vast majority were being treated for crack cocaine dependence and a few for heroin dependence. Some were polydrug users, but none were admitted to the programme for exclusive use of ganja. The duration of the programme is client-specific and determined by the court-appointed treatment provider. The project is still suffering from problems that are typical of the early stages of operation, including what appears to be a high drop-out rate. Thus far there are no graduates. It is therefore too early to evaluate the impact of these courts.

The difficulty is not that there are no evaluations, but rather that, despite some effort from the Ministry of Justice, there are no evaluative mechanisms. This de-emphasizing of the importance of proper evaluations may have many sources, including a fear that the courts may not be 'working', but of these, the view that these courts are morally right and just is perhaps a decisive factor in accounting for this disinterestedness in evaluation. It is regarded as being right in itself regardless of the instrumental outcomes, as simply the right thing to do. Drug courts are largely viewed as representing a break with the past in responding to the drug use problem. They represent a break with the traditional brand of adjudication – from an adversarial approach to a cooperative methodology, from the repressive penalty with which the system has been associated historically and which was primarily concerned with punishing the offender, to a more humane treatment of the offender. This new approach has energized the officers of the court and elicited a new response from the drug dependents and their families. Similarly, the outcomes in terms of reduced crime rates may be somewhat discounted because of the great importance and immeasurable value of these courts in terms of their legitimacy dividends. Finally, we wish to suggest that evaluations may be somewhat discounted because the courts are a foreign innovation and it is expected that the innovators will undertake the necessary evaluations in order to further perfect their creation. It would follow from this that there is no need for evaluations to support Jamaican adaptations and innovation. These are somewhat unpleasant but real difficulties which at present serve to retard the evaluation processes and the success of the courts in the Jamaican setting.

The Jamaican dilemma

The underlying rationale for the implementation of drug courts is that drug use causes crime and that reduction in illegal drug use will reduce crimes. Consequently drug courts have utility only for crimes associated with a drug-using lifestyle, in which individuals both use drugs and commit crimes or are driven to committing crimes because of their drug use. The increase in violent crimes in Jamaica is in part due to drug trafficking and drug dealing, not the prevalence of a drug-using lifestyle. The population of hard-drug users is still quite small. The most recent Survey of Drug Abuse in Jamaica (2001) estimates it to be some 0.5 per cent of the general population within the age range of 12–55 years. The same survey estimates that some 8.5 per cent of the survey population are users of cannabis. These are not lifetime users but rather current users, or those who used ganja during the year of the survey.[13] This drug is readily available, however, at an affordable price. In the Jamaican context, cannabis use therefore hardly ever drives one to commit other crimes in order to support the habit. The returns from the drug courts in terms of reducing crimes associated with a drug-using lifestyle are thus likely to be low, but the project may nevertheless be useful as an early response in anticipation of a growth in the number of hard-drug users.

Another reason for lowering the expectations of the drug courts as a crime control instrument is the limited resources that are available to develop an effective triage of medical/treatment, criminal justice and social services facilities and programmes. Elements of this are present but are not well articulated or systematically pursued.

Table 3.1 Arrests for drug-defined crimes, 1995–2001

YEAR	MALES		FEMALES		TOTAL
	Jamaican	Foreign	Jamaican	Foreign	
1995	83% (3,928)	4% (203)	9% (420)	4% (200)	4,745
1996	72% (2,666)	16% (576)	9% (336)	3% (103)	3,681
1997	81% (2,831)	6% (220)	9% (315)	3% (101)	3,467
1998	90% (6,625)	3% (242)	6% (460)	1% (109)	7,444
1999	88% (5,898)	3% (201)	7% (483)	2% (132)	6,714
2000	90% (7,957)	2.5% (221)	5.5% (491)	2% (194)	8,863
2001	86% (5,568)	4% (226)	7% (455)	3% (196)	6,445

Notes: 1 These drug-defined crimes include cultivating, trafficking, dealing and possession.
2 The rows may not sum to 100 per cent due to rounding.
3 There are differences between the figures in this table and those in Table 3.3. These are due to honest errors in the frequency counts provided by the Jamaica Constabulary Force (JCF) – which are based on manual counts taken at different times but using the same source data.
Source: Computed from data provided by the Narcotics Division of the JCF.

There is very little empirical evidence to indicate the value of the programme in terms of crime control outcomes. Assessment of data from Correctional Services of Jamaica and Jamaica Constabulary Force (JCF) statistics – covering arrests for dangerous drugs (use, possession or export) or incarceration for drug offences – indicate that the majority of Jamaicans arrested on Dangerous Drugs Act charges are for possession, dealing and trafficking offences. No evidence is available in the official statistics to suggest that drug abuse is giving impetus to the commission of serious crimes (see Tables 3.1 and 3.2). Indeed, the JCF statistics indicate that drug use is not a primary factor in criminal activities; instead, drug dealing and access to illegal guns (which are facilitated by the drug trade) are the most problematic criminal aspect of the drug problem.

It is currently posited that Jamaica's crime and violence are driven by the drug trade, with more recent reports indicating that Colombian cartels may

Table 3.2 Arrests for possession by type of drug 1995–2001

Year	Ganja	Cocaine	Other
1995	3,680	452	4,132
1996	3,285	396	3,681
1997	3,112	362	3,374
1998	6,703	649	7,352
1999	6,007	711	6,718
2000	8,004	859	8,863
2001	5,522	923	6,445

Source: Narcotics Unit, Jamaica Constabulary Force.

be establishing their presence in order to better facilitate drug activities being routed through the island. For example, Jones notes that recent changes in Jamaica's domestic environment include an increasing volume of cocaine transiting the island, the 'Colombianization' of Jamaica's drug trade and the possibility of a transition from political tribalism to narco-political tribalism in Jamaica (Jones 2002). The increase in cocaine transshipment through Jamaica has also increased women's participation in the drug trade, with an increase in Jamaican and foreign nationals incarcerated in Jamaica and also Jamaican women incarcerated abroad (see Table 3.3).

Table 3.3 Males in prison for drug-related offences, 1995–1998

Year	Age			Total drug offenders	Total prison population	% Drug
	17–20	21–25	26–30			
1995	16	215	116	347	2,119	16
1996	23		90	117	230	
1997	196	167	199	562	2,347	24
1998	112	136	99	347	2,271	15

Source: Compiled from Correctional Services of Jamaica Statistics.

This raises the question as to whether Jamaica's problem of crime and violence could be better addressed through alternative strategies. As indicated earlier, most of the persons convicted of drug possession are ganja users (see Table 3.2). Jamaica's recently concluded Commission on Ganja recommended the decriminalization of marijuana. The rationale is that such action would free up considerable criminal justice resources, thereby allowing criminal justice personnel to address more serious criminal justice issues.

For Hoffman (2000: 1475) current response to drugs fuels two unpalatable policy choices – either continue to fill prisons with drug users or legalize drugs. However, MacCoun and Reuter (2001) note that by focusing on extremes of prohibition or legalization, the current debate ignores the usefulness of more 'finely differentiated control options' such as those found in the control of licit substances. Acknowledging that criminalization may increase drug problems and that legalization would possibly lead to increase in drug use, MacCoun and Reuter suggest that a mid-range policy would be most effective. Since drug policy makers should work toward diminishing the adverse effects of prohibition, instead of legalization or decriminalization, depenalization, it is suggested, would reduce penalties without significantly increasing use. Depenalization refers to 'a substantial reduction of penalties for possession of modest quantities of prohibited psychotropic drugs' (MacCoun and Reuter 2001: 74). Thus, if a significant proportion of Jamaica's drug offenders are convicted of marijuana-related offences, drug courts become moot if decriminalization/depenalization is introduced.

Violence appears to be entrenched in Jamaican society. Thus issues of crime and violence within Jamaica need to be urgently and systematically addressed. Most drug court programmes target individuals charged with possession or trafficking of either cocaine or heroin, no history of violence, and clear signs of dependence. Since, as noted earlier, the more serious drug crimes are trafficking or are associated with trafficking rather than use and minor possession, drug courts are not likely to ameliorate Jamaica's drug problems. Hence the implementation of drug courts is primarily of symbolic value; it addresses the appearance rather than the essence of Jamaica's problems and simply results in the allocation of resources without the attendant crime control returns. Thus, a notable issue within the Jamaican context is: what is the degree to which alternative processes can meet Jamaica's long- and short-term drug control needs?

Conclusion

Despite the difficulties and imperfections, the non-adversarial character of the drug courts represents an advance in the response of the Jamaican criminal justice system to drug users. There must be an ongoing search for better solutions to the drug problem. However, if the drug court is taken as a given reality, there is still considerable scope for innovations designed to make it more effective. One problem is that it is profoundly paternalistic in dealing with the offenders brought before it. The interested family member(s) tend to be treated as the responsible party whose views are taken into account by the judge and his committee. This raises issues of responsibility and the place of responsibility or self-ownership of the problem of drug dependence in treatment and 'curing' of the participants in the programme. While the coercion of the court may be useful in initiating the process of breaking drug dependence, if the outcome is to be successful, at some point in the process the subject will have to freely wish to escape their enslavement to drugs. This transition should not be left to chance, or be seen as a post-treatment development, but rather must be built into the design and management of the process.

The drug courts may not turn around the drug problem, or significantly reduce drug-related crimes, but may be useful for the image of the courts and serve an important legitimating function. They contrast with the old image of the courts as places of harsh punishment with little consideration for the 'fallen'. The importance and value of this legitimating function should not be underestimated. It makes the drug courts worthwhile even if they yield very little in terms of crime control, as they point to the need to re-examine aspects of the present justice system. The drug court experience may yet open up a debate on the applicability of the method of the courts, of the non-adversarial, non-penalizing approach of the court, to other types of problems. The Jamaican family court could perhaps be re-examined in the light of this experience, and there is no good reason why a similar method, perhaps more explicitly informed by the principles of restitutive justice, could not be applied in dealing with some categories of violent crime.

The drug court may be seen as an important first step in depenalizing drug dependence, but the problem of ganja (cannabis) remains. In the Jamaican setting the societal pressures to legalize it will remain. In Jamaica, it is difficult to medicalize this issue by arguing that its users should be treated (as for an illness). And successful repression is too costly, does too much harm to police–citizen relations, and is unlikely ever to be successful. Increasing attempts by police officers to enforce the law are leading to violent conflicts with members of the public – resulting in tragedies that only harm the reputation of the police. At some point it will be difficult to avoid a legislative review – regardless of new discoveries on the degree of physical harm inflicted by ganja on its users.

NOTES

1   Executive Summary: Treatment Services in Adult Drug Courts, Report on the 1999 National Drug Court Treatment Survey.
    <http://www.ojp.usdoj.gov/dcpo/NCJ188086exec.pdf>, [2002-04-21].
2   < http://www.ncjrs.org/drug_courts/drug_courts.html>
3   International Association of Drug Court Professionals (IADCP) holds International meeting,
    < http://www.problemsolvingcourts.com/Newsletter3/t4.html>[19 April 2002].
4   See Press Release 91/2002, Communiqué Issued at the End of the CARICOM Heads of Government Meeting, Guyana, July 2002.
    <http://www.caricom.org/pressreleases/pres91_02.htm#STATEMENT%20ON%20REPORT%20OF%20THE%20REGIONAL%20TASK%20FORCE%20ON%20CRIME%20AND%20SECURITY>
5   See Introduction and Executive Summary. www.ojp.usdoj.gov/dcpo/monitor/introex.htm
6   *Ibid.*
7   See General Accounting Office (1997), cited in Miller 2001.
8   For an example of this kind of argument, see the article 'Drug Courts are Popular – Will They Be Good?', *Digest of Addiction Theory and Application*, 20, 7 (July 2001), Brown University.
9   *Ibid.*, pp. 7–8.
10 The Substance Abuse and Crime Prevention Act, also known as Proposition 36, was passed by 61 per cent of Californian voters on 7 November 2000. This initiative allows first- and second-time, non-violent, simple drug possession offenders the opportunity to receive substance abuse treatment instead of incarceration. Proposition 36 allocates $120 million annually for five and a half years to pay for treatments services.
    See <http://www.prop36.org/>

11 http://www.scotland.gov.uk/cru/kd01/green/courts03.htm
12 This is based on a personal interview with Justice Gayle, the judge in charge of the drug court in Kingston. He was reluctant to give an exact figure as this was constantly changing due to the high drop-out rate.
13 See the *Daily Gleaner*, 26 November 2002, p. A9.

REFERENCES AND SELECT BIBLIOGRAPHY

Andrade, X. (1995) 'Drug Trafficking, Drug Consumption, and Violence in Ecuador', in B. Bagley and W. Walker (eds.), *Drug Trafficking in the Americas*, New Brunswick: Transaction Publishers.

Belenko, S. (1988) 'Research on Drug Courts: A Critical Review', *National Drug Court Institute Review* I (1) 1–42.

—— (1999) 'Research on Drug Courts: A Critical Review – Update', *National Drug Court Institute Review* II (2) 1–57.

Burdon, W. M., J. M. Roll, M. L. Prendergast, R. A. Rawson (2001) 'Drug Courts and Contingency Management', *Journal of Drug Issues*, 31, 1 (Winter): 73–90.

California Association of Drug Court Professionals (1997) *Survey of Current Drug Court Programs in California*. San Francisco, CA: California Association of Drug Court Professionals.

Chevannes, B. (2001) *Report of the National Commission on Ganja*, Kingston, Jamaica: Government Printing Office, August.

Cooper, C. S. (1995) *Drug Courts: A Profile of Operational Programs. Paper presented at the State Justice Institute of Justice*, New York: Narcotic and Drug Research Inc.

—— (2001) 'Drug Court Survey Report: Programme Operations, Service and Participant Perspectives, Executive Summary', OJP Drug Court Clearing House and Technical Assistance Project, American University, November 2001, draft, <www.american.edu/justice/publications/execsum.pdf> [08-12-02].

DCPO (Drug Court Program Office) (1998) 'Looking at a Decade of Drug Court', find at <www.ojp.usdoj/dcpo/decade98.htm> [12 October 2002].

Drug Court Clearing House (1997) *1997 Drug Court Survey Report*, National Criminal Justice Office, US Department of Justice. <www.american.edu/academic.depts/spa/justice/publications/exel.htm> [2004-05-07]

Evans, D. G. (2001) 'Canada's First Drug Treatment Court', *Correction Today*, 63, 3: 30–1.

Gebelein, R. S. (2000) 'The Rebirth of Rehabilitation: Promises and Perils of Drug Courts', US Department of Justice, National Institute of Justice, NCJ 181412.

Gerstein, D. R. and H. J. Harwood (1990), *Treating Drug Problems*, Vol. 1, Washington DC: National Academy Press.

Goldkamp, J. S. (1994) *Justice Treatment Innovation: The Drug Court Movement*, Washington DC: Office of Justice Programs, US. Department of Justice.

—— (2000) 'What We Know about the Impact of Drug Courts: Moving Research from "Do They Work?" to "When and How They Work"', testimony before the Senate Judiciary Subcommittee on Youth Violence,
<http://www.cjri.com/PDF/testimony.PDF> [12 October 2002]

—— (2001) 'Do Drug Courts Work? Getting Inside the Drug Court Black Box', Journal of Drug Issues, 31, 1 (Winter): 27–72.

Goldkamp, J. S., M. D. White and J. B. Robinson (2002) *An Honest Chance: Perspectives on Drug Courts*, Crime and Justice Research Institute, 4/2002, NCJ 193403.
<http://www.ojp.usdoj.gov/dcpo/publications/honestchance/references.html>

Goldstein, P. J. (1985), 'Drugs and Violent Behaviour', *Journal of Drug Issues*, 15, 493–506.

Griffith, I. L. (1997) *Drugs and Security in the Caribbean: Sovereignty Under Siege*, University Park, Pennsylvania: Pennsylvania State University Press.

Harriott, A. (1996) 'The Changing Social Organization of Crime and Criminals in Jamaica', *Caribbean Quarterly*, 42, 2—3 (June/September).

Hoffman, M. (2000) 'The Drug Court Scandal', *North Carolina Law Review*, 78, 5: 1437–1534.

Hubbard, R. L., S. G. Craddock, P. M. Flynn, J. Anderson and R. M. Etheridge (1997)

'Overview of 1-Year Follow-up Outcomes in the Drug Abuse Treatment Outcome Study (DATOS)', *Psychology of Addictive Behaviours*, 11 (4), 261–78.

Inciardi, J. A. and C. A. Saum (1996) 'Legalization Madness', *The Public Interest*, 123 (Spring), 72–82.

Jones, M. J. (2002) 'Policy Paradox: Consequences of US Drug Control Policy For Jamaica', *Annals of the American Academy of Political and Social Sciences*, 582 (July): 117–33.

Longshore, D. (2001)'Drug Courts: a Conceptual Issue', *Journal of Drug Issues*, 31, 1: 7–26.

MacCoun, R. and P. Reuter (2001) *Drug War Heresies: Learning from other Vices, Times and Places*, New York: Cambridge University Press.

Maingot, A. P. (1989) 'The Drug Menace to the Caribbean', *Current Issues: The World and I*, 7.

Miller, J. M. and J. E. Shutt (2001) 'Considering the Need for Empirically Grounded Drug Court Screening Mechanisms', *Journal of Drug Issues*, 31, 1: 91–106.

National Association of Drug Court Professionals, *Defining Drug Courts: the Key Components*, Washington DC: US Department of Justice, Drug Court Program Office, 1997 NCJ 165478.

National Institute of Drug Court Review (1999) 1, 1 (Summer), find at <ndci.org/admin/docs/ndcir21.doc> [10-09-02].

Office of the National Drug Control Policy (ONDCP) (2002) 'National Drug Control Strategy', 2003 Budget Summary. Executive Office of the President, US. <www.whitehousedrugpolicy.gov/publications/policy/03budget>

Ostrow, R. J. (1998) 'Drugs, Alcohol Linked to 80 per cent of Those behind Bars', *Los Angeles Times*, 9 January 1998, p. A17.

Peyton, E. A. and R. Gossweiler (2001) 'Treatment Services in Adult Drug Courts', Report on the 1999 National Drug Court Treatment Survey.

Robinson, J. J. and J. W. Jones (2000) 'Drug Testing in a Drug Court Environment: Common Issues to Address', OJD Drug Court Clearinghouse and Technical Assistance Project, American University: Issues Paper Series.

Saum, C. A., F. R. Scarpitti and C. Robbins (2001) 'Violent Offenders in Drug Court', *Journal of Drug Issues*, 31, 1 (Winter): 107–28.

Schrest, D. K. (2001) 'Determinants of Graduation From a Day Treatment Drug Court in California: a Preliminary Study', *Journal of Drug Issues*, 31, 1 (Winter): 129.

Shicor, D. and S. Dale (2001) 'Introduction', *Journal Of Drug Issues*, 31, 1 (Winter): 1–5.

Simpson, D. D., G. W. Joe, G. A. Rowan-Szel and J. M. Greener (1997), 'Drug Abuse Treatment Process Components that Improve Retention', *Journal of Substance Abuse Treatment*, 14 (6) 565–572.

Spohn, C., R. K. Piper and T. Martin (2001) 'Drug Courts and Recidivism: the Results of an Evaluation Using Two Comparison Groups and Multiple Indicator', *Journal of Drug Issues*, 31, 1(Winter): 149–76.

Tauber, J. (2001) 'Drug Courts Under Attack', *Christian Science Monitor*, 93, 201: 11.

Terry, W.C. (1999) *The Early Drug Courts: Case Studies in Judicial Innovation*. Thousand Oaks, CA: Sage Publications.

'Treatment Services in Adult Drug Courts: Report on the 1999 National Drug Court Treatment Survey', 5/2001, NCJ 188085, find at <www.ojp.usdoj.gov/dcpo.NCJ188086exec.pdf>

Walker, S. (1998) *Sense and Nonsense about Crime and Drugs: a Policy Guide*, Fourth Edition, Albany, N.Y: Wadsworth Publishing Company.

White House, Office of the National Drug Control Strategy (2002) Budget Summary, Fiscal Year 2003, Washington DC.

Wolfe, L. (1993) *Report of the National Task Force on Crime*, Kingston, Jamaica: Government Printing Office.

Young, D. and S. Balenko (2002) 'Programme Retention and Perceived Coercion in Three Models of Mandatory Drug Treatment', *Journal of Drug Issues*, 32 (1), 297–328.

CHAPTER 4

Drugs and the Prison System

Impact of Legislative Changes on the Prison Crises in the Commonwealth Caribbean Region

WENDY SINGH

The English-speaking Caribbean is plagued by structural poverty, which affects some 12–40 per cent of the population, with the highest percentages in Jamaica, Guyana, St Lucia and St Vincent & the Grenadines. According to official government data and regional institutions such as the Caribbean Development Bank, unemployment ranges from as low as 5 per cent in Antigua–Barbuda to a high of 14–25 per cent in St Vincent & the Grenadines.[1] These high rates of poverty and unemployment have led to increased consumption and trafficking of illegal drugs, which provide a source of claimed 'comfort' for users (rich or poor), and seasonal income for many poor and marginalized in both urban and rural communities.

Structural poverty in the region is aggravated by continued international pressure for governments to meet the high rates of payment of external debt; the dismantling of preferential trade agreements, an example of which is the World Trade Organization rulings on bananas; falling prices for commodities exported from the region, which can be obtained in other countries at lower cost; and severe reductions in foreign aid from the United States of America and the European Union, in keeping with a declining interest in the region (Bernal 2000: 308).[2]

In cooperation with the United States of America and Europe, Caribbean governments have been intensifying their 'war against drugs'. Despite this, it is estimated that as much as 40 per cent of illicit drugs to North America and Europe pass through the Caribbean region. An analysis by the United Nations Drug Control Programme (UNDCP) in Barbados shows that the illicit drug cycle in the Caribbean, from production to trafficking and distribution, represents nearly 10 per cent of the income of the illicit drug industry for the year 2000.[3] This estimated US$3.3 billion contributes to an increase in corruption system-wide, further worsening the social and economic problems of countries in the region, where government attempts to control the activities of drug lords and their local/regional agents are often frustrated.

The illicit drug trade has undoubtedly generated financial gains and employment, but these have been outweighed by the negative impact of violence, corruption, political and social instability, the loss of investment in legitimate businesses and human capital, and future costs to the quality of the workforce. Poverty, unemployment and the harsh consequences of globalization, especially on small island states, accompanied by the adoption of an imposed strategy of a war against drugs that has diverted scarce resources from social investment, have all contributed to the serious problems of corruption, crime and violence. Inevitably, they have impacted negatively on the criminal justice administration system, with the greatest impact being felt by the prison system.

Effects on the criminal justice system

This social policy of confinement is graphically expressed by US criminologist Elliott Currie when he describes prison as having become

> the first line of defence against the consequences of social policies that have brought increasing deprivation and demoralization to growing numbers of children, families, and communities ... It is a self-fulfilling stance, and it will bring us a society we should not want ... a society in which a permanent state of social disintegration is held in check only by the creation of a swollen apparatus of confinement and control. (Currie 1998: 11)

Efforts by governments in the region to combat the smuggling of illegal drugs have resulted in a human security policy that is unjust, or what Noam Chomsky in *Deterring Democracy* (1992) defines as 'population control' of the poor and marginalized. The worst effects are felt in prisons – the final destination of those charged, awaiting trial, or serving a sentence for trafficking drugs or, in most cases, for possession of small quantities of drugs or for committing an offence to feed a drug habit.

Perverse outcomes of the war against drugs on the criminal justice system include: legislation which has resulted in overcrowded prisons and cluttered courts; harsher sentencing laws with longer prison terms for people who are for the most part drug users, not traffickers; large-scale arrests of those found in possession of small quantities of drugs; and the inappropriate incarceration of drug users who need treatment rather than detention. This policy has disproportionately affected women and children, as evidenced by the spiralling number of these vulnerable groups in prisons throughout the region.

Legislation

With regard to legislation at the international level, countries are encouraged to take legal measures against the trafficking and usage of illegal drugs.[4] The

United Nations Convention against Illicit Traffic in Narcotic Drugs and Psychotropic Substances (1988), Article 3, specifically requires countries to:

> adopt such measures as may be necessary to establish as criminal offences under its domestic law, when committed intentionally: (i) The production, manufacture, extraction, preparation, offering, offering for sale, distribution, sale, delivery on any terms whatsoever, brokerage, dispatch, dispatch in transit, transport, importation or exportation of any narcotic drug or any psychotropic substance contrary to the provisions and the 1961 Convention, the 1961 Convention as amended or the 1971 Convention.

At the national level, all Caribbean countries have on their Statute Books some variation of a Dangerous Drugs Act with harsh penalties for breaches thereof. There are very draconian laws on possession of as little as a gram of cocaine or a stick of marijuana, and the consequences of these laws are increasingly being recognized by policy makers across the region. In a Parliamentary debate in Guyana during 1999, parliamentarians argued for a revisiting of the 1988 Narcotics and Psychotropic Substances (Control and Amendments) Act, which stipulated a mandatory three-year jail sentence for anyone caught smoking or even in possession of one stick of marijuana, a crime for which other countries were increasingly applying less stringent measures in order to divert resources to tackling demand reduction, while reserving imprisonment in overcrowded jails for more serious offences.

To be caught in possession of a trafficable quantity of drugs means committing an indictable offence. Definition of a 'trafficable quantity' varies from country to country in the Caribbean. However, the quantities of drugs trafficked are usually so low 'that most of the people arrested, charged and sentenced, are users or small-time peddlers' (Klein 2001: 211). In Guyana, for instance, the quantities specified are one gram for cocaine and 15 grams for marijuana, while in the Bahamas the quantity is defined by packaging of the drug, not by its weight. 'Where a defender is found with two or more "packages", be these rocks of crack cocaine, or of marijuana, he/she is charged with trafficking'. During 2000, the legal weight was raised from 'one gram of cocaine to ten grams in Trinidad & Tobago' (Klein 2001: 212). In Barbados, the Drug Abuse (Prevention & Control) Act (1990), Cap. 131, defines 'trafficable quantity' as 15 grams of cannabis, one gram of cocaine, two grams of heroin, 55 grams of opium and three grams of morphine. In Belize, a person caught with more than one gram of cocaine or 15 grams of marijuana is presumed to be in possession with intent to supply; the burden of proof lies with the defendant.[5]

The harsh legislation has resulted in a flawed human security policy. Often indigents, unable to post bond when caught with a spliff of marijuana, are held in pre-trial detention for as long as a year. In some cases, prisoners awaiting trial remain in prison beyond the maximum time imposed for the relevant offences. For instance, among the Commonwealth Caribbean countries, the Bahamas and Trinidad & Tobago had the highest rates of prisoners awaiting trial at the end of 1997: 42 per cent and 34 per cent respectively.[6]

Imprisonment has increased the stigmatization and marginalization of drug users, many of whom need treatment but instead are criminalized by contact and association with others who have committed serious offences. Not only do they rarely receive treatment, but they are often able to obtain drugs in prison and subsequently increase their dependency.

Increasing rates of arrests

Increased trafficking of illegal drugs through the region has resulted in more drug use. This growing trend is undoubtedly linked to the increase in drug-related crime. For instance, in October 1996 then Prime Minister Basdeo Panday of Trinidad & Tobago told journalists at a gathering in New York that an estimated 75–80 per cent of all crimes in Trinidad & Tobago were drug-related. He also pointed out that the police lock-ups were full of persons on drug charges, and that the legal process involved in resolving these cases had led to a very clogged court system.

Statistics presented by the Inter-American Drug Abuse Control Commission for seizures of illegal drugs, and the corresponding arrests made in 2000, are reproduced in Table 4.1 below. The rates of arrest for illegal drugs per 100,000 inhabitants were calculated based on this Commission's statistics and other relevant data. The rates ranged from 96 in Guyana to 809 in Belize. These rates of arrest stand in sharp contrast with rates in the non-English speaking independent Caribbean countries (except for Cuba): Haiti at 0.8 per 100,000; Suriname at 32; the Dominican Republic at 52. The average rate of arrest for the Commonwealth Caribbean is 337 per 100,000 inhabitants.

Since statistics are incomplete, it is difficult to make conclusive statements, but judging from the make-up of the prison population (as established below), it could be inferred that in the Commonwealth Caribbean there may be a tendency to arrest and charge those in possession of small quantities of drugs as required by law, for this is usually an indictable offence. For instance, in St Kitts/Nevis, the Royal St Christopher and Nevis Police Force reported that the number of offences for possession of controlled drugs totalled 77 in 1999, 84 in 2000 and 115 in 2001; whereas importation of controlled drugs totalled 3 in 1999, 4 in 2000, and 1 in 2001.[7] Many of these persons are drug users, and they are filling up the prisons.

Table/Figure 4.1 Seizures of illegal drugs and corresponding arrests, 2000

Country Year 2000	Seizures of illegal drugs			Totals of illegal drugs		Total arrests	Rates of arrests per per 100,000 inhabitants*
	Cannabis leaf (kg)	Cocaine (kg)	Cocaine salts (kg)	Subtotal (kg)	Subtotal (UN) Cannabis plants		
Antigua–Barbuda	126	25		151	9,317	185	261
Bahamas	3,800	2,740	2,740	9,280		1,811	607
Barbados	2,641	59		2,700	1,078	933	338
Belize	203	13		216	43,000	2,072	809
Dominica	468			468	123,032	257	338
Grenada	103	96	96	295	2,091	225	223
Guyana	98	144	139	381	31,698	747	96
Jamaica	55,900	1,624	1,624	59,148		8,659	325
St Kitts–Nevis	119	53		172	34,057	64	162
St Lucia	1,596	71		1,667	9,314	339	217
St Vincent & the Grenadines	1,709	51		1,760	28,375	490	424
Trinidad & Tobago	8,287**	203	203	8,693	7,200,000	3,200	248

Source: CICAD 2001.*Calculations also based on population statistics provided by the Caribbean Community and the CIA Factbook 2000. See ‹http://caricom.org/expframes2htm› ‹http://www.odci.gov/cia/publications/factbook/geos/ac.html›
** Year 1999.

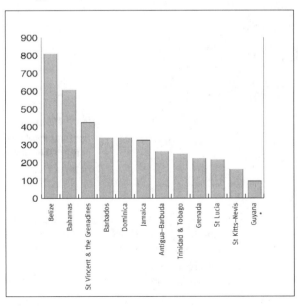

Increasing rates of imprisonment

Over 8 million men, women and children are being held in penal institutions throughout the world. In 1999, more than half of them were in the United States of America (1.7 million, now over the 2 million mark), 1.4 million in China, and 1 million in Russia (Walmsley 1999). In the wider Caribbean, prison populations range from 109 in St Kitts–Nevis to 33,000 in Cuba (Walmsley 1999). The Commonwealth Caribbean countries imprison a total of 14,981 persons. Research shows that Russia takes the lead in imprisoning its citizens (685 per 100,000), with the United States of America running a close second (645 per 100,000).[8] However, Belize and the Bahamas, small island states in the Commonwealth Caribbean, rate sixth and seventh respectively worldwide, with populations of 490 and 485 per 100,000 (Walmsley 1999). Walmsley goes on to say that whereas the median rate for South American countries is 110 per 100,000, for Caribbean countries it is as high as 330. For the Commonwealth Caribbean countries only, the median is 320. When we look at the rate of imprisonment per 100,000 in Caribbean countries, it looks like this.

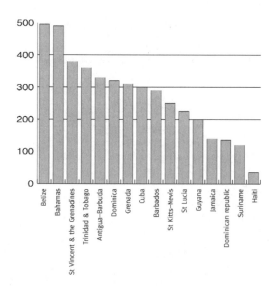

Figure 4.2 Rates of imprisonment per 100,000 in some Caribbean countries

One needs to bear in mind that prison conditions are worsening as the prison populations continue to spiral. The majority of prisons in the Caribbean were built a century ago to accommodate 20–33 per cent of their current population. Overcrowding, together with the squalid conditions, is making the situation unbearable for prisoners and staff.

Profile of the prison population

Young drug offenders

Research data indicate that the majority of those in prison are not there for the trafficking of illegal drugs, but for being caught in possession of drugs or committing an offence to feed their drug habit. A significant percentage of the population consists of juveniles and other young offenders, and of women, the latter often used as 'drug carriers'.

In Barbados, a survey carried out by the National Task Force for Crime Prevention revealed that 24 per cent of the prisoners interviewed at the main prison, Glendairy, had committed their offence in order to buy drugs to feed their drug habit, while 86 per cent of the respondents had used illicit drugs (NTFCP 1997: 53–4). An estimated 57 per cent of prisoners were below the age of 30 at the time of the survey (NTFCP 1997: 43).

Also in Barbados, a UNDCP survey carried out in 2000 showed that 77 per cent of 286 prisoners used marijuana, whereas 36 per cent used cocaine (mainly crack). Twenty-seven per cent of these had been imprisoned twice, 10 per cent three times and 25 per cent 4 times. Twenty-seven per cent had committed their first substance use when under 11 years old, 23 per cent when 11–14 years old, and 50 per cent when they were over 14 years old.[9]

In Guyana, 401 prisoners (an estimated 25 per cent) out of a nation-wide prison population of 1,697 were incarcerated during 1997 for being caught in possession of drugs.[10] The Minister of Home Affairs estimated that of the 822 prisoners at the Georgetown prison, 371 were serving sentences for drug trafficking and possession of narcotics; 345 more were on remand for the same offence; and a majority were young offenders.[11] This means that an estimated 60 per cent of the population at the Georgetown prison were incarcerated for a drug-related offence.

A 1997 report by the United Nations Centre for International Crime Prevention revealed that an estimated 50 per cent of the Jamaican prison population used illegal drugs, and that 53.8 per cent of the prison population in the Cayman Islands tested positive when the first mandatory drug test was undertaken. Estimates place persons convicted of minor drug-related offences and possession of small quantities of illegal drugs as constituting the bulk of prison populations in Caribbean Commonwealth countries (approximately 33–60 per cent), most of whom are categorized as young offenders).[12]

In Grenada, official figures for 1994 showed that a total of 14.4 per cent of prisoners – and 21.6 per cent during 1995 – served time for drug offences. In 1994, 84 were serving time for being found in possession of illegal drugs, while only 7 were in prison for trafficking (NDAC 1995). Also, a survey of the juvenile population in Grenada in 1995 sponsored by the United

Nations Children's Fund, revealed that 80 per cent of the group were drug users (UNICEF 1995).

In 1997, a sample of 323 prisoners at Hattieville Prison in Belize revealed that 61 per cent used marijuana at some point and 40 per cent had used crack or cocaine. A third of the population had continued to use marijuana and 7 per cent were still using cocaine. One out of three persons was in prison for drug possession or trafficking, and 41 per cent committed a crime while under the influence of drugs. A similar percentage committed the crime of purchasing drugs. Fifty-eight per cent identified drugs as their primary reason for serving time in prison.[13] In 1999, it was reported that 400 of the total population at that time (1,061) were young people aged 17 to 21 years old.[14]

Recognizing that imprisonment is inappropriate for drug users, the report of a regional governmental meeting hosted by the UNDCP in Barbados in 1996, acknowledged

> that conviction for offences related to drug abuse resulted primarily in custodial sentences, and noted the absence of appropriate sentencing alternatives. Consequently, the Meeting recommended the development of programmes geared towards alternative methods of sentencing, such as probation, community service orders, counselling and rehabilitation in accordance with international standards. (UNDCP 1996)

Likewise, at the recent July 2002 CARICOM Heads of Government Summit, the Heads acknowledged that drug addiction and use should be treated primarily as a 'public health issue'.[15] The United Nations Office on Drugs and Crime (UNODC) report on *Global Illicit Drug Trends* (2002) acknowledged that the increase in the prison population is mainly related to the war on drugs policy and a lack of effort in the area of demand reduction experience.

Many feel that drug abuse is better dealt with inside the health or social welfare care system rather than within the criminal justice system, especially where there is no violence involved. Drug-addicted offenders need to be dealt with in a more humane manner and not be put in prison if they cannot be treated there, especially since, as indicated earlier, prisoners somehow continue to have access to drugs while incarcerated. The establishment of professionally staffed drug rehabilitation centres is urgently needed. Governments, the UNDCP, the International NGO community and other agencies need to bolster resources and efforts to increase treatment and rehabilitation services throughout the region, and to increase funding for treatment programmes being run by qualified NGOs.

The region's governments have to be more sensitive to what is being done to young people in prison. Recidivism rates are high among these offenders, who pose a new threat to their communities upon release as a consequence of their exposure to hardened criminals and prison life in general. The National Task Force for Crime Prevention in Barbados reported that 56.3 per cent of the young offenders interviewed at the main prison had committed offences more than once within a two-year span, while two-thirds of those who had been convicted as juveniles had been confined previously at the Government Industrial School as a result of their offences (NTFCP 1997: 51). There is an urgent need for more research in this area to determine a more appropriate approach to young offenders.

Women

There is a spiralling number of women in prisons in the Commonwealth Caribbean. Most of them are poor; often they are single heads of households or victims of physical abuse; and many of them have been charged and convicted after being caught with trafficable quantities of illegal drugs. While specific data are unavailable at present, it is evident from the author's experience and anecdotal information from the criminal justice sector that the rising female prison population in the Caribbean mirrors the experience of the USA. One study shows that women constitute the fastest-growing population of people being imprisoned for drug offences in the USA. It states that, 'since 1986 the number of women in prisons has increased 400 per cent'.[17] A report by The Sentencing Project, a non-profit US group, highlighted the following points on 'Gender and Justice':

- Drug offences accounted for half (49 per cent) of the rise in the number of women incarcerated in state prisons from 1986 to 1996, compared to one-third (32 per cent) of the increase for men.

- The number of women incarcerated in state prisons for a drug offence rose by 888 per cent from 1986 to 1996, in contrast to a rise of 129 per cent for all non-drug offences. (The Sentencing Project 1997)

Women in the Caribbean also constitute a large part of the workforce. As an increasing number of female heads of households are incarcerated, children are dealt a double blow, being left without parental care and with limited financial provision. Increasingly the risk of juvenile delinquency among those children whose mothers are incarcerated is having a destabilizing effect on Caribbean societies, with prisons churning out violent young men who, anecdotal evidence has shown, commit worse crimes on their release.

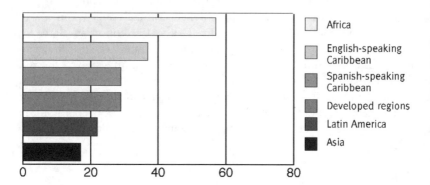

Figure 4.3 Percentage female-headed households (1985–96)
Source: Compiled by development researcher M. Abarca-Diaz from the UN Database

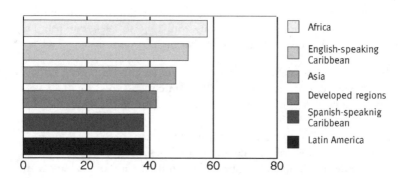

Figure 4.4 Economic activity by regions: women's participation in the labour force as a percentage (1995)
Source: Compiled by development researcher M. Abarca-Diaz from the UN Database

A more appropriate approach

Repeal mandatory sentencing for the possession of drugs

The July 2001 Report of the National Commission on Ganja to the Honourable Prime Minister of Jamaica states:

> The criminalization of thousands of people for simple possession for consumption does more harm to the society than could be done by the use of ganja itself. The prosecution of simple possession for personal use and the use itself diverts the justice system from what ought to be a primary goal, namely the suppression of the criminal trafficking in substances, such as crack/cocaine, that are ravaging urban and rural communities with addiction and corrupting otherwise productive people.[18]

Of course the necessary amendments will have to be made to the Dangerous Drugs Act, and a careful study done to ensure that this depenalization for possession and use will not breach the United Nations Drug Conventions which have been ratified by Jamaica.[19] As established earlier on in this paper, the Single Convention on Narcotic Drugs (1961) seeks to limit the possession and use of all narcotic drugs, while the Convention Against the Illicit Traffic in Narcotic Drugs and Psychotropic Substances (1988) requires states to adopt measures to establish as a criminal offence any activity related to narcotic drugs.

The UNODC notes in its 2002 report *Global Illicit Drug Trends* that the Netherlands took the lead in inserting the principle of expediency into the penal code empowering the public prosecutor to refrain from the prosecution of criminal offences if this is deemed in the public interest. Possession of cannabis up to 5 grams is accorded the lowest priority, and *de facto* decriminalized. It is up to the mayor of each municipality to license regulated outlets, known in Holland as coffee shops, for the sale of cannabis. There are over 400 of these shops in Holland, where up to 5 grams of cannabis can be purchased by adults over 18 years of age without fear of victimization by criminals or police intervention. Despite this ready availability, the prevalence rate for cannabis in the Netherlands is less than half that of the US, where cannabis users face imprisonment and career-threatening criminal records, losing their access to college loans along with their right to vote.[20]

According to the Dutch Ministry of Justice, if drug addicts were simply imprisoned, some 25,000 addicts (0.3 per cent of the population group aged 15–60) would be added to the prison population. Instead, records show that almost 90 per cent of this population is in contact with care providers.[21] The police are entitled to confiscate small amounts of hard drugs and to put persons in contact with a care organization. If the person is arrested and brought before the court, the case is usually dismissed but the drugs are confiscated.[22] Drug use in itself is not a criminal offence; however, if a person under the influence of drugs is repeatedly arrested – for disturbing the public peace and order, for instance – the Public Prosecutor may confront this person with a choice: detention or an addiction clinic (with a dismissal of the case). Treatment is also offered to pre-trial detainees and to persons wishing to serve the remaining part of their sentence in such a clinic. This approach 'is aimed at having as many criminal addicts as possible undergo treatment by providing them with care under dissuasion'.[23]

Other countries are taking steps to repeal mandatory sentencing for drug possession and use. A recent report from the Advisory Council on the Misuse of Illicit Drugs proposed that the British Home Secretary should downgrade marijuana to a 'low-risk' Class C status. It noted that marijuana posed less risk than alcohol or tobacco. This proposal was made shortly after a study released by the Criminal Policy Research Unit of the South Bank University found that 'decriminalizing marijuana would save roughly $71 million a year and free up the equivalent of 500 police officers' who could instead focus on 'violent crime'.[24] It was recently estimated that some five million people in Britain use marijuana regularly.[25] On 10 July 2002, Britain announced that it would relax its laws on marijuana smoking. The United Kingdom would keep the practice illegal theoretically, but would no longer arrest persons making private use of discreet amounts.[26]

A number of other European countries have also relaxed their drug laws. Marijuana possession no longer leads to imprisonment in Spain, Italy, Germany, the United Kingdom, Belgium, the Netherlands or Portugal. Some of these countries have extended this policy to the possession of all drugs.

More recently, a study by The Sentencing Project in the USA showed that an increasing number of states are scaling back their tough sentencing policies for drug offenders. The group reported that 'five states expanded drug treatment as a form of sentencing'.[27]

Reduce the length of sentence for drug use and possession

Guyana has come up with a potentially very appropriate response that would have the effect of both reducing the penalty for possession of small quantities of marijuana as an illicit drug, and helping to ease its problem of overcrowded prisons. The Guyana Parliament amended the 1988 Narcotic Drugs and Psychotropic Substance (Control and Amendments) Act, to allow the courts to impose smaller fines (US$17–34) and community service not exceeding 6–9 months for possession of no more than five grams of marijuana for personal use. Under the old law, convicted persons were heavily fined (as high as US$282) and sentenced to 5–10 years' imprisonment.

At the time of writing this chapter, it could not be determined to what extent community service was actually being utilized in Guyana as an option for drug offenders.

Use discretionary powers to promote treatment as an alternative to custody

In many Caribbean countries, even though there is no provision in the law for treatment and/or rehabilitation for persons found in possession of illegal drugs for personal use or for those who commit drug-related offences to purchase drugs, a magistrate could use his or her discretionary powers to send the person to a centre for treatment. This would require centres that function and that are willing to accept the person. However, in most countries existing centres are private; they reserve the right to accept or refuse admittance of an individual, and require payment. This situation poses a problem to the courts in utilizing this option as opposed to confinement.

In St Kitts–Nevis, the judge or magistrate makes decisions about eligibility for a rehabilitation programme of drug users who have been arrested for drug-related offences. This is based on recommendations from the police, or the prosecutor of a relevant health care body. This is not an option that is being used, however, 'since there are no qualified persons to deal with drug addicts and the prison system does not have a specific drug programme'.[28]

In Jamaica, prior to the establishment of the drug court, domestic legislation did not provide for treatment and/or rehabilitation. As in the other Commonwealth Caribbean countries, this was allowed by a magistrate or judge who was willing to use his or her discretionary powers. At the moment, there are three public institutions and four private institutions, including psychiatric services, that deal with treatment and rehabilitation in that country. The public institutions have a 90 per cent average occupancy rate, whereas the private institutions average a rate of 96.6 per cent. This limits the courts in utilizing treatment as an alternative to custody.[29] However, the Chairman of the Treatment and Rehabilitation Sub-committee of the National Council of Drug Abuse attributes this limited usage not only to a lack of resources, but also to a negative attitude on the part of some court officials who think that law has priority over treatment for drug users; a lack of specific training and expertise among drug court administrators and professionals; and too little understanding of the reality of the problem facing drug users.[30]

According to the UNODC 2002 Report, research has shown that treatment works. It states that follow-up studies in the United Kingdom found that, two years after completing a treatment programme, regular heroin use and acquisitive crime were both reduced by half; in the United

States, weekly heroin and cocaine use were down by two-thirds one year after the end of treatment. The report also states that the global average of people receiving drug treatment was 584 per million inhabitants in the late 1990s, but it also points out that the availability of drug treatment is rather limited in most developing countries.[31] It is obvious that more treatment centres will have to be established and financed throughout the region for this option to be effectively utilized by the courts. This may be accomplished either through a discretionary use of their powers or through mandatory legislation, as in the case of drug courts, or through a Community Service Act that allows drug offenders the option of treatment as opposed to a custodial sentence.

Implement in-prison treatment programmes

Some positive steps have been taken to assist drug addicts with treatment and rehabilitation while in prison. The regional office of the UNDCP implemented a drug rehabilitation programme within the prison in Barbados to assist prisoners addicted to drugs. The team reported that the programme, which was instituted as a pilot project, has now expanded and works with various referrals and support groups.[32]

No formal treatment and rehabilitation programmes exist within the prisons in Jamaica. Prisoners who require treatment for their drug habit may be assisted by specialists. During 2000, a proposal was submitted for the establishment of a substance abuse treatment facility at the main high security prison at Tower Street.[33] In Antigua–Barbuda, an in-prison programme on drug education was scheduled to begin in 1998 but it never got started.[34] In Grenada, no treatment or rehabilitation programmes exist in prison, but some prisoners are visited by counsellors, doctors or psychiatrists. This is managed by organizations such as Friends Forever and the National Drug Avoidance Committee. The Richmond Hill Prisoners Welfare, Rehabilitation and After Care Foundation was set up in July 1999 by the Commissioner of Prisons and his staff.[35]

In Europe, the Dutch drug policy seems to be the most advanced in relation to in-prison treatment programmes. It is based on harm reduction, supply reduction, and demand reduction. Enforcing this policy is done in cooperation with the Ministries of Health, Justice and Home Affairs. The main premises of this policy are:

> Further development of an accessible and differentiated supply of facilities for care and assistance, social integration and better use of the possibilities within the criminal justice system. This involves an integrated policy in which the police, justice authorities and organizations for the care of addicts work closely together. Central aspect of this policy is the 'compulsion and dissuasion' approach.[36]

The current prison drug policy of the Netherlands has three major objectives, according to the Dutch Ministry of Justice:

> Improving control; providing medical care (including methadone maintenance treatment for drug addicts, screening for TB, voluntary testing for HIV, hepatitis and STD and prevention programmes for staff); and preparation for continued drug addiction treatment upon release. In some cases, the vicious addiction cycle is not broken while in prison. In this case, a more forcible and intensive treatment was developed which is carried out at the Penal Care Facility for Addicts (Strafrechtelijke Opvang Verslaafden, SOV). The law regulating this facility came into force on 1 April 2001.[37]

It is expected that the Facility will house drug addicts who repeatedly commit crimes because of their addiction and with whom voluntary treatment has failed; they will be placed in a penitentiary treatment institution for a maximum period of two years. An evaluation has not yet been carried out to determine whether this experiment is successful, but one will be carried out after a few years.[38]

Introduction of new laws

Caribbean governments have made progress in the area of introducing alternatives to custody for non-serious criminal offences. For instance, Barbados enacted a comprehensive Penal Reform Act, Act No. 50 of 1998, which includes legislation for both attendance centres and community service. Jamaica was the first Commonwealth Caribbean country to implement a Community Service Scheme under its Criminal Justice Reform Act (1978). Grenada and St Lucia are considering introducing legislation for the implementation of community service for adult offenders and attendance centre orders for juveniles and other young offenders. Belize and Antigua are in the process of drawing up plans to reform their penal systems. Trinidad & Tobago enacted the Community Mediation Act, Act No. 13 of 1998.

However, except for Guyana as mentioned earlier, and Trinidad & Tobago, these alternatives do not pertain to drug addicts and users who are routinely confined. The Trinidad & Tobago Community Service Orders Act, Act No. 19 of 1997, allows the courts to grant a non-custodial sentence to drug offenders. Given the large number of persons in prisons in the region who commit offences to feed their drug habit, there is an urgent need to deal with this problem as a health care issue, not as a criminal offence requiring imprisonment.

The most serious attempt to deal with the problem so far is through the establishment of drug courts as was first done in the Bahamas, then in Jamaica and Trinidad & Tobago. According to Klein, the drug court in the

Bahamas which was the first to be established (1986) has been the most successful in the Commonwealth Caribbean (Klein 2001: 215). Sentencing guidelines established for the courts promote non-custodial alternatives such as fines, community service and treatment.

The regulations for the Drug Court (Treatment and Rehabilitation) Act in Jamaica have been prepared and implementation provisions are being made. If an individual is arrested and charged with an offence under the magistrate's jurisdiction, and the arresting officer has reason to believe that he/she is dependent on any drug, the magistrate can recommend that the individual be referred to the drug treatment court. The consent of the offender to participate in such a programme is required. Sanctions are imposed by the court for failure to abide by the terms of the programme. However, Jamaica seems to be experiencing difficulty in working with treatment centres owing to their high occupancy rates, as pointed out earlier, and this has resulted in under-utilization of the drug court. Additionally, managers of the treatment centres are refusing to treat anyone sentenced by the court since they feel that treatment should not be forced on drug addicts, but must be a voluntary act since forced treatment often results in failure. Trinidad is focusing on bolstering existing rehabilitation centres prior to implementing treatment as a sentence by the drug court.

It is time to recognize that drug abuse is better dealt with inside the health or social welfare care system rather than the criminal justice system, especially when there is no violence involved.

Conclusion

The trafficking of drugs presents a threat to more than consumers and traffickers. It has emerged as a serious threat to national/regional security, with grave implications for good governance and democracy. As can be ascertained from this chapter, it fosters corruption and criminal violence, and generally weakens the very fabric of societies. It leads to a breakdown in family life, contributes to overcrowded prisons, adds to the problems of already stretched police services and undermines good governance.

Policies adopted by Commonwealth Caribbean governments so far have for the most part focused on the confinement of large numbers of persons convicted primarily of possession of small quantities of drugs, or those who commit an offence to feed their drug habit. This has resulted in a crisis in the criminal justice system, with the worst impact being felt in the prisons where most of these persons are left to languish with their drug addiction.

Dependency on drugs is a health problem and has to be treated as such. It must be removed from the criminal justice domain. If this is not done, the crises being experienced in prisons in the region will never end. It is time to change this policy. Perhaps Caribbean governments are beginning to recognize the necessity for this as acknowledged during the July 2002 CARICOM Summit. Maybe governments will now adopt progressive steps towards the decriminalization of drug addiction.

As already pointed out in this paper, significant progress has been made mostly in Europe, where efforts have been made to find an alternative along the lines of harm reduction policies – measures that reduce the harm drugs do, both to users and to society at large. We cannot continue to focus solely on drug law enforcement, but should give more attention to health and development, which are a fundamental aspect of drug control policy.

The United Nations Declaration of the Guiding Principles of Drug Demand Reduction (1998), which provided the first global standard-setting in the area of harm reduction, emphasizes the need for adequate resources for achieving this. This does not only mean financial resources, but building solid partnerships. In keeping with this, the United Nations Declaration calls for the need for partnerships to be created between governments, NGOs and community-based organizations, especially with target groups such as youth, and to develop culture- and gender-specific interventions.[39] Effective and lasting solutions to the problem will come about through care and cure, not confinement and criminalization.

NOTES

1   Interview with a noted Caribbean journalist, 9 August 2002.

2   According to Bernal, in 1994, aid from the United States of America fell by 72 per cent in Jamaica, 98 per cent in Barbados and 99 per cent in Trinidad & Tobago.

3   'The illegal drugs market in the Caribbean generates an estimated income of 3.3 billion US dollars' or some '3.1 per cent of the registered GDP in the region'. When one considers the 'hidden economy' in our countries, this could account 'for between 20 to 65 per cent of the total economy' (UNDCP Report 2001: 1). Comparatively, US consumers spent US$65.7 billion or 0.7 per cent of the local GDP on drugs, whereas US$10 billion or 0.7 per cent of the local GDP was generated by the drug trade in the United Kingdom (UNDCP Report 2001: 6). The highest *per capita* cocaine flow occurs in the Bahamas with 100 grams *per capita* in annual transit, while Belize has 90 grams per capita: both have largely uncontrolled coasts (UNDCP Report 2001: 6). In St Vincent, 'marijuana exports provide some 10 million US dollars, an income that represents 18 per cent of the Saint Vincent & the Grenadines' legal exports and 3 per cent of the local Gross Domestic Product. It also generates an average income of 85 US dollars for every Vincentian' (UNDCP Report 2001: 7).

4   The Single Convention on Narcotic Drugs (1961) aims to combat drug abuse by coordinated international action. There are two forms of intervention and control that work together. First, it seeks to limit the possession, use, trade in, distribution, import, export, manufacture and production of drugs exclusively to medical and scientific purposes. Second, it combats drug trafficking through international cooperation to deter and discourage drug traffickers.

    The Convention on Psychotropic Substances (1971) establishes an international control system for psychotropic substances. It responded to the diversification and expansion of the spectrum of drugs of abuse and introduced controls over a number of synthetic drugs according to their abuse potential, on the one hand, and their therapeutic value on the other.

The Convention against the Illicit Traffic in Narcotic Drugs and Psychotropic Substances (1988) provides comprehensive measures against drug trafficking, including provisions against money laundering and the diversion of precursor chemicals. It provides for international cooperation through, for example, extradition of drug traffickers, controlled deliveries and transfer of proceedings.

<http://www.undcp.org/un_treaties_and_resolutions.html>

5   Belize, Misuse of Drugs Act, 7 September 1990; Act 22 of 1990.
6   See 'Penal Reform in the Caribbean', a presentation by the author to the Caribbean Drug Control Coordination Mechanism, Barbados, May 2000. Apart from newspaper clippings, prison statistics and other relevant publications, information in this paper draws on 'site visits' and interviews with Prison Superintendents/Commissioners and prison staff.
7   St Kitts-Nevis Observer, 15–21 February 2002.
8   On 15 February 2000, the US prison population passed its two million mark. One in every 130 people is living behind bars (Village Voice, 22 February 2000).
9   UNDCP, Report on Drug Rehabilitation Programme by Drug Team, Barbados, December 2000.
10   1998 Survey for the United Nations by the author.
11   See note 6.
12   Based on estimates from the 1998 Survey for the United Nations by the author.
13   Belize Times, 23 March 1997.
14   Belize, The Reporter, 11 April 1999.
15   <http://www.caricom.org/expframes2.htm>
16   See UNODC, 2002, Global Illicit Drug Trends 2002, New York: United Nations.
17   Lynn Paltrow, 'Women and Drug Use', National Advocates for Pregnant Women, March 2000, <http://www.lindesmith.org/lindesmith/library/focal_women2.html>
18   <http://home2.netcarrier.com/~aahpat/ganja.htm>
19   In relation to narcotic drugs, Jamaica is also a signatory to the Inter-American Convention Against Corruption (1996) and the Inter-American Convention Against Illicit Manufacturing of and Trafficking in Firearms, Ammunition, Explosive and other Related Materials (1997).
20   See note 16.
21   Michel Amoureus, 'Dutch Drug Policy: The Role of the Prison System', a presentation to the Drugs Coordination Unit, Directorate-General Justice and Home Affairs, European Commission, Brussels, September 2001.
22   Ibid.
23   Ibid.
24   Drug Policy Alliance, 14 March 2002,
     <http:// www.drugpolicy.org/news/DailyNews/03 14 02UK.html>
25   New York Times, 11 July 2002.
26   Ibid.
27   Wall Street Journal, 7 February 2002.
28   'Country Profile of St Kitts–Nevis', a presentation to the Caribbean drug control Coordination Mechanism, Barbados, May 2000.
29   'Country Profile of Jamaica', a presentation to the Caribbean drug control Coordination Mechanism, Barbados, May 2000.
30   Correspondence with Mr Howard Gough on 27 September 2002. Mr Gough is also a member of the National Council of Drug Abuse.
31   See note 16.
32   See note 9.

33 See note 29.
34 'Country Profile of Antigua–Barbuda', a presentation to the Caribbean drug control Coordination Mechanism, Barbados, May 2000.
35 'Country Profile of Grenada', a presentation to the Caribbean drug control Coordination Mechanism, Barbados, May 2000.
36 See note 21.
37 *Ibid.*
38 *Ibid.*
39 Stephen Baranyi, 'Drugs and Human Security in the Americas', a presentation for the Department of Foreign Affairs and International Trade Peacebuilding and Human Security Division, Ottawa, December 1998.

REFERENCES AND SELECT BIBLIOGRAPHY

Bernal, R. (2000) 'The Caribbean in the International System: Outlook for the First 20 Years of the 21st Century', in Kenneth Hall and Dennis Benn (eds.),Contending with Destiny: the Caribbean in the 21st Century, Kingston: Ian Randle Publishers, pp. 295–325.

Chomsky, N. (1992) *Deterring Democracy*, New York: Hill and Wang, p. 455.

Currie, E. (1998) *Crime and Punishment in America: Why the Solutions to America's Most Stubborn Social Crisis Have Not Worked – and What Will*, New York: Henry Holt and Company Inc., p. 230.

Griffith, I. L. (1997) *Drugs and Security in the Caribbean: Sovereign Under Siege*, Pennsylvania State University Press, 1997.

Klein, A. (2001) 'New Directions for Drug Control in the Commonwealth Caribbean', *New West Indian Guide*, 33, 3–4: 193–228.

NDAC (1995) *Summary of Drug-Related Statistics for the Year 1994*, St Georges, Grenada: National Drug Avoidance Committee.

NTFCP (1997) *Report on Criminal Risk Factors*, Barbados: National Task Force for Crime Prevention, Office of the Attorney-General.

Steering Committee on Penal Reform (1997) *Report on Alternatives to Imprisonment in Barbados*, Barbados: The Steering Committee On Penal Reform.

The Sentencing Project (1997). *Report on Gender and Justice: Women, Drugs, and Sentencing Policy*, Washington DC: The Sentencing Project.

UNICEF (1995) *Trinidad & Tobago: Juvenile Justice Survey*, Trinidad & Tobago: United Nations Children's Fund.

—— (2000) *Towards a Rights Approach for Children,* Report on Juvenile Justice in the Caribbean, Bridgetown, Barbados: United Nations Children's Fund.

UNDCP (1996) *Barbados Plan of Action*, Bridgetown, Barbados: United Nations Drug Control Programme.

—— (2000) 'Conclusions of the 3rd CCM Task Force Meeting, Final Report', CCM Task Force Meetings 2000, Bridgetown, Barbados: United Nations Drug Control Programme.

—— (2001) *Illicit Drug Market in the Caribbean*, Bridgetown, Barbados: United Nations Drug Control Programme.

UNODC (2002) *Global Illicit Drug Trends 2002*, New York: United Nations Office on Drugs and Crime.

Walmsley, R. (1999) *World Population List*, London: Home Office.

CHAPTER 5

Rethinking Privatization, the State and Illegal Drugs in the Commonwealth Caribbean

PHILIP NANTON

The problem

A recent paper on illegal drugs in the Caribbean outlined the following scenario:

> The traffickers move their cargo across different staging posts, hopping from island to island until the destination is reached. Fast boats leave from the Venezuelan coast for Trinidad, and on to St Vincent. From there, on to St Lucia or Dominica, before entering French waters. At each stage a new group of traffickers can become involved, often receiving payment in the form of merchandise. (Klein 2001)

As well as the regional and international issues of trafficking, there are local dimensions. The increasing and diversified supply and use of a range of illegal drugs – predominantly heroin, cocaine, marijuana and synthetics like ecstasy – have become so extensive and continuous that, beyond the more short-term concerns for political stability, the loss of integrity of individually small, open economies has appeared to be under threat. These problems have been increasingly recognized as unprecedented. One specialist has gone so far as to express the view that 'Drug criminality has no economic, social or political boundaries'(Griffith 2000: 143).

An understanding of the nature and extent of the historical relationship between the public and the private sector and how this relationship has changed and developed in the Caribbean is essential to the formulation of any analysis that links the state, privatization and illegal drugs. In the latter part of the twentieth century, when privatization became a ubiquitous policy concern, its conceptualization in the Commonwealth Caribbean appeared similar to privatization as understood in Western Europe. That is, at first it seemed a more narrowly defined concept, addressing the transfer by sale of the ownership and control of state-owned assets to the private sector.

It also involved the sale of state-owned enterprises, the leasing of state-owned assets and the contracting out of services performed within the public sector. In practice, however, the goal of privatization in the Caribbean context has been debt reduction and fiscal survival.

We need to begin, however, by recognizing the influence on the ebb and flow of privatization of (1) a number of historical factors, and (2) the way in which state authority is exercised. Both these broad influences have profound implications for any conceptual framework of illegal drug trafficking in the Caribbean. In the two sections which follow (on historical and contemporary perspectives), I develop this fundamental principle by demonstrating: first, that the Caribbean region has had a long experience of accommodating privatization (in its widest sense, that of pertaining to the private sphere) in tandem with illegality; second, that the role of the state as a force for regulation in the society has long been circumscribed by migration, systems of belief (particularly Pentecostalism and Rastafarianism) and traditional economic practices that include marijuana growing; and, last, that under late capitalism the Caribbean political economy is being forced to come to terms with new forms of marginalization, including the mixed fortunes which follow from the widening of international market competition and the retrenchment of government and its services. I conclude, in the third section, by suggesting a new and alternative framework within which to examine these issues.

Historical perspectives on privatization and regulation in the Caribbean

The production of sugar by means of plantation slavery, driven by private capital with limited state intervention, was a long-term reality of the region, whose territories – comprising partially carved out, private plantations in the early colonial period – have remained far from clearly delineated states. A common form of revolt against the social restrictions of these amorphous entities was to escape to areas where planters were reluctant to enter without protection, called the 'summits', 'heights', or maroon settlements, after the Spanish term cimarrones (or people of the heights).[1] According to Curtin, 'maroon settlements existed on every sizeable Caribbean island' (Curtin 1990: 104).

Where to draw the boundary of legitimate regulation between one territory and the next in the region has remained an unsettled issue, subject to contestation. In the early colonial period, the islands were traded like booty. It was in this context that St Lucia, which was traded back and forth between France and Great Britain, became known as the Helen of the West

Indies (see also Swanson 1991). At a more prosaic level in the Anglophone Caribbean, boundaries within the British area of rule were also regularly redrawn. This process has continued after the territories obtained political independence. After a brief flirtation with a federal structure in the 1950s, island-based political independence followed in various amalgamations (Trinidad & Tobago, St Vincent & the Grenadines, Antigua–Barbuda, St Kitts–Nevis, and others). Many of these island nation-states, based on uneasy alliances, have been subject to regular threats of secession and the redrawing of state boundaries. Nevis's dispute over its association with St Kitts is the latest illustration of this trend, with the Nevis island assembly voting for a referendum to decide on secession.

A weak regulatory role on the part of the state has gone hand in hand, historically, with disputed boundaries, uncertain scope and privatization. In the seventeenth century, the Caribbean islands seized by Britain quickly became a combination of frontier settlements for the soldiers who expropriated them. In Jamaica, for example, the social historian Pares noted that when the colony was founded, 'It was laid out regiment by regiment; here we are told the regiment of Colonel Barry planted, and there the regiment of General Doyley' (Pares 1960: 3). Central to this period, as noted above, is the early fashioning of the region as a locale of lawlessness, piracy and gangsters, for example through the tradition of the privateers and buccaneers who were at their height in the 1660s. Curtin attests to their longevity when he notes that 'the last Caribbean pirate was hanged in the 1830s, the decade that brought emancipation to the British islands' (Curtin 1990: 96).[2]

The history of plantation slavery has cast a long shadow in the region. There were few regulations to inhibit this privatized process of 'wealth creation'. In the case of Jamaica, Patterson has noted of plantocratic slavery institutions that: 'Power was completely diffused ... state and society were poorly developed, a bureaucracy hardly functioned and when it did was extremely inefficient' (Patterson 1967: 93). Another commentator has drawn attention to the essential characteristics of slave society as revealed by census and other official data between the years 1807 and 1834. Higman demonstrates the extensive ways in which the society was for the most part privatized, harsh and unregulated. That most basic feature of public regulation, a professional police force, was a post-emancipation development. Prior to that period, the policing function of the local militia was aimed at the prevention of rebellion and disorder. With a few exceptions – St George's (Grenada), Port of Spain (Trinidad) and George-town (Guyana) – urban sanitation remained essentially a private matter, public authority confining itself to occasional exhortation. Publicly sponsored education was banned and when introduced was for a long time provided by religious denominations.[3]

Higman's overall assessment of plantation slavery for this period, using census data, is an indictment of the absence of regulation. He demonstrates that once supplies of slaves from West Africa were reduced, the population declined to such an extent that it was threatened with extinction. As he points out for the period 1807–34: 'The central feature of the experience of the British Caribbean slave population was the general failure to achieve a natural increase, to show more births than deaths.' Although Higman identified significant variations in the level of natural increase in a few islands, he argues that: 'The continued harshness of the regimes under which the slaves laboured after 1807 made ultimate extinction a real possibility' (Higman 1984: 4–5).

By the mid-eighteenth century, the massive if short-lived windfalls that accrued from sugar plantations in the islands were being flaunted by white West Indian planters 'at home' in England. Their behaviour became characterized for the English population of the day by the maxim 'as wealthy as a West Indian'. Indeed, during the nineteenth century, the islands appear to have existed in the British mind as centres of British wealth creation. According to John Stuart Mill: 'The West Indies … are places where England finds it convenient to carry on the production of sugar, coffee and a few tropical commodities' (Mill 1868).

Although Mill emphasized the closeness of the business relationship between the Caribbean and Britain at this time, this reality was undergoing change. After the 1820s and the collapse of the second boom in the price of sugar, the fear of increasing costs resulting from the abolition of slavery, growing difficulties in obtaining property sales of plantations because of high mortgages encumbering estates, and with the abandonment of certain estates, a dramatic change occurred, both in perceptions of the fabulously wealthy West Indian and the value of a close relationship with the area. The change is once again to a less flattering view of the Caribbean. The view of the region was of a metropolis-dependent periphery, populated by various forms of colonial cheats and idlers, on whom 'civilization' (never a given in a frontier society) needed to be imposed. On his visit to the West Indies in 1859, for example, the British novelist Anthony Trollope, in his travel writing, made repeated reference to the region's want of 'civilization' and lamentable public institutions, 'of whose public honesty – I will say nothing. Of that I myself will say nothing, but the Jamaicans speak of it in terms which are not flattering to their own land' (Trollope 1859: 121).

One reason for increasing British suspicion was the worsening relationship between absentee landowners and the colonial community. Although this suspicion can be traced as far back as the seventeenth century, it intensified in times of economic decline. Thus, whenever absentee land-lords tried to make claims on their estates in the West Indian colonies, Pares notes, 'Nothing could altogether counteract the tendency of the colonial communities to favour the interests of the resident debtor against those of the creditor in Europe. Every creditor found that *les absents ont toujours tort*' (Pares 1960: 44).

Another important ongoing trend can be identified here. With the economic collapse of sugar and the decline of the West Indies as a region of strategic importance during the nineteenth century, a fundamental change can be identified in the underlying economic structure of the society as well as in the way that the region and its population were perceived. The private business sector, which for a long time relied on metropolitan protection for its export produce, became increasingly oligopolistic with core sets of families in each territory moving out of agriculture into (merchandising) business, controlling significant directorships and operating to influence the agenda of the state (Brown and Stone 1976; Reid 1980). With political independence this reliance on the state has tended to take the form of exclusive government contracts and import licences to prop up domestic markets (Henke and Marshall 2003).[4]

As already marginal Caribbean economies take a downturn, the usual cycles of depression and associated poverty appear to coincide with increased official anxiety over illegal practices (for example, smuggling, avoidance of excise duty and illegal emigration) and the need for regulation. As a result of the West Indies Royal Commission Report (1889), a form of minimum welfare ideology became established in the last twenty years of the nineteenth century. The first locally initiated land settlement policy in the British West Indies, aiming to provide land for the landless, was put into effect in St Vincent in 1885 and subsequently officially sanctioned in the Report. This was one practical response arising from the first of many official enquiries into what was increasingly identified as 'the West Indian problem': poverty, unemployment and maladministration. Among many such reports, the Report of the Moyne Commission, compiled in the 1930s, but embargoed till 1945 because of fear of social unrest, was the best known. This welfare ideology was to expand, with the state taking increasing responsibility for 'development', after island states became politically independent from the 1960s (the result of this expansion is examined below).

Welfare ideologies promoting the legitimacy of the state are, however, overshadowed by a number of privatized traditions and institutions that centre on the individual, that are common throughout the Caribbean and that marginalize the state's regulatory function. One important tradition that increasingly demonstrates this process is emigration. The earliest pressures on migration involved attempts to restrict the outflow of labour, in an attempt to maintain an adequate supply of cheap manpower in the islands. In the nineteenth century, many islands had passed local Emigration Acts, imposing financial penalties on ships' masters for transporting passengers without the requisite certificates. However, given the geographical complexity of the region, with innumerable small cays throughout, for example, the Bahamas, Virgin Islands and Grenadines, implementation was not a simple matter. In the vicinity of St Vincent, the Grenadines became notorious as offering an easy route for ships to pick up illegal emigrants undetected. Many Leeward and Windward Islanders sought to migrate to more wealthy islands such as Trinidad to the south (Richardson 1992). The lament of the Lieutenant-Governor of St Vincent on the difficulties of controlling the illegal migration of 1874 could easily be mistaken for that of a twenty-first century regulator of illegal trafficking. In his dispatches he noted: 'The existence of these scattered islands with sheltered harbours stretching from St Vincent to Grenada makes it difficult to keep control over the Grenadines trade and hence the movement of vessels there' (Public Records Office Rennie to Lawson 30 March 1834, St Vincent Archive, no. 37).

Far from being a problem requiring control and restraint, despite occasional anxieties over the extent of loss of population to some island nation-states, in the twentieth century out-migration became an essential safety valve, offering relief from high levels of under- and unemployment in the region, cheap labour for the metropolis and substantial invisible export earnings. In Jamaica, unemployment was estimated at about 15 per cent of the labour force in 1953 and by the early 1960s emigration from Jamaica had probably reduced unemployment both relatively and absolutely (Tidrick 1973: 191). At this time some aspects of the organization of the out-migration were taken over by metropolitan and local political elites through state institutions. However, the decision to migrate has been that of the private individual. Unemployment has remained a significant problem, though varying in extent from state to state in the region. In the Eastern Caribbean in 2003, for Dominica, St Lucia and St Vincent unemployment rates were estimated to be 23, 19 and 22 per cent respectively but, even though high, unemployment rates were considerably lower for Barbados (10 per cent) and Grenada (12.2 per cent) (see Table 5.1, p. 144).

One result of emigration has been that a defining characteristic of late twentieth century Caribbean societies is the growth of large (in proportion to the size of the remaining 'home' populations) island diasporas in Western metropolitan cities. This phenomenon was region-wide. Premdas has collated Cohen's data to demonstrate that by the 1980s in the UK there was a community of some 650,000 'Black Britons'. By 1990 the French Antilles sent to France 337,000 migrants and to the Netherlands went about 250,000 Dutch Antilleans (Premdas 2002: 58). Nearly half as many of the people of Puerto Rico, Suriname, Martinique, Guadeloupe, and Jamaica as live at home are now located in the traditional metropolitan centres of the USA, the Netherlands, France and the UK (Grosfoguel 1995). Unofficial estimates suggest that nearly as many Barbadians, Vincentians and Dominicans live outside the 'home' society as within it.

Where the state has become politically independent, this population is, in practice, outside the sanction and regulation of the 'home' state. Premdas suggests that this extensive migration requires nothing less than a reconceptualization of the role of the state. He notes that 'the practices of Caribbean peoples are at great variance from the exclusive claims for singular loyalty to the state ... Caribbean peoples share a common deterritorialized imaginary. This requires the reconceptualization of the notion of sovereignty' (Premdas 2002: 60). However, at the same time, many people in Commonwealth Caribbean states rely on remittances from migrants abroad as essential private economic supplements. Remittances to Jamaica are estimated to amount to 4 –5 per cent of GDP per annum; those to Guyana have recently been estimated (probably erring on the low side) at over US$90 million per annum or around 13 per cent of GDP (Orozco 2002). The small numbers who return 'home' to the region after many years are often culturally and socially dislocated. However, despite some unpopularity,[5] they exercise sufficient economic influence for island governments in Jamaica and Barbados to offer formal inducement packages of concessions on their return.

Another phenomenon demonstrating the marginalization of the state is the recent growth of the Pentecostal church in the Anglophone Caribbean, where church attendance and claimed denominational adherence had shown considerable decline in each ten-year census for the past thirty years.[6] The Pentecostal churches are the sole exception to this trend, in showing rapid growth. These churches are most popular with the poorest in Caribbean society. Among their smaller gains, the Barbados census report for 1990 notes an increase for the Pentecostals from 7.7 per cent of church-attending congregations in 1980 to 12.8 per cent in 1990. However, the report also notes that when all branches are combined, 'The largest congregations in Barbados are now found among the Pentecostals.' The report continues: 'The biblical principle of tithing means more money available to support their programmes, including building' (Forte 1996: 26). This simplistic view of its organizational prowess and community appeal greatly underestimates the extent to which Pentecostalism in the region has been able to marginalize the secular state. It should not be overlooked, for example, that those whose incomes are too low to be subject to state taxation are the very people who willingly pay tithes to the church.

In other, less wealthy, societies in the region, the growth in Pente-costalism, particularly in the past ten years, has been dramatic. In St Vincent,

Pentecostals now represent the third largest single religious group. Their growth increased in the ten years from 1981 to 1991 at an estimated rate of 181.3 per cent, achieving 10 per cent of the church-going population. In her study of the history and influence of the church in Jamaica, where Pentecostals comprise the largest single category of religious affiliation, Austin Broos has pointed out the implication of this growth for the state and its role. In terms of both the belief system and practical support, the church has supplanted the state and secular politics.

One of the largest Pentecostal groupings in Jamaica, for example, is the New Testament Church of God. In 1990, from a census population in Jamaica of 2.3 million, the two Pentecostal categories 'Pentecostal' and 'Church of God' totalled around 663,223 – the largest category of religious affiliation. In 1996, the Pentecostals supported 337 churches and maintained assets equivalent to around US$16 million. In that year, the church was also sustaining 62 basic or pre-school centres and two old-age homes. The church further maintained a retirement plan for ministers, funeral assistance and life insurance programmes. In 1991 it maintained 53 retired ministers on pensions. The international links enable members from the Caribbean to obtain access to congregations in other countries (from accommodation to various forms of professional help), particularly in the UK and the USA, where the church is well established. Links with Pentecostal church headquarters enable subsidized study for high achievers up to university level at its own church-affiliated university in Cleveland. Of equal importance to the avoidance of state involvement is the ideological basis on which the world of Pentecostalism is constructed. While adherents do recognize the secular state and politics, these are viewed as peripheral. In Austin Broos's words: 'They leave in their wake a distance from the state, and a quietistic response to politics. This response, moreover, is sustained and encouraged by links with the metropolitan world' (Austin Broos 1996: 63).

The rise and decline of the illegal marijuana crop in the region provides a third illustration of both the continued dominance of the private sphere and the marginalized role of the state. A central feature of most twentieth-century Caribbean economies is their 'openness' and thus their vulnerability to world economic trends. This situation applies to legally grown cash crops as much as to those which are illegal. The pattern of economic expansion and contraction in the traditional cash crop sector of Caribbean economies appears to have been duplicated among marijuana growers. Agricultural production for export has dominated the region from the outset, with small economies shifting over the centuries from one export cash crop to another, as they are overtaken by higher marginal costs because of their smaller scale of production compared with producers elsewhere. One important cause of the demise of sugar production in the nineteenth century, for example, was the availability of cheaper mass production of sugar beet in Europe. In the Eastern Caribbean, typical island products, such as finely woven sea-island cotton, cocoa and arrowroot, were each in turn threatened and then overtaken by more economical Egyptian cotton, West African cocoa and Egyptian arrowroot.

In the context of this pattern of early exploitation of a cash crop followed by its demise as larger producers enter the market, the recently attractive marijuana crop is about to become the latest casualty in this Caribbean cash crop cycle of expansion and decline. This crop appeared to reach a peak of production in the 1970s and is reported to have been in decline for the past two decades. By 2000, Caribbean marijuana growing and exports were replaced in their traditional export markets – the United States, Canada and the United Kingdom – by high-quality local, Mexican or Moroccan production. The United Nations Office on Drugs and Crime (UNODC) 2000–1 Report argues that, in real terms, the value of Caribbean marijuana exports has plummeted by 80 per cent since the early 1980s. In the UK, herbal cannabis from the Caribbean is now estimated to represent less than 2 per cent of the market (UNODC Report 2003: 10).[7]

The historical context traced above thus points to the long tradition of the importance of the private sphere and the underlying peripheral nature of the Caribbean state, both at the level of capital and among the poorest in the labour force. The examples demonstrate why, for fundamental structural reasons associated with traditional patterns of migration, belief systems and economic practices, regulation in the region is likely to be weak, and the role of the private sphere to be uppermost.

Contemporary perspectives on privatization and regulation

In the second half of the twentieth century, as the Anglophone countries obtained political independence, the state appeared to become a more important influence in these societies. Public sector spending increased dramatically, both in manufacturing and government service provision. Micro island governments became part of the world system of international relations. For a while relatively high rates of economic growth were achieved. By the 1970s internationalization of illegal drugs began to affect the region and, as the Caribbean became recognized as a point of transshipment, the use of illegal drugs by the local population was increasingly identified by officialdom as a threat to society. How significant have these changes been and to what extent have the historical patterns re-emerged?

First, the natural vulnerability of these countries, given their location and resources, has been increasingly recognized. The Commonwealth

Vulnerability Index for Developing Countries has assessed the capacity of small island states to withstand economic shocks and natural disasters, and has noted of Commonwealth Caribbean states in particular that: 'They are very dependent upon a small number of exports such as bananas, sugar and tourism for employment and foreign exchange earning ... imminent and future market changes in the world economy may have quite severe implications for their economies – both in terms of their vulnerability and their resilience' (Atkins *et al.* 2000: 32). Of 111 countries evaluated, five Caribbean island countries were rated among the 15 most vulnerable.

Second, vulnerability has been compounded by poorly executed state economic intervention policies in the latter half of the twentieth century. At the height of their expansion in the 1970s, Jamaica operated over 200 state-owned enterprises, Trinidad operated close to 100 and in Guyana the number of public enterprises increased from 18 in 1977 to over 50 by 1980 (McBain 1996; Knight 1997). While there have been important exceptions to the ways in which these enterprises have been managed, Ramsaran has examined the nature and results of Commonwealth Caribbean state interventions and concluded that for the most part they were less than successful and in many instances economically disastrous, with high levels of inefficiency, overcapacity and lack of profitability. Knight adds that many state enterprises were also characterized by patronage and the recruitment of political supporters (Knight 1997). These internal weaknesses were exacerbated by economic shocks and downturns that the region was unable to withstand, starting with oil price increases in the 1970s and continuing through international economic retrenchment in the 1980s and again in the late 1990s. Ramsaran suggests that there is as yet no apparent means of alleviating the internal conditions reinforcing economic decline (Ramsaran 1997).

During the decades after political independence, many state-owned or state-supported enterprises in the Caribbean accrued substantial debt, which the state could not continue to support through public funds. For a time the state had little difficulty in borrowing from commercial banks when official sources were not available. But, as debts increased, if the state wanted to borrow additional funds it was faced with international lending agencies hostile to state expansion. Since the dominant international lending institutions, the World Bank and the International Monetary Fund, have been invited into the Caribbean, they have imposed severe restrictions on Caribbean borrowing. Specifically, the World Bank argued in 1991 that: 'It is better not to ask governments to manage development in detail', but instead, 'governments need to do less in those areas where markets work reasonably well. In many countries it would help to privatize many of the state-owned enterprises' (World Bank 1991, cited in Ramsaran 1997).

It was primarily the concern over debt reduction that was the impetus for the privatization of much of Caribbean state enterprise. In McBain's survey of privatization in four countries in the Caribbean (Jamaica, Trinidad & Tobago, Guyana and Grenada), for example, she argues that, from the perspective of governments, 'Privatization was seen as an end in itself rather than as a means to an end.' As a result, where enterprises were sold, most, she notes, 'were sold to achieve fiscal objectives'. She also notes that there was little sign of a coherent regulatory strategy in tandem with the drive to privatization (McBain 1996).

The more draconian demands of the international regulatory regimes which many Caribbean countries experienced in the 1980s have been tempered, to some extent, by the Second Generation of Reforms. These emerged from the Monterrey Conference in Mexico (2002) and have focused on issues of inclusion, partnership and poverty reduction. Important regulatory standards for such activities as data dissemination, fiscal policy transparency and corporate governance have been identified as the responsibility of the International Monetary Fund and the World Bank; but Marshall suggests that in essence these measures amount to an emerging intricate web of surveillance and discipline that will amount to control over both the public and private spheres in the South (Marshall 2002).

It would be misleading to suggest that after forty or more years of political independence Commonwealth Caribbean states have become totally subservient to international regulatory demands, or to suggest, for that matter, that they have been passive in areas of public policy such as social welfare provision, public sector education, health care and national insurance provision. While many Caribbean states have achieved middle to low ranking in the United Nations Development Programme (UNDP) *Human Development Report* for their efforts at inclusive public provision, a handful, notably Barbados, achieved high ranking (among the top 30 countries internationally), and the Bahamas led the 'medium' range of countries.[8]

As laudable as these achievements are, it is nevertheless important to recognize that the Caribbean states' battle for hearts and minds remains far from won. In the informal sectors there is considerable civic disengagement, which many identify as a lack of confidence in the prevailing social order. Among the youth of the region, Hilaire notes that 'attitudes to the functioning of the state are now characterized by open deviance and, in most cases, subtle rejection through deviance and opposition to traditional social norms and values. And it is among the poor youth – urban as well as rural – that this finds its most poignant expression (Hilaire 2000: 1). This is graphically illustrated by Rohlehr's analysis of what he calls the youth 'culture of dread' and 'culture of terminality' (Rohlehr 1994), and the establishment of 'garrison' communities, essentially urban ghettoized islands of self-regulated communities policed and managed by gang lords (Henke and Marshall 2003). Increasingly, then, an important test for these countries is the way that public sectors perform and the effectiveness with which initiatives are implemented. In a region where skill levels, educational attainment and economic performance do vary widely, so will effectiveness and implementation of public sector policy. The issue of illegal drugs perhaps provides one of the severest tests for all states, and even the more astute face severe contradictions in their attempt to bridge the gap between promises made internationally and their local delivery.

Indeed, international relations have provided one of the main contexts within which security and law and order preoccupations over illegal drugs have come to be discussed during the latter quarter of the twentieth century. This framework prioritized national security in Europe, the USA and the politically independent countries of the region. 'Normal' debate in this context has been articulated as a moral panic about how to improve cooperation against a menace that threatens to overwhelm legitimate government and states and bring about the total destruction of the local population. For example, it is the often-cited view of the West Indian Commission that: 'Nothing poses greater threats to civil society in CARICOM countries than the drug problem; and nothing exemplifies the powerlessness of regional governments more' (West Indian Commission 1992: 343).

A recent volume bringing together practitioners and theorists to report on 'several years reflection' on security in the region, was exercised as to how to solve the problems of illegal drug trafficking and illegal migration. According to the co-editors, 'cooperation has become the predominant theme in discussions of security in the Caribbean Basin' (Tulchin and Espach 2000: 1). The precise nature of this cooperation and the questions to which it gives rise – are there dominant and compliant partners? Do they necessarily always have the same goals or give the goals the same priority? Where are the boundaries of cooperation? – have sorely tested both metropolitan and Caribbean governments. Attempts to answer these questions have suggested solutions on an *ad hoc* basis that may appear to be of more benefit to US than Caribbean interests. This view has been represented by the recent State Department Report on International Narcotics Drug Control as not uncommon in St Vincent (US State Department 2002). Also, in the Eastern Caribbean more widely, progress on initiatives (for example National Joint Headquarters or registration of small craft and crew members) has been hampered and the absence of investigative leads has been associated with 'the lack of personnel, rivalries between law enforcement bodies, and in some jurisdictions, an apparent lack of political commitment'. The result has been 'costly and of limited effectiveness' and, in the euphemistic language of the State Department's 2002 Strategy Report, 'there appears in some cases to be a less than aggressive maritime drug law enforcement posture' (US State Department 2002).

Attempts by the USA to gain a common agreement with regional governments to obtain the unhindered right to pursue suspect air and sea craft in all waters controlled by Caribbean nation-states came unstuck with the objections lodged by Barbados and Jamaica and their renegotiation of the Maritime Interdiction Treaty (Ship-rider Agreement). Watson has outlined the different terms that Barbados negotiated with the USA. He offers a critique of the Agreement as a form of post–Cold War imperialism (Watson 2003). Both countries requested that issues of aid, immigration, anti-gun smuggling and trade be linked to the version of the agreement they would sign with the USA. When joint USA 'advisers' and Caribbean forces conduct operations on sovereign territory it is not unknown, as in the case of St Vincent, for marijuana growers to form a union and conduct public protests concerning the destruction of their crops.

The Caribbean Regional Office of the UNODC presents the illegal traffic in drugs as an extreme form of privatized activity. The Office has been producing data aimed at 'better understanding of regional drug-related issues' based on 'open sources of information, seizure data and interviews'. The implications of their monitoring reports lead to conclusions balefully similar to those drawn by the international relations experts. For example, a recent report estimates that 'with the total illicit drug exports transiting the region estimated at approximately $4,800 million in 2001, this figure almost triples total CARICOM petroleum export earnings (also the number one export income earning sector) for 2000 and in fact surpasses the total of the top five CARICOM domestic exports in 2000' (UNODC 2003: 7).

Klein has drawn attention to the *ad hoc* nature of the establishment of this UN office in the region and raised questions concerning the utility and lack of its data-gathering exercises (Klein 2001). The purpose of these data has also been questioned by Harriott, who has challenged their data-gathering methods. He suggests that

> [t]here may be double counting of volumes transshipped via more than one Caribbean country, thereby inflating the regional totals (the same shipment may be moved via Trinidad and Jamaica), controlled shipments are often added to the totals and they may be subject to political manipulation by various bureaucratic interests. For these reasons different sources may yield different estimates and even different trend lines. These difficulties make it difficult to determine the meaning of the data. (Harriott 2000: 110)

These two streams of thought, focusing respectively on security and trade, and their separate concerns of coercion and incorporation, have in common a framework of social regulation. At the same time the stumbling blocks to effective regulation have been identified as a lack of resources and commitment, an important aspect of the latter being corruption within the ranks of certain governments in the region (Griffith and Munroe 1995, Griffith 1997, Maingot 1994) among certain of the police forces in the region often associated, Harriott suggests, with shifts in drug trafficking activity (Harriott 2000)[9] and in particular industries, for example tourism, where illegal earnings are interwoven with a major regional industry (Pattullo 1996: 91–5). The possibility that some of these issues suggest different priorities – at the individual and community level and between governments in the region and metropolitan governments – that may account to some extent for this shortfall in resources and commitment appears to have been ignored or identified as a sort of weakness of moral fibre rather than real differences of interest.[10]

The state in the Caribbean now finds itself on the horns of a dilemma. On the one hand outside pressures have been forcing Caribbean states to reverse their interventionist policies in the name of 'privatization' – as if the notion is a relatively new one to the region. On the other hand, pressure is great for the state to participate in illegal drug regulation. Both of these things are done. Neither of them is done well. Many of the contradictory features that emerge from this dilemma suggest, in the context of the Caribbean region, the need to rethink the relationship between what has become the conventional late-twentieth-century notion of privatization and state regulation as applied in the Caribbean. Simultaneously, as the role of the state shrinks and it is required to ignore contradictions – like the convenient, *ad hoc*, notion of privatization and subverted notions of cooperation – the state has neither the capacity nor the willingness to carry out effective regulatory practices relevant to illegal drugs. The historical experience of the region does not fit it for either of these roles.

An alternative framework

The evidence presented so far suggests the need to reconceptualize the problem of illegal drugs, the Caribbean state and privatization in a different context. The context that I wish to apply takes account of both historical and contemporary approaches to illegal drugs and provides a way to pay greater attention to local realities.

It is useful to recognize first that both local and metropolitan states appear equally involved in the issue. Pratt has offered a perceptive observation on the nature of this relationship. 'The metropolis,' she notes, 'habitually blinds itself to the ways in which the periphery determines the metropolis, beginning, perhaps, with the latter's obsessive need to present and represent its peripheries and its others continually to itself' (Pratt 1992: 6). In the context of illegal drugs, these presentations and representations centre on the notions of 'civilization' and the 'wild'.

Thus the question that underlies these concerns, I want to suggest, is how to achieve 'civilization'? This question has been a constant in the region from the time of European settlement and colonization through to political independence and has taken different forms in different periods of the region's history. For a considerable time, 'civilization' implied the imposition of external values, including the imposition of labour and industry on a colonial and subject labour force by means of taxation. In the words of a former Colonial Secretary, Lord Grey, proposals for 'civilization' were designed to 'substitute for the direct coercion of the whip by which Negroes had hitherto been impelled to labour' (Grey 1853: 19). According to Grey, 'civilization' was advanced by the establishment of a locally supported public service, to maintain order and security and to establish the infrastructure of roads, schools, places of worship and hospitals. In return for bringing 'civilization' to the colonies, each territory had its part to play in the Empire, for which it would obtain the protection of the 'mother' country. The concern about civilization also has a contemporary form. Courses are regularly taught at the University of the West Indies on 'Caribbean civilization'. They appear to struggle with issues of type and categorization (see for example Gutzmore, n.d.). The term 'Caribbean civilization' has also been revived in a different context by Prime Minister Ralph Gonsalves of St Vincent and the Grenadines. He has chosen to identify a variety of features specific to contemporary Caribbean society that are underpinned by the attainment of identified levels of social development and what he calls 'ennoblement' (Gonsalves 2001).

An important but often ignored feature of civilization, implicit as much in the historical as in the contemporary view, is that civilization's proponents find themselves in an unspoken dialectical relationship with the 'wild' or 'wilderness'. In the contemporary context, 'drug trafficking', like the terms 'under-' or 'less developed', are ideological terms implicitly imbued with civilization's polar opposite: that is, states of wilderness with which civilization contends, whether socially, culturally, politically or economically.

Nash has illustrated how, in the early days of European penetration of the Americas, exposure to wilderness was met with fear and hatred on the part of those who saw themselves as contending with it for survival or success. These frontier-based ideas of wilderness involved the notion of untouched geographical territory where savages roamed, or, in more interventionist language, locations which needed to be pacified (Nash 2001). The Caribbean has had a distinctive tradition of 'wild' places which, historically, have included Maroon areas of Jamaica and the habitations of 'Bush Negroes' in Suriname, while 'pacifying' has also involved no less than the extermination or relocation of those opposed to European penetration – as happened, for example, to the Caribs who held parts of St Vincent and Dominica in the two 'Brigands' Wars' at the end of the eighteenth century.

The title of a source book about Caribs, *Wild Majesty*, points clearly to this notion of a region outside the pale of civilization. In that epigraph, Hulme and Whitehead observe: 'Wilde Majesty was a phrase used by the writer Samuel Purchas in the margin of his seventeenth-century compilation of English voyages. He was commenting on John Layfield's description of a native king on the island of Dominica, wild by nature, majestic in appearance'. The region was a complex of conflicts and interests involving many European national interests and groups who met fierce resistance from islanders referred to as 'Caribs' in the English sources. 'These islands were only finally pacified at the end of the eighteenth century, when several thousand so-called Black Caribs were transported to the coast of Central America' (Hulme and Whitehead 1992: 1).

The notion of 'wilderness' is important to my argument not only as a physical location, but also as a state of mind; not so much what a place is but what men think it is. Nash has observed: 'The New World was also wilderness at the time of discovery because Europeans considered it so' (Nash 1967: 7). Today this aspect of the wild is perhaps exemplified in a modified way by ambivalence to non-human environments (the ocean, for example, or outer space) that in the past were identified as wild and inhospitable.

But why should we care a fig about ancient colonial perceptions of the Caribbean, or even contemporary notions of civilization and wilderness? What relevance might they have to our understanding of the illegal drug trade in the Caribbean in the early twenty-first century? I propose that these historical and conceptual features of the wild are useful because they demonstrate continuities rather than breaks, revealing at particular historical moments parallels and crossings between legal and illegal, official (state) and unofficial (popular) boundaries. For example, 'reading' the international relations perspective on illegal drugs through the ideological lens of 'civilization' and 'wilderness' suggests that manifestations of the wild now include 'drug lords', 'growers' and 'pushers' who corrupt domestic society. In 2000, Attorney General Ramesh Lawrence Maharaj of Trinidad & Tobago made the link thus:

> There is a direct nexus between illegal drugs and crimes of violence, sex crimes, domestic violence, maltreatment of children by parents and other evils. Our citizens suffer from drug addiction, drug-related violence, and drug-related

corruption of law enforcement and public officials. The drug lords have become a law unto themselves. (Cited in Griffith 2003: 213)

The drug lords and the growers, as elements of the modern wild, become both a physical presence and – along with either their powerful speedboats or their locally grown marijuana cash crops – are, in official terms, returning parts of the regional environment to a state of wilderness. Thus, the modern wilderness has identifiable geographical locations, for example substantial acreages of land where illegal drugs are grown, or sea and air routes through which illegal substances are spirited. In the urban context, ghetto areas with high crime rates, illegal drug associations and illegal shootings – notably parts of Georgetown (and more recently Buxton) in Guyana, Kingston's Trench Town and Port of Spain's Laventille – have attained this status. They have become places that the state only periodically polices effectively (even though local stations may be located in these areas) and then predominantly with the intention to subdue (a role not dissimilar from that of the pre-police force militia at the time of slavery). Simultaneously, in a rural, traditionally more agriculturally oriented country like St Vincent, an attempt, in 2000, to eradicate the 'wild' involved the destruction of some 171 out of 263 acres identified as marijuana-growing (Klein 2001). In 2002, some108,758 marijuana plants were reported to have been eradicated in that country (US State Department 2002).

There is always a boundary between wilderness and civilization. The problem of locating this boundary in the context of illegal drugs is that it is at the same time easily identifiable, and also shifting, contested, crossed and re-crossed. It is easily identifiable because, as I have indicated, specific fields of marijuana can be set alight and plants destroyed, slums and beaches can be periodically raided. But the boundary is also shifting by time, depending on whether it is day or night. For example, a beach, housing district or a city street, which may be legal territory by day, may be transformed by periodic raids at night into a 'war zone' when representatives of the 'civilized' world cross into a location which becomes, for a time, a wilderness. This is illustrated by the following extract from a newspaper report of a recent night raid conducted by Bahamian law enforcement officials.

> Bimini was rocked by a sudden state of frenzy when drug enforcement officers swooped on this island, creating what [other] residents called a 'war zone' in this tight-knit community. A team of police and defense force officials along with Customs and Immigration officials descended on approximately 20 homes, vehicles and other premises on the island during the undercover project, dubbed 'Operation Blue Marlin'.

The newspaper report goes on to cite a local government official who commented:

This was forthcoming. I just didn't know when and how these guys would strike. Bimini really needed shaking up and they certainly stormed through the community. But people were left frightened. Who wants to live in a war zone? In fact, to tell the truth, I thought I was in Kuwait. I haven't seen action like this since watching the Gulf War on television. (Pinder 2003)

The boundary also shifts according to both practice and belief, where various forms of 'herb' consumption are involved. The consumption of marijuana, for example, has been recognized to be 'widely prevalent in the lower socio-economic groups in Jamaica for more than one hundred years' (Thorburn 1974: 19). During this time it has acquired a long history of use as a 'spiritual herb' among the Rastafarian religious sect and in more recent years its use has spread across the range of social classes in the society. Moreover, there exists an entire institutional basis of alternative medicine directed by 'bush-men' or 'herbalists'. They believe that the spiritual body can fight off all possible ailments if strengthened by 'herbs'. The practice is carried out through a 'church' called a 'Mission' which is led by a 'Mother' or 'shepherdess' in the institution called a 'Balm-yard'. While many herbal teas they use have been reported to be harmless and not illegal, 'several harmful examples' have been reported on in Caribbean scientific literature. One of the best known of these is the 'white back' or 'consumption bush' (*crotalaria fulva*) which is widely consumed in Jamaica and causes vero-occlusive diseases of the liver (Lowe 1972: 21).

These privatized and unofficial religious and health-related practices represent alternative belief systems. In the past some belief systems – for example, the practice of obeah, which encouraged the charge of sedition – have been interpreted as a direct challenge to officially sanctioned authority (Chevannes 1971). At other times, particular practices may be ignored or tolerated. In the context of the use of specifically illegal drugs, only particular elements of the practice, for example the consumption of marijuana, may be declared 'illegal'; for the adherent of the practice, however, the illegal behaviour often provides an essential element of the alternative belief system. In this way, considerable areas of the privatized social world of Caribbean belief and practice have continuously existed parallel with, or at times may have crossed, the boundary between legal and illegal, official and unofficial, wild and civilized worlds.

This ambiguity highlights once more the fact that, historically speaking, the state, as regulatory local government imposed by metropolitan governments, was neither particularly active nor particularly strong. Furthermore, with political independence, local state intervention policy has been for the most part ineffective and at best variable, its capacity for regulation weaker and more circumscribed than many of the conventional and official paradigms of illegal drug policy analysis are willing to recognize. Indeed, moves towards state intervention were rapidly confronted by the need for severe restraint. The failure of analysts to acknowledge this has meant that the conventional framing of the discussion of privatization, illegal drugs and the state in the Caribbean has been narrow and simplistic. The form of international cooperation that has emerged, therefore, one which emphasizes a managerial process with prescribed objectives and measures of achievement, fails to take account of the specificities of the Caribbean context. Without closer attention to popular and alternative structures, beliefs and practices, an ever-widening gap appears between state exhortation and concrete action, and between concrete action and the popular perception of that action as legitimate.

Implications of the alternative framework

Reverting to the scenario with which we began – of fast and efficient powerboats plying the Caribbean sealanes with their cargoes of illegal drugs – I would now like to offer an alternative vignette. It is not unusual to see, lying at anchor in Calliaqua, St Vincent, the country's state-of-the-art coastguard boat, supposedly the scourge of illegal drug traffickers. Perhaps it is a mere coincidence that my regular trips to the island have coincided with this state of inactivity, which may be due to the perpetual problem of obtaining spares and the lack of financial resources to operate and maintain such expensive equipment. But my personal experience, it appears, is not all that unusual. In its 2002 Report, the US State Department noted that 'the Royal Bahamian Defence Force's own fast response boats … were frequently out of service and were not able to respond to any OPBAT (Operations Bahamas, Turks & Caicos) requests for assistance in pursuits' (US State Department 2002). But the contrast between a highly effective, high-powered illegal transportation network, and an ineffective, albeit willing, challenger, confronts us with the cold reality of the limitations of regional policing capabilities.

I invoke these contrasting images not only to dramatize the distance between the official discourse about drugs in the Caribbean and the actuality, but also to suggest the urgency of making some uncomfortable links between the two.

Underlying the seemingly intractable problem of illegal drugs and their control are the fundamental realities of historical myopia, inadequately explored patterns of poverty and the nature of belief systems in the region. Klein has observed that specialists who examine the issue of illegal drug trafficking tend to ignore the function of the trade as a strategy for escaping or counteracting poverty. Similarly, the professionals who have been assessing poverty in the region have also failed to accord significance to the undeniable link between an individual's poverty and his poverty alleviation strategy, a part of which may include dealing in illegal drugs. Undoubtedly, for the individual, a part of this will be the lure of considerable amounts of cash. However, analyses of two recent country poverty assessment reports indicate that one (for Dominica) restricts its view of illegal drugs by categorizing them exclusively as a health hazard (Halcrow Group Ltd 2003). The other (for St Vincent) notes simply that: 'There has been a long tradition, especially in the Southern Grenadines, of an unregulated informal trade of goods with non-residents. More recently, there has been detected evidence of illegal cultivation of marijuana in parts of the country, and the authorities have been destroying large quantities of marijuana. There are signs that these flows are being monetized into the economy in indirect ways' (Kairi Consultants Ltd 1996: 31). In neither case is there any attempt to suggest reasons for the growth of illegal drug use or trafficking, or to make the link with wider structures of trade and the free market.

By making the claim that the influence of popular belief systems needs to be assessed more rigorously by those wishing to enforce regulation of illegal drugs, I am suggesting the need to accept that, in the absence of state welfare or other poverty alleviation programmes, or where they are seen as partial, biased or irrelevant, alternative structures like Pentecostalism and Rastafarianism will continue to provide substitutes.[11] The key factor, which the state discusses much but is relatively powerless to influence, is the underlying poverty of many of these small island societies and the intractable poverty of urban areas of the more developed countries (MDCs). Those who lack other resources must find solutions for themselves. At the same time that the Barbados Labour Party administration led by Owen Arthur, with a refreshed mandate in 2003, recommits its efforts to 'poverty eradication', across the region, the Rastafari 'brethren' resolve the problem by redefining the social system, deliberately distancing themselves from the formal establishment, or 'Babylon', which designates all aspects of the state, from education to policing.[12] The Pentecostal 'saints', similarly, see the state for the most part as irrelevant to their economic and religious 'salvation'.

While these two belief systems are notable for their diametrically opposed views on illegal drugs, they are united nevertheless in their recognition of the need to subvert or bypass the state as part of a strategy of poverty alleviation. The same pattern as manifests itself through these belief systems can be detected in an even more fundamental area: that of agriculture. The decimation of the banana-growing sector, resulting from the banning of preferential markets for Caribbean bananas, has guaranteed a firmer commitment to the already established practice of marijuana growing in the islands. With nothing to fall back on but the land itself, a significant number of farmers are driven to exploit it in whatever way they can to support their families and ensure the continuance of their communities. It is plain to see, therefore, that the issue of poverty and its avoidance is an important associated factor in the increasing acreage devoted to marijuana growing in the Eastern Caribbean.

What emerges from this discussion is the gap between indigenous beliefs and practices and those of the dominant actors on the stage of illegal drug control. The United States and the European Union appear to share the vision of the Caribbean as a 'wild' place, and have convinced local regimes to adopt this view.[13] The perception of the region as inhabiting a state of wilderness enables metropolitan interests also to divert resources to other localities or priorities (for example, the 'war on terrorism') should these suddenly become more pressing. Simultaneously, the contradiction implicit in a partnership between essentially marginal economies and globally power-ful ones has permitted the ascendancy of an overbearingly antagonistic posture by both sides of the partnership towards the issue of illegal drugs, and by metropolitan elements of the partnership towards the region. An important by-product of this contradiction is that the local state, in seeking the approval of its powerful mentors, makes statements that the metropolis wishes to hear, but is somewhat more ambivalent in implementation. The outcome is that the local state inevitably distances itself further from the popular reality, and in turn contributes to restricting the framework for the discussion of illegal drugs. The mismatch between metropolitan interests and those of local states – the latter less than powerful, anyway, in their articulation – is at the basis of this contradiction.

It is possible that this mismatch could be resolved by the negotiation of a trade-off between metropolitan support for legitimate activities in small societies on one hand and more active Caribbean cooperation extending beyond gestures on the other. This would require far more local state awareness of its limitations and a more thorough engagement with the underlying social dynamics of these societies. Most political parties in government in the region have mastered the art of populism, ably manipu-lating colour, class, national and racial loyalties, to either gain or retain power; far fewer have come to terms with effective social intervention, in particular to effect more widespread poverty alleviation.

In the context of what appears to be a situation of substantially buoyant illegal drugs activity in the Caribbean, and in the absence of externally caused and unexpected changes, failure to rethink these issues suggests that the Caribbean countries will remain centres of throughput, cultivation and use of illegal drugs.

ACKNOWLEDGEMENT

I am grateful to Don D. Marshall and Mark Wilson for reading and commenting critically and helpfully on an earlier draft of this essay. Errors and omissions are those of the author.

NOTES

1 In the domestic sphere of plantation slavery, another weapon of resistance, which was greatly feared, was the use of poison by black nannies and cooks against children and adults in white planter households. Beckles notes that '(M)any lived with the fear that nannies would murder their children, and as a result, infant mortalities were commonly enveloped in suspicion of foul play. Poisonings were rarely detected by white doctors ... When in 1774, for example, a slave nanny described by her owners as a "favourite" was convicted of poisoning their infant, it was discovered that this was not the only occasion on which she had done so' (Beckles 1989: 69).

2 Piracy in the region has not disappeared. The London-based International Maritime Bureau identified 8 attacks on merchant ships in the Caribbean Sea in the first three months of 2003 (*Guardian Weekly* 26 June 2003; 2 July 2003, p. 7).

3 The state has, admittedly, taken more and more welfare responsibilities, including the provision of schooling in most of the politically independent countries. However, after some 40 years of political independence many primary and secondary schools continue to be managed by religious denominations. At the level of teacher training, even in the 1980s half the elementary teacher-training colleges in Jamaica were still managed by church organizations (Miller 1986: 11–12).

4 Gayle has observed: 'In the case of the manufacturing sector, particularly in the smaller member countries of CARICOM, business enterprises still rely more upon government for assistance in protecting local markets while maintaining and expanding export markets' (Gayle 1995: 149).

5 Those who return from the United Kingdom, for example, are often characterized as socially 'mad' (Thomas-Hope 1992).

6 The 1990 Jamaica census estimated the number with no church affiliation to be 554,564, the largest registered category. Anglicans comprised the largest single denomination at 81,000 in the Barbados census for 1990; the number claiming no religion was 49,564.

7 It has to be remembered, however, that the loss of market share that the Caribbean experienced is in a substantially increased market.

8 The index, used by the report to rank countries according to their quality of life, is based on income per head, life expectancy and educational attainment. In 2000, Canada was ranked first and Sierra Leone 174th. The countries of the Commonwealth Caribbean achieved the following rankings: Barbados was ranked 30th, the Bahamas 33rd, Antigua–Barbuda 37th, St Kitts 47th, Trinidad & Tobago 50th, Dominica 51st, Grenada 54th, St Vincent and the Grenadines 79th, Jamaica 83rd, St Lucia 88th, and Guyana 96th.

9 See also, for different countries in the region, Scott 1987, O'Dowd 1991, and Lee 2001.

10 Corruption in the public service, for example, when identified as the antithesis of activity designed to be in the public interest, is a form of boundary crossing that sacrifices collective interest for individual aims.

11 In some island countries, notably Barbados, where state welfare provision is more developed, church provision is more of an alternative to state provision; in many of the societies, church provision is the main option available.

12 Chevannes (1999) suggests that they are kept at arms length by the state in such matters as the formal acceptance of Rastafarianism as a recognized religion.

13 This view of the 'wild' may be contested. It could be argued that, as the periphery is absorbed into the metropolis, the Caribbean, particularly through the marketing of

tourism, blends itself into a metropolitan imaginary projecting the notion of 'wild' more in the sense of freedom from convention and work, and with a paradisiacal climate. I am not denying that this view of the region may exist; but 'wild' in the sense of dangerous and untamed is the conventional mindset that more readily links the Caribbean with illegal drugs. This coupling, presenting a region riddled with drug trafficking, money laundering and political instability, is also promoted by agents projecting US and EU power in the region.

REFERENCES AND SELECT BIBLIOGRAPHY

Atkins, J. P. *et al.* (2000) (for the Commonwealth Secretariat) 'A Commonwealth Vulnerability Index for Developing Countries', London: Commonwealth Secretariat, Economic Paper 40.

Austin Broos, D. J. (1996) 'Politics and the Redeemer: State and Religion as Ways of Being in Jamaica', New West Indian Guide, 70, 1 and 2.

Beckles, H. McD. (1989) *Natural Rebels: a Social History of Enslaved Black Women in Barbados*, London: Zed Books.

Brown and Stone, C. (1976) Essays on Power and Change in Jamaica, Kingston: Kingston Publishers.

Caribbean Development Bank (1999) Barbados: Annual Report, CDB.

Chevannes, B. (1971) 'Revival and the Black Struggle', *Savacou*, 5.

—— (1999) 'Coming in from the Cold: Native Religions and the Problem of Democracy in Jamaica' (mimeo).

Cohen, R. (1998) 'Cultural Diaspora', in Mary Chamberlain (ed.), *Caribbean Migration*, London: Routledge.

Curtin, P. D. (1990) *The Rise and Fall of the Planter Complex: Essays in Atlantic History*, Cambridge: Cambridge University Press.

Forte, A. G. (1996) *Population and Housing Census of the Commonwealth Caribbean*, Barbados: National Census Report.

Gayle, D. J. (1995) 'The Evolving Caribbean Business Environment', in Anthony T. Bryan (ed.), *The Caribbean: New Dynamics in Trade and Political Economy*, Miami: North–South Centre Press.

Gonsalves, R. E. (2001) *Politics of Our Caribbean Civilization: Essays and Speeches*, Kingstown, St Vincent: Great Works Depot Ltd.

Grey, E. (1853) *The Colonial Policy of Lord Russell's Administration*, Volume 1, London: Richard Bentley.

Griffith, I. L. (1997) *Drugs and Security in the Caribbean: Sovereignty Under Siege*, Pennsylvania State University Press, University Park.

—— (2000) 'Drugs and the Emerging Security Agenda in the Caribbean', in Joseph S. Tulchin and Ralph H. Espach (eds.), *Security in the Caribbean Basin: the Challenge of Regional Cooperation*, Boulder: Woodrow Wilson Centre and Lynne Rienner.

—— (2003) 'Security and Sovereignty in the Commonwealth Caribbean: Probing Elements of the Local Global Nexus', in Cynthia Barrow-Giles and Don Marshall (eds.), *Living at the Borderlines: Issues in Caribbean Sovereignty and Development*, Kingston: Ian Randle Publishers.

Griffith, I. L., and T. Munroe (1995) 'Drugs and Democracy in the Caribbean', *Journal of Commonwealth and Comparative Politics*, 33, 3.

Grosfoguel, R. (1995) 'Colonial Caribbean Migrations to the Metropoles in Comparative Perspective', paper presented at the Conference 'Comparative History of Migration Within the Caribbean and Europe', Oxford Brookes University, England.

Gutzmore, C., n.d. J*ourneying After Arrival*, Volume 1, a provisional inter-disciplinary text and documentary reader for the Foundation Course, Caribbean Civilization, Faculty of Arts and Education, University of the West Indies, Mona, Jamaica.

Halcrow Group Ltd., for Caribbean Development Bank and Government of the Commonwealth of Dominica (2003) *Country Poverty Assessment: Dominica*. Volume 1.

Harriott, A. (2000) 'Police Reform in the Commonwealth Caribbean', *Caribbean Dialogue*, 6, 1 and 2 (January, June).

Henke, H. and D. D. Marshall (2003), 'The Legitimacy of Neo-Liberal Trade Regimes in the Caribbean: Issues of "Race", Class and Gender', in C. Barrow-Giles and D. Marshall (eds.), *Living at the Borderlines: Issues in Caribbean Sovereignty and Development*, Kingston: Ian Randle.

Higman, B. (1984) *Slave Populations of the British Caribbean 1807 – 1834*, John Baltimore: Hopkins University Press.

Hilaire, E. (2000) 'Shaping the Future for Youth', *Caribbean Dialogue*, 6, 1 and 2 (January, June).

Hulme, P. and N. L. Whitehead (eds.) (1992) *Wild Majesty: Encounters with the Caribs from Columbus to the Present Day. An Anthology*, Oxford: Clarendon University Press.

Kairi Consultants Ltd., in association with the National Assessment Team of St. Vincent (1996) *Poverty Assessment Report: St Vincent and the Grenadines*, Main Report, Volume 1. Port of Spain, Trinidad.

Klein, A. (2001) 'Between the Death Penalty and Decriminalization: New Directions for Drug Control in the Commonwealth Caribbean', *New West India Guide*, 75, 4.

—— (2004), 'The Ganja Industry and Alternative Development in St Vincent', (this volume).

Knight, G. (1997) 'The Public Sector in the Caribbean: an Historical Overview', *Caribbean Dialogue*, 3, 1 (March).

Lee, G. (2001) 'Crime in the Caribbean', *The Washington Post*, 4 August 2001.

Lowe, H. I. L. (1972) 'Jamaican Folk Medicine', *Jamaica Journal*, 6, 2.

Marshall, D. D. (2003), 'Governance and Reregulation of Offshore Financial Centres: (Re)Framing the Confines of Legitimate Debate and Protest', in C. Barrow-Giles and D. Marshall (eds.), *Living at the Borderlines: Issues in Caribbean Sovereignty and Development*, Kingston: Ian Randle.

Maingot, A. P. (1994) *The United States and the Caribbean*, London: Macmillan.

McBain, H. (1996) 'Privatisation Experiences and Perspectives in the English-Speaking Caribbean', paper for the Caribbean Studies Association Conference, San Juan, Puerto Rico.

Mill, J. S. (1868) *Principles of Political Economy* (People's Edition), London: Longman, Green, Reader and Dyer.

Miller, E. (1986) 'Marginalization of the Black Male: Insights from the Development of the Teaching Profession', Kingston: Institute of Social and Economic Research.

Nash, R. F. (2001) [1967, 1973, 1982], *Wilderness and the American Mind*, New Haven: Yale.

O'Dowd, D. (1991) 'Review of the Trinidad and Tobago Police Service', unpublished report.

Orozco, M. (2002) 'Remitting Back Home and Supporting the Homeland: the Guyanese Community in the USA', cited in *Stabroek News*, 11 August 2002.

Pares, R. (1960) *A West India Fortune*, London: Longman, Green and Co. Ltd.

Patterson, O. (1967) *The Sociology of Slavery: An Analysis of the Origin, Development and Structure of Negro Slave Society in Jamaica*, London: MacGibbon and Kee.

Pattullo, P. (1996) *Last Resorts: the Cost of Tourism in the Caribbean*, London: Cassell and Latin American Bureau (Research and Action) Ltd.

Pinder, M. N. (2003) *Bahama Journal*, 24 June 2003.

Pratt, M. L. (1992) *Imperial Eyes: Travel Writing and Transculturation*, London: Routledge.

Premdas, R. R. (2002) 'Self-Determination and Sovereignty in the Caribbean: Migration, Transnational Identities and Deterritorialisation of the State', in Ramesh Ramsaran (ed.), *Caribbean Survival and the Global Challenge*, Kingston, Jamaica: Ian Randle.

Public Records Office, St Vincent Archives no. 37, 1834, Rennie to Lawson, 30 March 1934, London.

Ramsaran, R. (1997) 'Reflection on Development and Structural Adjustment in the Commonwealth Caribbean', in John Gaffar LaGuerre (ed.), *Issues in the Government and Politics of the West Indies: a Reader*, St Augustine, Trinidad : School of Continuing Studies, University of the West Indies.

Reid, S. (1980) 'Economic Elites in Jamaica: a Study in Monistic Influence', *Anthropologica*, 22, 1.

Richardson, B. (1992) *The Caribbean in the Wider World 1499–1992*, Cambridge: Cambridge University Press.

Rohlehr, G. (1994) 'Folk Research: Fossil or Living Bone?', *Massachusetts Review*.

Scott, G. (1987) *Report of the Commission of Enquiry into the Extent of the Problem of Drug Abuse in Trinidad & Tobago*, San Fernando: Unique Services.

Swanson, C. E. (1991) *Predators and Prizes: American Privateering and Imperial Warfare, 1739–48*, Columbia, SC.

Thomas-Hope, E. M. (1992) *Explanation in Caribbean Migration Perceptions of the Image: Jamaica, Barbados and St. Vincent*, Warwick University Caribbean Studies, London: Macmillan Caribbean.

Thorburn, M. J. (1974) 'Jamaican Bushes and Human Chromosomes', *Jamaica Journal*, 8, 4.

Trollope, A. (1859) (republished 1960), *West Indies and the Spanish Main*, Pall Mall: Dawson.

Tidrick, G. (1973) 'Some Aspects of Jamaican Emigration to the United Kingdom 1953–1962', in Lambros Comitas and David Lowenthal (eds.), *Work and Family Life: West Indian Perspectives*, New York: Anchor Press/Doubleday.

Tulchin, J. S. and R. H. Espach (2000) *Security in the Caribbean Basin: the Challenge of Regional Cooperation*, Boulder, Colorado: Woodrow Wilson Centre and Lynne Rienner Publishers Inc.

UNODC (2003) *Caribbean Drug Trends 2001–2002*, Bridgetown, Barbados: Caribbean Regional Office, United Nations Office on Drugs and Crime.

UNDP (2000) *Human Development Report*, Washington, DC: United Nations Development Programme.

US State Department (2002) *International Narcotics Drug Control Strategy Report*, Washington DC: United States of America State Department.

Watson, H. (2003) 'The "Ship rider Solution" and Post-Cold War Imperialism: Beyond Ontologies of State Sovereignty in the Caribbean', in Cynthia Barrow-Giles and Don Marshall (eds.), *Living at the Borderlines: Issues in Caribbean Sovereignty and Development*, Kingston: Ian Randle Publishers.

West Indian Commission (1992) *Time for Action: Report of the West Indian Commission*, Barbados: Black Rock.

World Bank (1991) *World Development Report*, New York: Oxford University Press.

Appendix: Table 5.1   Comparative Economic Indicators

	Anguilla	Antigua	Dominica	Grenada	Mont-serrat	St Kitts	St Lucia	St Vincent
Area (sq.km.)	91	442	750	345	103	269	616	388
Population ('000, 2001)	11.6	75.8	71.2	102.6	4.3	46.1	157.8	112.0
Average pop. growth (%) (1996–2001)	1.6	2.0	0.4	0.7	11.2	1.7	1.3	0.1
GDP (US$m, 2002)	95.9	591.4	216.4	340.3	25.0	354.8	579.6	271.2
GDP per head (US$, 2001)	8,105	7,706	3,696	3,316	5,690	7,450	3,662	2,421
Real GDP growth (%) (2002)	0.4	2.1	0.8	0.6	4.4	1.5	0.4	0.8
Consumer Price Inflation (2001)	2.9	1.5	2.5	2.0	4.7	1.8	3.0	0.6
Average Unemployment (%) (2001)	8.6	7.0	23	12.2	n/a	4.5	19	22

Source: Economist Intelligence Unit, Country Profile, OECS 2003.

PART 3

INTERVENTIONS ON THE GROUND

Putting Demand Reduction into Practice –
'I Have Plenty of Nothing, and Nothing Is Plenty for Me'

CHAPTER 6

Drug Abuse Treatment and Rehabilitation in Jamaica and the Caribbean

HOWARD GOUGH

During a break at a recent meeting of drug abuse treatment & rehabilitation (T & R) workers, a small group of participants was overheard discussing the drug problem in Jamaica: its history; its causes; its effects; its management; and the role of external influences with their impact on local trends.

The quality of the material that comes out of these informal, 'off the air' discussions is always impressive. Efforts to reprise the contents of these mini-conferences when the break ends and the meeting reconvenes cannot recapture the intensity and spontaneity that characterize these intra-break sessions. Members of these small informal groups use the relative safety engendered by the group's size to share strong and controversial views that may not be as easily shared in the large group.

The small group in question made some statements that could be considered politically incorrect. Some members expressed their disagreement, without making the proponents any less vocal. This little informal group took hold of topic after topic and fearlessly turned them inside out. The non-stated but obvious consensus was, 'let the chips fall where they may'.

This chapter tries to capture highlights of the contents of the several unofficial mini-conferences on drug abuse treatment and rehabilitation in Jamaica and, to some extent, the rest of the Caribbean. These meetings had no designated recorder but mental notes were taken and later transformed into minutes. Those issues that were considered insignificant and those of which the writer was not fully supportive have conveniently been forgotten. The minutes that you are about to read, then, reflect the writer's thinking and are indicative of his own contributions as a member of the small groups in question.

My hope is that you will read analytically, make notes uninhibitedly, and, when the next formal meeting comes around, be ready to look more closely at 'matters arising from the minutes' as well as a few 'new items under discussion'.

Some say, 'nothing is what it seems to be'

The first major controversial statement was that the National Council on Drug Abuse (NCDA, 1983) was not set up primarily to address a local drug problem. Development of a comprehensive and culturally sensitive programme, based on existing needs and designed to serve Jamaicans, was secondary to reducing the amount of ganja reaching the shores of the US. This topic triggered an animated discussion that needed more time than the 15-minute break allowed, so it continued in subsequent informal sessions throughout that day and after. The richness of the material made listening very tempting and yielding very easy. It got even more interesting when the stronger members of this small group directed the proceedings toward their area of specialty – T & R.

It is well known that the early-to-mid-1980s saw one of the most successful anti-ganja campaigns in Jamaica. The government of the day was forced by external pressures to institute vivid measures to curb the supply of illegal drugs originating in and passing through Jamaica to our Big Uncle up north. The source of the pressure was willing to contribute and/or facilitate the availability of substantial amounts of resources to apply these measures; the government, in turn, needed new coordinating bodies. The NCDA was set up as one such body. It was only in later years that this entity began to address the drug problems of Jamaica and Jamaicans.

The small group argued, correctly or incorrectly, that for the first several years of the NCDA the major concern was supply control and to a lesser extent prevention education, making the two relevant committees the most supported and hence the most active. Despite a glaring need for T & R, it was not until the late 1980s that this issue started to get the attention it deserved. Thanks to the EU and the Private Sector Organization of Jamaica (PSOJ), the plight of Jamaican drug users who had difficulties with control of use was finally to be addressed. And so the late 1980s to early 1990s saw the beginning of a focus on and development of T & R facilities.

The birth and development of T & R in Jamaica

Prior to 1989 the management of alcoholism was basically what T & R of drug addiction problems was about in Jamaica. The distinguished Michael Beaubrun, arguably the father of addiction treatment in the region, must be credited for his pioneering work in this regard. In the mid-1960s he began paving the way for medical practitioners, particularly psychiatrists, to diagnose and manage alcoholism as the chronic, recovery–relapse–recovery illness that it is. His caring, professional and – perhaps most importantly – non-moralistic approach to managing the condition invited closet and other alcoholics from all walks of life to come forward and experience the hope of better days.

The monumental legacies of his work are many and include the Department of Psychiatry in the University Hospital of the West Indies at Mona, the development of Alcoholics Anonymous groups locally, and the establishment of the Caribbean Institute on Alcoholism and Other Drug Problems (CARIAD) – an ongoing annual two-week institute that is fully supported by UWI and the University of the Virgin Islands (UVI, St Thomas). His work basically laid the foundation for the development of drug abuse T & R facilities more than two decades later.

Leading the way was the Addiction Alert Organization (AAO). In 1989, through the sponsorship of the PSOJ, the AAO started a 12-step non-residential programme that would soon succumb to the harsh realities of setting up and maintaining a T & R facility. Someone has to pay, and pay consistently. The users of the service are unlikely to be that 'someone', as they very often have no resources of their own – and the erratic nature of their condition is likely to have already destroyed relationships with others who might have been able to pay on their behalf. Some good corporate citizens will always be there to assist, but this source is far too unpredictable to form the basis on which sound financial projections can be made. AAO learned all this very quickly and, by 1993, had made a paradigmatic shift to focus on the relatively less expensive but no less challenging prevention education, which now represents the bulk of its work.

The matter of who should pay for T & R threatened to break up the small group, as some members thought that government should pay while others claimed that service users and/or their relatives should pay. The small group survived this controversial 'who should pay' issue only because the informal agenda was far from exhausted.

One group member was eager to look at the challenges that confront the T & R sector – but this was not to be, at least not yet, as another member with more leadership skills got the group to return to programme development.

By April 1991 three other T & R facilities with a total of about 58 bed spaces had come on stream. The Salvation Army set up the William Chamberlain Memorial Rehabilitation Centre (about 25 beds – male), with Christianity and vocational skills training as the foundation of its therapeutic programme. The Detoxification and Assessment Unit of the University Hospital of the West Indies (eight beds – male and female) offered treatment based on the usual medical approach of an in-hospital detox unit. This was followed by Richmond Fellowship Jamaica, which opened Patricia House (about 25 beds – male and female), with its 'psychosocial rehabilitation in a therapeutic community setting' approach.

T & R services: the obstacles

The advent of T & R facilities in the early 1990s should have meant the beginning of good quality service for problem drug users, but this was a long time coming. The lack of readiness generally, and in relation to the human resources in particular, plagued the field then and continues to do so today. Some saw the management of drug abusers as a specialty but it could not have been treated as such, as the appropriately trained persons to staff the facilities were simply not available.

This led to several very interesting ways of determining who was qualified to work with problem drug users. The most vocal of those at the front of the line was a group of people who called themselves 'recovering addicts'. They came highly recommended by themselves, on the grounds that 'the therapeutic value of one addict helping another has no parallel'. This set could be safely regarded as anti-academia as they launched verbal attacks on all professionals who did not have a history of out-of-control drug use. Many professionals who became victims of the onslaught from this group found themselves regretting that they had not developed a drug abuse problem so as now to be 'in recovery' – and 'reputed' as the institution through which a diploma in drug abuse management could be had.

No better than this group of 'recovering addicts' was another set made up of burnt-out, tired, and frustrated professionals mainly from the fields of nursing, teaching, and social work. They too came highly recommended. Many claimed that their friends and family members considered them 'good listeners' and were always coming to them for advice, hence counselling should not be too difficult for them as they had the 'natural ability'.

A few were honest enough to say they just wanted a change from careers that had become mundane. It was from this 'honest set' that some of the most trainable candidates eventually emerged.

Training – what a need!

Since the stock of qualified people was in reality non-existent, no one disputed the great need for training. The disputes were about who was qualified to conduct the sessions, what T & R modality should be emphasized, and how the training programmes should be structured. Some of these disputes are ongoing and have spread from training *per se* into the areas of T & R modality and general programme background and style. The sad story of these disputes is that many of the proponents of the different schools of thinking are not prepared to accept the immeasurable value of variety in the field. Some have taken these disputes to levels where they openly slander programmes that are different from the ones they promote.

Networking, collaboration and cooperation – essential ingredients for success in drug abuse T & R – are hindered in some instances and seriously affected in others because of the unhealthy competition fostered by personalization and attempted monopolization of the field by some professionals. It is not unusual after an experience with these people to wonder where among their priorities the clients come: the top of the list is obviously taken up by very personal issues. They themselves are primary and secondary beneficiaries of their involvement, with clients coming in a distant third.

The need for formal training in all aspects of drug abuse management and the related areas such as administration, resource management and public relations continue to be at the top of the agenda in Jamaica and the rest of the Caribbean. The field/industry is full of people with good hearts who are willing to give but who do not know how, what, when, where or why they are giving. So many are giving 'until it hurts' both themselves and those receiving. Among this group of good-hearted givers is a set of humble former problem drug users (recovering addicts) who would make excellent growth facilitators (counsellors) with the appropriate training and exposure.

In the absence of the necessary resources to effect these preparations, we continue to have a flood of 'instant experts' and a trickle of appropriately trained persons. Perhaps donors and others interested in impact studies should be aware of the limitations that we are forced to work with in the Caribbean. The same set of criteria used to evaluate the effectiveness of a programme costing X amount of dollars in a resource-rich country cannot be used to evaluate the same programme in countries such as ours. Something has to be done to ensure that the output of these evaluations reflects the realities of the context in which they are being conducted.

Let's formalize and standardize, not rationalize

Another major threat to regional T & R in general and to the clients/service users in particular is the absence or ineffectiveness of systems geared to ensuring that service users get the high quality and standard of service that they deserve and to which they are entitled. In Jamaica, for example, after one decade of service provision in this area, the field is still wide open to anyone/any group from anywhere to come in and set up T & R facilities without prior consultation with any local body. Those facilities in existence are under no obligation to report to a national coordinating body responsible for overseeing their work.

Whilst this 'no-bureaucracy' situation has some advantages in that it allows for easier development of services, the disadvantages are too great to be allowed to continue any longer. Those seeking to break free of the chains of addiction are usually desperately searching for help, and so are willing to accept almost anything that will get them off the risky streets and out of the state of general bankruptcy in which their drug use (usually crack cocaine) has landed them. So they accept admission into these facilities without questioning the philosophical contents of the programme to which they are to be exposed. In a matter of days/weeks the 'self' begins to recover and they begin to see that the programme contents have strong religious, cultural, and other dissonances.

These clients are not at liberty to question the regime to which they are now subject. Any attempt at doing this is usually met with defensive responses from the protectors of these programmes. Instead of an opportunity to air their grouses freely and responsibly, clients get sub-poenaed to so-called 'therapeutic sessions' in which their views are ignored and all kinds of programme jargon used to rationalize the programme's position. Some get diagnosed and labelled as resistive, rebellious, ungrateful, and may even suffer consequences (learning experiences) for their so-called defiant behaviours. Many of these frustrated clients will leave programmes prematurely and their behaviours will consolidate the view that crack cocaine users in treatment have a high relapse rate.

While this is happening, these programmes continue their high-threshold, low-tolerance policies that put protection of philosophical backgrounds first, staff members second, and everything and everyone else after. It is no wonder, then, that the few T & R centres (less than 100 beds) are not always bursting at the seams under the pressure of long waiting lists. Instead, there are almost always empty beds in these centres, while the street population of out-of-control drug users is showing no sign of reducing.

Harm reduction

This brings into sharp focus the great need for unconventional programmes geared to reaching out to needy drug users where they are – on the streets, or certainly outside T & R programmes. The relatively new (to Jamaica) concept of harm reduction must now be given sufficient attention to ensure careful examination and passage through a cultural and contextual filter with a view to appropriately implementing potentially useful components. This is currently being done with limited support, as the true value of the programme is not yet fully appreciated and sceptics are just doing what sceptics do.

Harm reduction (HR), like most other concepts/ideologies, includes extreme views and positions that may be detrimental to its growth and development. Much more harmful than these extremes, however, are intellectually dishonest opponents who conveniently magnify and distort HR's grey areas, usually in a bid to defend and/or promote another approach that they perceive to be under threat. Thus it is not unusual to hear HR being aligned with the unpopular 'legalize all drugs', and other similarly potent views.

One of the beauties of HR theory and practice is that there is room for people with a range of views and who uphold these views with different levels of intensity. No one is locked into a cognitive box, unless they wish to be. Opponents of HR, particularly those in the Caribbean, are hereby implored to step outside their boxes – because we can't afford the luxury of that comfort zone any longer. With a heroin epidemic in the Caribbean on the horizon and a large pool of HIV+ persons already in place, we have the rudiments of a disaster. We also have the good fortune of being in a position where we can take proactive steps to limit the impact of such a disaster. Several countries were not so lucky. Let us learn from their experiences. Let us explore this concept of HR that is primarily about enhancing the quality of life of marginalized people who may not be (and may never be) ready to do what we think they should be doing.

Because of the religious (and sometimes hyper-religious) nature of the Caribbean, HR may best be viewed from an abstinence-based perspective, wherein the ultimate aim of all interventions is to achieve a drug-free lifestyle. Whatever the definition or configuration we want to give it, HR in the Caribbean can't wait. HIV+ and other crack abusers on our streets are selling sex to support their habits. Then there are commercial sex workers, some of whom use/abuse crack to help them cope with the trade. And maybe the most frightening part of all this is the fact that the larger percentage of the clientele is made up of non-drug users, so-called 'upstanding' citizens, with families and good jobs. HR is needed for today but more so for tomorrow.

The power of external influences

As this small informal group started showing signs of breaking up, one somewhat forceful member who would like to be seen as fearless decided to turn his attention to international funding agencies. He warned them not to seek to repeat the follies of the 1990s, when they came to the Caribbean with their own hidden and not-so-hidden agendas, exploited the relative lack of resources by first dividing us and then leading us off into different directions with the proverbial 'carrot and stick'. The outspoken group member made it clear that funding agencies that were not reaching out to the region with the primary motive of improving the quality of life of our people should keep their money or spend it elsewhere.

Effective use of these resources, he went on to say, would be best achieved when these resource-rich organizations begin to show respect for the region's cultures, professionals, and established organizations/institutions by involving them in proposed projects from conception through to delivery and after. Anything short of this, he said, would be like a pregnancy with little or no antenatal care, thereby increasing the risk of gestatory, prenatal, and postnatal problems. Such an unfortunate situation could easily produce a child (or project) with many defects, causing it to have major difficulties adjusting to contextual realities.

Having won a good measure of approval from other group members, the speaker made room for another. The new speaker, also recognizing that group interaction was in its closing stages, made a somewhat hurried remark about 9/11 and the subsequent American actions against Afghanistan. Acting on non-verbal signals from the group, he quickly qualified his comments by pointing out that he had no desire to express his views on the politics of the matter, but rather on some of the ways in which the movement and use of drugs in and through the Caribbean may be affected.

With the mayhem continuing in Afghanistan, one of Europe's largest suppliers of heroin, the outflow of the product will reduce, resulting in the upward movement of price at its destinations. This will attract traditional and non-traditional suppliers who will seek to cash in on a more lucrative market place. Such opportunists could include Mexico and Colombia. And given the resultant tightening of security throughout the access routes of our Big Uncle up north, the Caribbean is a likely route for Spanish-speaking heroin and more cocaine destined for Europe and Uncle Sam. The group went quiet for a while as each member pondered the obvious upshot: increased transshipment of heroin through the region. Thus the Caribbean heroin problems may be nearer than previously thought. The effects of the 9/11 disaster are truly multifaceted.

The end of a small group

One group member glanced at his watch and pointed out that the workshop's large group was about to reconvene. He drifted off to get rid of the empty napkin that once held the muffin he munched on during the break. Another member headed off in the direction of the ladies' room, saying something about fixing her hair. Meanwhile, as in the case of many of these small informal groups that form during breaks at workshops, a few members will linger until the workshop facilitator summons them to the larger group. This group was no exception. The lingerers stayed long enough to agree that, even after several 'sittings' of this small group, the list of issues relating to drug abuse treatment and rehabilitation in Jamaica and the rest of the Caribbean is far from exhausted. Therein lies the need for many more small groups of this nature.

CHAPTER 7

What's the Hook?

Diary of a Drop-In Centre or Rehabilitation before Abstinence

MARCUS DAY

St Lucia is located in the Eastern Caribbean (14.1N 61E) with the Atlantic Ocean to its east and the Caribbean Sea to its west. A former colony of the United Kingdom, it became an independent nation in 1979 and elected a Westminster-style parliamentary government.

The estimated mid-year population was 160,145 in July 2002, with females slightly more than half of the total and 31 per cent of the population under the age of 14 years. Life expectancy was 72.82 years during the same year (69.26 years for males and 76.64 years for females).

The only 'city' in this small island developing state, the capital Castries, has a population of approximately 60,000 and the social phenomena typically associated with its larger counterparts: homelessness, drug misuse, vagrancy, sex work, begging and abject poverty – all within the shadow of a multi-million-dollar cruise ship port and duty-free shopping complex welcoming tourists to the tropical paradise of 'St Lucia, Simply Beautiful', as the Tourist Board proclaims.

With the implementation of a single market in Europe and the economic attacks by the United States through the World Trade Organization on the preferential treatment of Windward Island bananas in the UK market,[1] the collapse of the mainstay of the rural economy has led to a migration of country people into the Castries basin in search of a better life of electricity, indoor sanitation and employment opportunities. Tourism, long the number two income earner, has surpassed agriculture and won the battle for economic dominance. What was once an economy driven by independent farmers producing a crop that harvested weekly and contributed to a regular infusion of cash in the local economy has now metamorphosed into an economy driven by enclaves of all-inclusive hotels populated by white tourists and serviced by local black workers paid a pittance in monthly salary.

The official unemployment rate in 1999 was 17.5 per cent, but that figure is defined as the percentage of people actively seeking employment.[2] An analysis of the employment figures on the same website shows that the true figure of people aged 15 and over without employment is more like 41 per cent.[3] According to the 1995 poverty assessment survey conducted by the University of the West Indies, 18.7 per cent of households and 25.1 per cent of individuals were categorized as poor (earning below US$65 per month).[4]

Even though by law school attendance is compulsory for all children aged 5–15 years, the 1990 literacy rate was only 54.1 per cent, with 27.2 per cent categorized as illiterate and 18.7 per cent as functionally illiterate. The cradle language of most rural students is a French Creole, which places them at a disadvantage when they enter a classroom where the language of instruction is English.

The many individuals who were unable to make the transition from semi-literate farm labourer to clean and polished hotel service worker have fallen through the cracks. This is particularly evident on the street corners where groups of under-educated young men congregate the day through, living on the margins, doing odd jobs and searching for the better life that daily smacks them in the face as the opulence driven by the tourist dollar goes on display in luxury automobiles, duty-free shops and manicured hotel grounds.

The mantra of an IMF-led post-communist world, privatization, has further exacerbated the plight of those living on the fringe. Privatization of the Water Authority was forced upon St Lucia in exchange for the internationally funded aid project that constructed a dam and reservoir. In close succession, water authority and electric company went from state-owned statutory bodies to private shareholder corporations, with the state maintaining majority shares in each. With privatization, their prime missions changed from providing services to the people to making a profit for shareholders. With privatization the newly formed water company commenced a drive to connect all residents to the water mains with metered feeds, a most laudable goal whose downside was the capping of most free public stand-pipes. The rationale was that if all homes had pipe-borne water there was no need for public standpipes. Of course that reasoning was flawed because it left the squatters, the shantytowns and others on the outer margins without access to water.[5]

A series of devastating fires in the late 1940s and early 1950s transformed the face of Castries from quaint nineteenth-century West Indian town to a city of housing projects and office buildings in the style of 1950s modern. Many of the prominent old families relocated to areas 1–2 miles outside the city centre, further changing the character of the city. The Botanical Gardens in the George the Fifth Park, once the favoured promenade of the city's elite, became progressively more run-down until at its nadir the city council used it as a place to park their garbage trucks. Neglected and blighted, the Gardens earned a reputation as a dangerous area frequented by drug addicts and criminals, the human refuse discarded by society sharing space with the vehicles used to cart away unwanted leavings. The Gardens became the home of a cadre of homeless men and women eking out a precarious living in the informal economy, performing menial tasks and sometimes venturing into criminal activities, surviving as best they could on the scraps society had discarded.

St Lucia's 'drug of choice' since the early days of colonial domination has been rum. The Caribbean, rum and pirates are three images intertwined in the thoughts of many a Caribbean marketing agent and tourist board. While there are no data on the prevalence of alcohol use and misuse in the general population, a 2000 study funded by the Pan American Health Organization (PAHO) found that 'Within the year preceding the survey, 63.3 per cent of the teens had taken an alcoholic drink, and almost 1 in 10 (8.6 per cent) drank alcohol on a monthly or more frequent basis.'[6] Daily alcohol use was found in 42 per cent of those surveyed by the author in an unpublished research project looking at primary health care among street drug-using populations in Castries. Anecdotal evidence of the widespread misuse of alcohol was provided by the director of Turning Point, the sole residential treatment and rehabilitation centre in St Lucia, who stated that most admissions were for alcohol abuse. Furthermore, while conducting a needs assessment of drug demand reduction with the CARICOM member states the author heard officials of every national drug council state that alcohol abuse was the single largest problem in their country.[7]

The use of cannabis became popular in the mid-1970s with the rise in popularity of the Jamaican reggae scene and the glorification of the Rastafarian culture and religion. Cannabis is grown locally and imported from neighbouring islands (previously Dominica and now St Vincent). Efforts by the US to eradicate local crops peaked in the mid-1990s and have all but stopped as nationalist governments become more sensitive to foreign US troops on their soil and to the environmental damage caused by eradication efforts.

In the same PAHO-sponsored study cited above, 5.5 per cent of males aged 10–19 reported using cannabis on a monthly basis. The author, while not advocating the use of any mood-altering substance, usually points out that there are no 'ganga whores or ganga jumbies' (vagrants) and that the limited resources devoted to drug demand reduction activities would be better allocated to teaching about harms related to specific substances than to generic anti-drug education efforts that bundle all drugs together and warn that 'drugs kill'.

Be that as it may, the concern over illicit drug use, misuse and abuse runs very high in St Lucia as well as in the rest of the Caribbean. St Lucia is a major transshipment port for cocaine from Colombia onward to Europe. With each shipment that passes through some 'skim' (a percentage of goods) stays behind as a payment in kind for the facilitation of the movement. As the facilitators have no need for the drug, most not being users, the cocaine is 'dumped' on the local market at prices well below metropolitan equivalents. Arriving as high-grade powder cocaine, it is mixed with baking soda and water, boiled dry and converted into the smokeable cocaine base commonly referred to as 'crack'. A 'crack' rock that costs US$10 in the US costs less than US$2 in Castries.

In the 1990s the government of St Lucia along with other Caribbean countries signed up to the various initiatives sponsored by the United States, the United Nations Drug Control Programme and the European Union to combat drugs. It is a signatory to the Barbados Plan of Action (BPA) of 1996, and the US–Caribbean summit of 1997 in Santo Domingo (referred to the Santo Domingo Declaration) that clearly stated as objectives the intensification of efforts to eradicate the cultivation of cannabis and the interdiction of cocaine transiting the region.

Following the signing of the BPA, the European Commission established the EC Drugs Control Office (ECDCO) in Barbados to coordinate the work of stemming the flow of drugs into Europe. More than just supply-side interventions, the EC sought to address the health and human cost of drug use in the transit countries, and commissioned a study of the state of drug treatment and rehabilitation in the Caribbean.[8] The study found a large number of high-threshold, abstinence-based residential treatment centres, primary prevention 'Just Say NO Campaigns', and virtually nothing in between. From that study grew a project to strengthen the capacity of non-governmental organizations and widen the scope of their service provision to include low-threshold, street-based interventions designed to reach that large pool of individuals who were not receiving any treatment because they did not fit into the narrowly defined entry criteria of the existing services. In the summer of 1999 a project was submitted by DOH International (DOHi) to address the gaps in capacity and service. The author was appointed regional project coordinator and, after trying to interest some local St Lucia NGOs in implementing a low-threshold, street-based intervention programme (SBIP), he took personal charge of setting up such a programme. It was envisaged that the drop-in centre would provide drop-in counselling services to the homeless crack-using population in its intake area.

The first challenge: location, location, location

In the real estate trade, they say there are three important considerations when looking for a place: location, location and location. The first challenge in setting up a low-threshold drop-in centre was to find an appropriate location and in this case the area that most people were running from was the area we wanted to be in. To put it in the colloquial, the 'shittier' the area – the more run-down, crime-infested and abandoned by 'polite' society – the better, when it comes to housing a drop-in centre targeting those very populations.

Observations of the author in the Castries area and throughout the Caribbean have shown that homeless drug users confine themselves to areas of comfort in which they operate. That is not to say that they do not move outside of that area but you can be pretty sure of seeing the same homeless people in the same area day after day, and in Castries if you move down the road a mile you will see a different set of homeless people occupying a different turf. Therefore, in looking for an appropriate site for the centre it became imperative to find a place located in an area that was home to individuals who would need and use the services provided.

It was clear from the beginning that there were four prime locations for this type of intervention in Castries: George Charles Boulevard Marchand, Grass Street/Wilton's Yard off Chaucee Road, The City Council housing project in La Clery (across the street from the author's house) and the George the Fifth Park mentioned above. There were abandoned buildings in all of these locations and a team made up of the author and a clinician, Carole Mullally, from the DOHi regional office, spent hours and days walking the area, speaking to potential clients and residents, and searching for the best location at the best price (and possibly at no cost at all).

In November 2000 word came to the office that the St Lucia Save the Children (LUSAVE) was going to close its offices for lack of funds to pay staff. The LUSAVE offices were located in the George the Fifth Park (G5P, commonly referred to as 'the Gardens'), in an area frequented by dysfunctional, chaotic – and mostly homeless – crack users, in a run-down building built by Canada Fund 30 years ago and owned by LUSAVE. It seemed as though the office was run by people under siege; the staff of two would lock themselves into the building daily for fear of being attacked by the homeless horde hovering on their doorstep. The LUSAVE staff managed a caseload of 18 children and administered the scholarships provided to them by individuals and the business community. An overture was made to the LUSAVE Board of Directors: in exchange for full use of the building as a drop-in centre, DOHi would manage the LUSAVE scholarship programme and pay for the utilities as well as the upkeep of the building.

On 18 December two elderly German cruise ship tourists were savagely chopped with a machete in broad daylight, robbed of their belongings and left bleeding on the threshold of an adjacent abandoned building, the man clutching the severed finger of his right hand in his left. The keys were handed over two days later on 20 December and it was decided that the first official working day would be 3 January 2001, after the Christmas break.

On Sunday morning, 31 December, at 6 am two dreadlocked men in flowing white robes, carrying torches and gasoline, entered a packed Cathedral of the Immaculate Conception in the centre of Castries and proceeded to set people afire. They bludgeoned to death a nun and burned the priest to death. They burned the Bishop's chair, the altar and the Bible, and later told police that 'on old year's night Babylon makes its covenant with the devil and we needed to cleanse the place with fire'.

Needless to say the nation was traumatized by the incident. It was clear that, with over 600 individuals witnessing such a horrific event, there would be much need for critical incident stress debriefing and counselling: as a result an announcement was made on the radio that we were there to help, and we opened the doors of the drop-in centre a few days earlier than planned. It soon became apparent that this was not to be the last time that the centre would respond to a need by providing a service it had not envisaged. In fact, this is the hallmark of an NGO, the ability to re-programme as necessary and to respond to the needs of its clients.

The hook!

Many have discussed what it takes to get crack users into a drop-in centre. Programmes targeting injecting drug users have a ready-made lure in the exchange of clean needles;[9] this by itself is frequently enough to get users into the centre, where other services on offer are available for the user to select at his or her own pace. Service providers who seek to operate a low-threshold drop-in centre in the English-speaking Caribbean have always looked for that attraction to use with crack users. Some programmes in North America give out smoking kits containing filters and other paraphernalia; a few have created safer crack use brochures.[10] The challenge is confining our basis of attraction to elements of users' lives that are most obviously drug-related. The harm that's brought about by drug use – especially in a society that doesn't approve of it – arises more from the disapproval than from the actual dependency. Public health problems and widespread social harm can be much more problematic then the actual direct consequences of drug use. The more interaction one has with the target population, and the more one thinks outside the box, the greater the likelihood of finding solutions that work for both the client and the service provider. The goal of this drop-in centre was to have a more practical impact on local users' lives – and to bring them into contact with the programme. In the case of the G5P drop-in centre the attraction became something not at all expected: a standpipe supplying free fresh water!

One of the challenges in setting up any programme to help drug users is that many of the targeted beneficiaries do not want to be helped. Kohler and

Moore found many programmes premised on the strong belief that the service provider knew best what was needed to solve the problems of drug users, and this remedy mostly revolved around abstinence. When asked what they needed, over 37.5 per cent of homeless drug users named job placement as the most important service that should be provided by a drop-in centre, while 8.8 per cent said food was the most important service.[11]

In the past LUSAVE had had a problem with homeless drug users breaking the water pipe behind the building. Within three weeks of taking possession of the building we found the building without water and the feed pipe broken. Enquires were made as to the reason someone would do this. A 'rapid assessment' of a few users quickly revealed that the pipe had been broken so that the homeless residents could draw water to bathe but more importantly to wash cars and taxis to bring in needed income.

Again a reprogramming took place. If access to clean water would attract people to the building it was possible that this could be the hook to attract people to use the centre. Once first contact was established, more meaningful contacts would follow. Rather than seal the pipe again, as had been done so often in the past, it was decided that a faucet would be installed in line. The services of one of the Garden's residents was enlisted and work commenced on modifying the building's feed line to allow for easy access to the water supply. By giving their clients access to clean water, the centre not only addressed their survival needs, but also expanded the definition of what was an appropriate harm reduction service.

Of course this decision met with some resistance from the neighbours, the people who keep the gardens clean, the police patrols – basically everyone. It was also clear that this would not be the last time decisions surrounding the formation of this drop-in centre were met with resistance. The usual comment was, 'If you do that (install a standpipe) it will just attract "them".' To which the staff usually commented, 'That's the idea.' You can imagine the looks we received.

In the first few weeks the standpipe was broken often. It was clear that the work would have to be up to heavy-duty industrial standards to stand up to the parade of individuals in various stages of intoxication. A purely practical decision was taken to add a concrete pillar and a permanent faucet, as the previous brass faucet had been stolen! After each adversity the 'nay-sayers' encouraged the centre to stop the noble experiment.

The needs of a developing world harm reduction programme are in some aspects quite different from those of the average urban harm reduction programme in the US or Europe. This account is useful in showing how creativity and the ability to re-programme as required may be used to bring in clients, while making a positive impact on their lives at the same time. Although it is unlikely that the route described here would be repeated in the developed world, substitute other services such as a shower and bathing facilities, or access to a washer and dryer, or even a place to cash in recyclable aluminium cans, and you can see the similarities.

After the faucet was installed the next step was promoting the availability of the pipe for general use. It was time to do some street work. As usual, when one has something concrete to offer it is much easier to make a meaningful contact. I walked out of the Gardens toward the public market and stopped at the first person I saw washing a vehicle, a fellow bent over with a bucket washing a taxi van on the adjacent avenue. Not knowing what kind of reaction I would get, I walked over and told him about the pipe. Obtaining clean water to ply their car wash trade was very difficult. It meant a long walk and was costly – fifty cents a bucket from the market standpipe two blocks away. His immediate enthusiasm surprised me. Apparently the gods of street work were smiling that day because I had selected at random a person who felt much ownership in the Gardens and who would turn out to be a key gatekeeper over the coming months. Morris explained how he and the other car washers got water and how difficult it was to find a toilet to use – or to get a bath. When I asked, he also told me how much crack he smoked and how often: 'two, three rocks a day and only at night'. Of course he wanted to be put in charge of the standpipe and collect the 'fee', which he promised to hold for the centre. He had a real problem accepting that the water was free, clean water being such a valuable commodity in St Lucia. He thanked us for the service we were providing and said he had to get back to washing the cars. Later he came by the centre and said he had organized a meeting of 'all' the car washers in the area on Saturday at 11 am to discuss the standpipe and its use. We had no expectation of what would happen, but planned to be there on Saturday just in case.

Of course the law of unintended consequences always takes over in situations like this. The next day the staff noticed that the rear of the building had become a mud hole, as we had provided no adequate drainage outlet to drain the run-off. To assist in the work I recruited another person, Dave, a crack user and a skilled wood carver and artist who lives in my neighbourhood. He was happy to have an employment opportunity that would also help his fellow users.

We drove directly to the Gardens to assess the project (all projects must have a needs assessment!). Being doers rather than talkers we picked up a piece of iron rail and began to dig a hole in search of the wastewater outlet. We promptly broke the water pipe in a new spot. The whole project promptly refocused on repairing the broken pipe, which then called for a reallocation of material resources – we needed a dollar fifty to buy two pipe couplings!

It was soon time to break for lunch. Dave's strength was waning and it was clear he wanted to pipe up (smoke some crack). I gave him some dates to eat, as a sugar buzz is better than nothing. We shut down the job and drove home for lunch. My wife's Montessori School (next to my home) prepares food for 50 children, seven staff members, my family and anyone else who wanders by looking hungry. There is always food for one more mouth. Dave got a very large helping from the kitchen and a big cup of strong coffee with lots of sugar from my private stash (not quite the same as piping a rock but my coffee has been known to cause at least a minor buzz in the unsuspecting).

After lunch we loaded up the pick-up truck with the necessary materials and tools, most of which were scavenged from around my yard. We begged (my main occupation as a drop-in centre administrator, begging resources) the pipe couplings from some water company workers and thus saved the buck fifty. Back to the job, while Dave and I worked on the 'fortification' of the water line, Greg dropped by to ask if it was true we were providing water. Our second client had arrived! About 3 pm Felix came by. In and out of jail, Felix is a homeless person who has used ganja and crack for years, but at 40 prefers rum as his drug of choice. A nice, soft-spoken fellow, Felix told me he had to go to court the next morning at 9 for stealing a jar of cashews from the supermarket. I asked him what he was wearing to court and he motioned to the clothes he had on – ragged short pants and a torn t-shirt. Giving in to my usual habit of overcommitting myself I told him to meet me at 8 the next morning for a shower at the centre – and that I would find him some clothes to wear, too. Felix then asked if he could also get a shave and a haircut. I smiled to myself: welcome client number three. I had been worried about how we would get clients, that no one would drop in on the centre – a bit like holding a party and worrying that no one would come. I was pleased to be wrong.

I began to realize that there was a small group of human beings who were beginning to have some expectations of receiving services from our new project. We now had an obligation to keep going – not so much for ourselves as for them. We were going to have to find some dependable funding sources. The salary of Carole, the drop-in centre's counsellor, was paid up until the end of July. My salary was probably paid until October, but with the European Community there are no guarantees without pen to paper. During the afternoon I had fielded a few phone calls, including one concerning a regional CARICOM meeting the following week in Antigua. There I would have an opportunity to advocate and lobby regional policy makers to include street and community-based intervention programmes in the regional policy response to the drug problem. As I stood in the Gardens in my knee-high wellies, short pants, dirty t-shirt covered in cement dust and mud, I laughed at the dichotomy of the scene. I was morphing into NGO man, responding to grassroots needs at local level, while with equal aplomb providing evidence with which I could hope to influence regional policy.

I had been encouraged to take this on, and I was feeling contented: service provision gave new purpose to what had been up to then primarily a project management position. Of course, the paper work was building up on my desk!

Dave and I were able to complete the first phase of the pipe repair job by 5.30 pm. We loaded up the truck and headed back to the school for dinner. By this time Dave really only wanted to get paid and go score. I told him that it would be good to fill up his belly before he went off to party, and gave him a big bowl of salt fish, green figs and spaghetti. I gave him a spare pair of shoes – and again wished I had a hundred pairs of men's shoes and workboots to give away to the guys I met daily. Women's clothing is much easier to get than men's – especially shoes. (If I can't help the guys curb their use at least I can help them look smart while they wander the streets.) I paid Dave his $50 for the day's work and he walked off into the sunset with a few mangoes he had picked from my yard and a hunger in his eyes.

It is an interesting question to muse over, paying people for service rendered when you know that they will most likely spend their money on drugs. During a recent research project conducted at the Centre we paid each person interviewed EC$20 (about US$8) for a two-hour interview. Many people thought this was wrong because of the implication that the recipient would spend the money on drugs. Much of what we do at the centre is to teach people how to function in society (while they are still using drugs). It is hoped that if they succeed in getting clean the transition into the non-drug-using world will be easier with these life skills, and that if they continue to use drugs their lives will not be so chaotic because they have learned some coping skills to get them through the day. One of the skills we try to instil is budgeting and the proper allocation of resources. So whenever we pay cash for services rendered we reinforce the discussion of budgeting with a small talk on spending some of the money on food and other necessities and not only on drugs. But we always pay for services and time rendered because it is important to let our clients know that we value their services and their time.

During the day spent with Dave and many days to come hanging by the pipe I had the opportunity to practise what has been referred to as 'rehabilitation before abstinence' (RBA). This philosophy goes beyond the traditional harm reduction (HR) approach. The Merriam Webster Dictionary defines 'rehabilitate' as 'to restore or bring to a condition of health or useful and constructive activity'. RBA believes that the reduction of harm can be taken further by working with drug users, assisting them to improve the quality of their lives while continuing their drug use. RBA assists drug users to deal with the underlying traumas of life and teaches them life skills that allow them to cope with the stress of everyday situations in the wider society.

Low-threshold drop-in centres like G5P recognize that drug use may be seen as a coping mechanism to assist an individual to mask the pain caused by trauma . By gradually introducing coping skills at the appropriate 'learning moment', and without requiring abstinence, service providers are able to assist drug-using individuals to make their lives less chaotic.

The importance of street-based work is supported from the bottom up. Previously cited unpublished research showed that 31 per cent of the clients self-reported a change in their consumption and 62 per cent reported a change in attitude toward their drug use.[12] With a change in attitude a change in behaviour is not far behind.[13]

The United Nations Office on Drugs and Crime (formerly the UN Drugs Control Programme) states on its webpage that outreach programmes are 'necessary to reach the many drug users who are not in contact with any medical or drug abuse treatment institutions'. It goes on to state that 'flexible, unconventional approaches developed outside formal health and social environments and aimed at accessing, motivating and supporting drug abusers can reach out-of-treatment drug users, increase drug treatment referrals and reduce illicit drug-use behaviour.[14]

People who are 'addicted' to drugs are a diverse group of individuals who are linked by their compulsion to use drugs. For many people drug taking is symptomatic of other problems. One theory that has held up to research is that individuals use illicit drugs as a form of self-medication to relieve the pain caused by some past psychological trauma. Studies have shown that substance abusers are more likely to have post-traumatic stress disorder than the general population.[15]

Of all the homeless, chaotic crack-using individuals the author has worked with, not one came to that state overnight. Their drug-taking career started as a gradual process, until one day they found themselves jobless, homeless and generally shunned by society. If asked, clients consistently describe the long road they travelled to their present state. I often wonder how a high-threshold, abstinence-based treatment service expects people who have taken years to reach the 'bottom' to reverse that position in 28 days.

Networking pays off

After Dave and I had completed the pipe job and had dinner it was 6.30 pm and I had to get ready to attend a posh farewell cocktail party for the British High Commissioner and his lovely wife – and to welcome his successor and *his* lovely wife. I would have preferred to sleep, but I knew that the opportunity to network with people who could help the centre was too valuable to miss. I dressed casually elegant and, as I looked in the mirror, recalled the expression of a dear old friend in St Thomas: 'Boy, you clean up real nice!'

It was actually a good evening. I got a local hotelier to donate 25 used bath towels to help with the shower programme and I was able to ask the French ambassador for support for the project. I also promised to take him to meet some of the other NGOs working in the social services field. It's an interesting fact that many of these diplomats never get to meet people doing real grassroots work. I take every opportunity I get to introduce people who can help to other NGOs. The more exposure for the sector, the more we work to uplift the people we are targeting.

As a result of that casual meeting with the French ambassador, the French government awarded a €40,500 grant to the drop-in centre for renovations, training and research. The research is completed and will be published shortly. A major focus of my work seems to be making connections: bringing together people who have something and people who need something. I got home after midnight and thought about my commitment to meet Felix at 8 the next morning. I asked myself what I had started and whether I would have the strength to continue.

Thursday, 7 June 2001

I woke up at 5.30 am, grabbed a cup of yesterday's coffee from the thermos flask and grimaced at the bitter taste. (I figure it's more for the buzz than the taste!) I had two and a half hours till my hair date with Felix, and I started to think about what I would need to assist him in his transformation. Hair clippers, towel, a shirt, pants. I asked Pinkie, my wife, 'Honey do you have an old pair of pants you don't need for Felix to wear to court?' Then I scrunched up my shoulders and waited for a barrage of 'Who's Felix? What did he do? Why you?' I paid the price in blood and guts, and in exchange got a great pair of jeans that I know he will like. At five minutes after eight I rushed off to the Gardens wondering if Felix would even be there. I have learned that these pre-planned liaisons sometimes never come off, but it is important for me to be seen as fulfilling my commitments, even when it is doubtful that the other party will. Time keeping and responsibility are not the strong points of homeless chaotic crack smokers. Three minutes later I arrived at the centre. There was Felix, waiting patiently under the eave of the building, sheltering from the pouring rain.

Unlocking the well-defended entrance we entered the building. 'Well, let's get on with it,' I told Felix, 'Sit here next to the outlet.' I fired up the clipper, which promptly stalled trying to eat through his thickly matted hair (Should he have washed it first?) I realized that I had better attack the job with scissors. Meanwhile I confessed to Felix that I had never cut another man's hair before. He grimaced and bowed his head. Anticipating a rough and dirty job I had worn my blue drill work coveralls and as the four-inch-thick locks fell to the floor I was relieved not to find any sign of parasitic inhabitants living in them. When all the locks were gone, I got the clippers going again and finished the trim job. When the hair was done, Felix asked for a shave. While I wished for a straight razor and one of those brushes with talcum powder, I made do with the hair clipper and removed his beard and moustache. For a moment, I had flashes that I'd turned into Floyd the Barber on Andy Griffith. Grooming completed, I sent Felix off to the shower and to change into his new clothes. He came out all clean and snazzy, a new man ready to meet the rigours of the St Lucian criminal justice system. The old saying is the clothes make the man: in this case we had taken Felix from a dirty street person with a drug problem to a clean, respectable person with a drug problem – only the 'problem' was not so apparent. I couldn't help but feel good about the whole affair, convinced that we would go a long way to making community life less crazy if we were able to assist the street-based drug-using population to clean up and change into fresh clothes.

At 10 am Carole called me from the drop-in centre to tell me she had collected the first dollar from the standpipe. Although Morris had indicated that he expected to pay for the water, and some of the other guys I ran into concurred, I hadn't thought this angle through. If they wanted to pay for the water – after all, they had to pay for it at the market – who were we to say no? They insisted, and we weren't going to deprive them of the opportunity to contribute. Carole described how Greg, another client with 'anger' issues, had asked what he should do with the money if no one was there to collect it. She had told him to keep track of the number of buckets he filled and pay later, and that we trusted him, after which he looked kind of confused. Apparently no one had said they trusted him for a while. Since we don't care if we collect any money it's easy for us to be cavalier about the bucket fee. It will be interesting to see how it turns out. Carole reminded me of the meeting of the car washers on Saturday. It's all the buzz around the market. The guys now want to form the Gros Islet Bus Stand Car Washers Association. 'Would this be considered a users' group?' I wonder.

It's interesting to muse that if you asked most people what the crack users in central Castries needed, they'd be unlikely to say 'water to wash cars'. And yet this was just the thing that these guys said they needed. The lesson for me is that when I ask a person 'What do you need?' I should be prepared to hear answers that are not necessarily in keeping with my expectations.

Saturday, 9 June 2001

Tim, aka Mufi, aka Coconut Man, stops by my house at 6.45 am. It is unusual to see Tim this early unless he has been up all night. I have known Tim for 10 years and have watched his physical deterioration from the crack.

He was a handsome young man when I first met him, but after a broken jaw, various cutlass wounds, and now a strange case of boils erupting all over his body (since diagnosed as leprosy and under control) he has a frightful appearance and is now known as the Troll. He lives in a very small and humble one-room squatter's house not far from my home. He built it out of scrap lumber; it has no running water, no electricity.

My kids are scared of him, which is sad because he is a nice guy. As much as I like him it is also 6.45 am. I have not had the first hit of my drug of choice yet. I muse to myself about the issue of 'boundaries and social work in small island states'. A great topic for a regional roundtable discussion; maybe I should post the question on the regional email list. This is a problem to which a person living in a large country may not be able to relate. In a large country like Trinidad or Jamaica, a person working with a homeless, drug-using populations can go home and be anonymous. In a small island state like St Lucia everyone knows where we live and unless it is far outside of town, clients will stop by the house. The guys I work with at the drop-in centre know where I live, what car I drive, that my wife owns a pre-school, everything about me including whatever myths are currently circulating.

Anyway, there is Tim with a big grin, looking slightly peckish. 'One more for breakfast, Pinkie,' I tell my wife, while my ten-year-old Minnie tells me not to feed him. This then leads to a discussion of the meaning of charity and the strong helping the weak. After some grilled cheese sandwiches and coco tea the purpose of the early call is revealed: Tim had helped me put on a new roof the week before and now wants some of the left-over galvanized roofing for his mother. I smile at the fact that he has asked for it rather than just taking it. Of course he wanted me to deliver it to her house, about ten miles away. Well that was the hook for me: this was taking our relationship to a new stage. He was comfortable enough for me to meet his mother and I of course really wanted to meet her and see what his home life was like before he moved out.

He loaded the galvanized sheets onto the truck while I got ready to leave. My son Bass came with me. When we arrived at the neighbourhood I still had visions of Mufi's mother being poor. Of course this is just a manifestation of my prejudice because, as I know but sometimes forget, drugs touch all. But I was surprised by how nice the house and yard were; it was all very middle-class. A very nice lady, Mufi's mom knew of me already. Apparently Mufi speaks about Pinkie and me often, and she thanked me for taking care of him. I was touched. I never suspected he told his mother anything about my wife or me and how we helped him. When I told Pinkie she changed her attitude toward him and became a bit softer. It is clear that the demonization of drug users had succeeded in brainwashing me to forget that even drug users were someone's children. Mufi's mom gave Bass a soft drink, a big bag of mangoes and some cuttings of a bougainvillea plant. We said our goodbyes and drove home.

The next time I was at the centre Johnson came by to fill his bucket and informed me of the 'raging' controversy over water rights and usage. There appears to be serious disunity between the guys who pay and those who don't – especially on weekends and evenings, when there is no one to monitor the situation. The root of the issue lies not in the water but in a class war between the various categories of users of the resource, guys who pay regularly vs guys who don't pay regularly vs guys who don't pay at all. Current crack users vs former crack users, crack users with shoes vs those without, those who can read vs those who pass as readers, and on and on. There was as much social stratification as at Her Majesty's Court. In real terms there is a problem between the guys who come and fill up many buckets (these guys are 'rich' because they own multiple buckets) and the guys who own one bucket and need to fill it fast and get back to washing cars or lose the job to someone else.

It looks as though one solution is multiple taps, one being the express fill-up line, one buck or less. Another solution is for an agreement that a multi-fill defers to a single bucket, or some such regulatory move. I hope to ask the guys about scheduling a next meeting so that this and other issues can be discussed. The meeting on the Saturday before last never came off; it was raining and no one showed up.

I start to wonder when everything falls into place so nicely, when everything is just meshing, that there is balance in the world. I can only feel that everything is going too well and that something is going to go wrong. I start to feel certain that things are going too well. It seems that the time was right for this initiative and that the pieces continue to fall into place – and of course this begins to worry me. When things are going too well I can't help waiting for the hammer to fall, and that feeling of 'impending doom' tickles my consciousness. Oh well. 'Always look on the bright side of life.'

I continue to purge myself of any expectations, so the small victories are that much sweeter and the setbacks not as devastating. It is kind of a Zen and the Art of Drop-in Centre Management philosophy. I regularly tell people that I have no false conception of the 'noble savage'. I realize very well that the people I work with are probably the most selfish, self-centred and self-absorbed people in the world. It's the drug, the crack, and the desire to feed that need for crack that greatly contributes to that cult of 'self'.

I went up to Al (one of the car washers) the other day, just to say hi and ask about him. He started to tell me how much the water has meant to him and how appreciative he is and that I should ask him if I need any help because he could give me a hand if I needed one. Well, I'll tell you what a difference this made to me. I had been in a slump. Al gave me just what I needed that afternoon, just a bit of TLC from him to me. That kind word really made my day.

That is not to say that there weren't any problems. There were people getting naked behind the building to bathe. Sometimes the guys have a heated discussion of some current event that sounds like a fight but is really just a 'discussion'. Our neighbours have never stopped begrudging us the water we provide for free to the needy.

Epilogue

While LUSAVE still operates in St Lucia, the George the Fifth Park drop-in centre is now closed. It operated for two years. At the height of its service provision it provided a daily hot meal at lunch, fresh water, used clothes and lots of love, understanding and respect to the people who came around and used our services.

Sustainability of projects of this type is always a problem. Funding for projects whose objectives are not black and white is hard to come by. Our focus was on increasing the quality of life of our clients and the non-drug-using people who lived in the community. Even while we thought we had strong verifiable indicators, like a reduction in violent crime, the community and government did not seem to be convinced. There was opposition from the neighbours who, despite having lived in proximity to the drug users for years, did not like a project that treated the latter with dignity and respect. The manager of the Gardens was more concerned with breaking down the cardboard 'housing' than seeing the benefits of coexistence.

It's a funny thing: as previously stated, the area where the drop-in centre was located, the Botanical Gardens, has seen better days. Located in the centre of a city that has been all but abandoned by the middle class, the Gardens over the years have attracted a homeless crack-using population. The place was pretty crazy before we started to operate, with violent muggings a usual occurrence. In the two years that we were open there, there was not one mugging. Now that the drop-in centre function has been discontinued, the violence has come back. Recently there were two machete choppings, gunshots have been heard and the LUSAVE staffers have again begun locking themselves in.

When the centre staff began the process of engaging the user population, reaching out to them with respect and treating them with dignity, they responded. The response was extraordinary: there were not any fewer homeless crack users, they were not any cleaner, nor were they using drugs more sparingly, but their attitudes toward life and the people around them had begun to change. They realized that there were people there who cared about them for no other reason than that they were there. They realized that they lived in and were part of a 'community' and had begun to act as members of that community. They cooperated better among themselves and with the neighbours. They had begun the process of rehabilitating themselves even before they contemplated becoming abstinent.

NOTES

1 According to trade statistics published by the Organization of Eastern Caribbean States, the total US dollar value of exports from St Lucia to the rest of the world dropped 38 per cent during the period 1994–8. OECS External Merchandise Trade Annual Report 1998, December 1999, Castries, St Lucia.

2 < http://www.stats.gov.lc/laba44.htm>

3 <http://www.stats.gov.lc/laba22.htm>

4 Kairi Consultants Ltd. in association with the National Assessment Team of St Lucia, *Poverty Assessment Report: St Lucia*, Main Report, Vol. 1, April 1996.

5 The 2001 Population and Housing Census conducted by the St Lucia Government Statistics Department showed that the distribution of water by standpipe dropped from 28 per cent in 1991 to 5.1 per cent in 2001.

6 T. J. Fountain, *Findings of the Caribbean Youth Health Survey: St Lucia*, Nassau, Bahamas: C Research Consultants, 2000.

7 A. Klein, M. Day, E. Oppenheimer and A. Harriot (eds.), *A Drug Demand Reduction Needs Assessment in the Caribbean Community and Market*, London: DrugScope, 2002.

8 U. Kohler and D. Moore, *Drug Treatment and Rehabilitation Needs, Report for the European Commission of the Assessment Mission for Drug Treatment and Rehabilitation Needs in the Caribbean*, Bridgetown, Barbados: European Commission, 1997.

9 G. V. Stimson, D. C. Des Jarlais and A. Ball (eds.), *Drug Injecting and HIV Infection: Global Dimension and Local Responses*, London: University College, 1998.

10 These kits were available for distribution at the Third National Harm Reduction Conference (October 2000) in Miami, Florida.

11 M. Day, 'Needs Analysis for Primary Health Care among the Street Drug-Using Community in Castries, St Lucia: 2002', 2003, unpublished.

12 *Ibid.*

13 J. Keller, *Attitude is Everything: Change your Attitude ... and You Can Change your life*, Tampa: INTI Publishing & Resource Books Inc, 1999.

14 My emphasis. United Nations Office on Drugs and Crime, Access to Treatment and Rehabilitation <http://www.undcp.org/odccp/treatment_toolkit.html?id=14>

15 L. M. Najavits, R. D. Weiss and S. R. Shaw, 'The Link between Substance Abuse and Posttraumatic Stress Disorder in Women', *American Journal on Addictions*, 6, 4, 1997: 273–83.

CHAPTER 8

Cayman Drug Council

Practising Harm Reduction in a Zero-Tolerance Society

CATHERINE CHESTNUT

The invitation to contribute to this book came after a chance meeting with one of its editors during Cayman's participation in the first conference on Demand Reduction for Caribbean Overseas Territories. As head of delegation for the Cayman Islands, it was my responsibility to overview the achievements of the National Drug Council of the Cayman Islands at the opening ceremony. As each country made its presentation, the diversity of policy responses and programme initiatives became apparent. Caribbean Overseas Territories are not well represented at many of the conferences and seminars held throughout the region and this was an opportunity for us to share and learn from each other's experiences.

Genesis of a national drug council

An Advisory Council on the Misuse of Drugs was established in the Cayman Islands in 1989. Based on the structure of the UK Council of the same name, it remained in existence for a number of years and provided the government with advice on matters related to substance abuse. As it was an advisory body, there was no secretariat to conduct the work of the council and membership was for the most part on a voluntary basis. By 1996, tackling drug issues was elevated to ministerial status, and the Ministry of Health and Social Welfare was expanded to include Drug Abuse Prevention and Rehabilitation. The Ministry's mandate was to identify the problems associated with drug abuse in the community and develop a master plan to address them.

In 1995 the Cayman Islands government decided to use the strategic planning model to develop a comprehensive plan for drug abuse prevention and rehabilitation, including both demand and supply reduction. An alliance, consisting of the stakeholder agencies and the wider community, was created to undertake the task of developing the master plan. The establishment of a national co-ordinating body, the National Drug Council, a statutory body mandated by law (NDC Law 1997) came directly from the plan and was deemed critical to implementing the plan over time.

Developing a master plan

The Ministry decided that a collaborative approach based on strategic thinking would yield the best results and provide the ownership necessary to ensure implementation. With this in mind, an alliance of associated governmental and non-governmental agencies was formed to oversee the process. The 30-odd member alliance debated what its mission, objectives, beliefs and parameters were before developing its list of strategies to address the drug problem. The process involved was exhausting, but resulted in consensus. It was then up to the action teams, which represented a microcosm of the community, to develop action plans that would realize each strategy. The entire process involved approximately 250 members of the community, out of an estimated population of 34,000 at the time. The resulting plan was then presented to the government as the wishes of the people and adopted in the Legislative Assembly.

The process of developing our master plan is dynamic in the sense that each year the alliance meets to review its implementation and examine whether the underlying premises, practices and action plans themselves are still appropriate or should be either removed or changed. It is this process of annual updating that breathes new life into our master plan and each year reaffirms our commitment to the cause. But that is not to say that the process is flawless. A good plan and the best intentions are not enough to ensure implementation. Political will and funding are key components of a successful plan. In the changing environment of the political cycle, priorities change and funding varies accordingly. For long-term plans this sometimes means actions may have to be shelved mid-stream.

The NDC therefore has the task of taking both external and internal factors into consideration before developing policies and programmes that are consistent with the plan. In a society that has experienced rapid economic growth over a relatively short span (approximately 30 years) the changing views of the expanding populace must be considered very carefully. For example, public opinion is divided between those who want perpetrators of drug-related crimes removed from society and those who think that treatment and rehabilitation should be used to address the chemical dependency issues, which in turn will constrain the likelihood of repeated offences and reduce harm to the individuals, their families and society at large. The art of balancing the needs of both sides of public opinion becomes a serious consideration in making decisions about public policies. Public information is the main tool by which we are able to educate the public about various approaches to substance abuse issues and how these approaches may or may not suit our society.

Zero tolerance

'Zero tolerance' is a common expression in the Cayman drug abuse vernacular. It is often used to describe the vigilant approach the law enforcement agencies have taken towards reducing the supply of drugs on the streets: in essence, using criminal laws with stringent penalties to deter drug use. Many argue that to maintain social order we must take a firm stance against drug users. By that they usually mean that they should be locked up so that they cannot use or sell drugs on the streets. Although this view is quite popular among the general populace, there is also acknowledgement of the burden that this approach places on the criminal justice system. The prison is overcrowded and there has already been a major uprising that resulted in a significant portion of the prison being ravaged by fires set by inmates.

Rightfully, the public is now questioning what needs to be done to reduce the recidivism rate, which is exacerbating existing constraints on the justice and welfare systems. Indeed, the public is now more aware of the inherent problems that can arise when we seek to punish all drug-related offences by use of traditional custodial sentences. Incarceration is no longer viewed as the only desirable outcome, and slowly is being replaced by notions of restoration and rehabilitation. In September 2002, the Chief Justice announced the implementation of the drug court legislation, having spent the past three years introducing the concepts in the courts under the discretionary powers of the magistrates. This initiative will ensure that treatment and rehabilitation services are used by the criminal justice system to provide a more holistic approach to dealing with drug-related offences that are non-violent in nature. Drug courts are but a part of a more comprehensive campaign to provide alternative sentencing options.

We seem to be in the process of a paradigm shift towards a more liberal understanding of drug abuse in the criminal justice context. Zero tolerance has not been totally abandoned. Instead its meaning has changed to convey the determination inherent in drug control strategies. A more practical approach has therefore been adopted towards implementing programmes more accurately described as reducing the harm associated with drug use.

Reducing harm vs harm reduction

If we start by making a distinction between 'reduction of harm' and 'harm reduction' we can minimize the ambiguity inherent in the latter term.

'Reduction of harm' is then defined as any measure that reduces the negative consequences of drug use. These measures range from supply reduction to interventions that reduce demand, and also include measures specifically intended only to reduce adverse consequences. 'Harm reduction' then applies to those specific measures that prevent the adverse consequences of drug use without addressing drug consumption. So, conceptually, our definition of reducing harm includes measures that could be classified under our definition of zero tolerance, which is based on prohibition.

The past seven years of planning and implementing strategies aimed at reducing the harm associated with drug abuse have not been easy. Initially, the stakeholder agencies had to grapple with differing definitions of drug abuse before they could move on to formulating demand and supply reduction strategies. It was only through a process that focused on total consensus that they were able to agree on a philosophy, which then formed the basis of the master plan that has remained unchanged over time. This philosophy reflects many positive attributes of the human mind and spirit and how it can be nurtured to resist the negative influences of drug abuse.

It is from this perspective that the concept of 'reducing harm' developed although the term itself has never been stated as public policy. Perhaps the failure of stakeholders to use the term has been due to the fear of resistance by segments of the community likely to argue that such an approach was a 'soft' option in contrast to zero tolerance, which seems to have more public appeal. There may also have been concerns that using the term 'reducing harm' could be taken as encouraging or condoning drug use, promoting legalization, or conflicting with law enforcement and with traditional or religious beliefs, and so leading to increased levels of drug use.

However, it has been recognized by the stakeholders that this approach would in fact attract more problem users into the existing services, provide more user-friendly services for non-abstinence goals, increase the capacity of outreach services to connect with target audiences, and minimize high-risk behaviours, while protecting the community from drug-associated harms. The case history will demonstrate the coexistence between 'reducing harm' and 'zero tolerance' in the context of planning and implementing a successful campaign against drinking and driving in the Cayman Islands.

Purple ribbon bus

A local radio station and the Cayman Islands Road Safety Advisory Council started the Purple Ribbon Campaign several years ago. The campaign targets drunk drivers during the Christmas holidays, which have a significantly higher number of traffic accidents related to drinking and driving. The idea was to increase road checks by police while raising awareness about drinking and driving, using public service announcements and purple ribbons attached to vehicle antennae and bumper stickers, all of which demonstrated a pledge by drivers not to drink and drive and had the added bonus of making them eligible for prizes if spotted by radio announcers. Recognizing the success and importance of this national campaign, the NDC decided to pilot a project to contribute to it. The project had two components, a designated driver programme that involved all the local restaurants providing free drinks to appointed drivers wearing special bracelets, and the introduction of a Purple Ribbon Bus, which provided free transportation across the island of Grand Cayman on New Year's Eve. The latter was accomplished using an elaborate schedule and ten buses identifiable by purple ribbons and sponsored by local businesses. The programmes were promoted as part of the national Purple Ribbon Campaign and have been very successful. The Purple Ribbon Bus, which was supported by over two thousand people on New Year's Eve, is particularly interesting because it epitomizes the concept of reducing harm.

In its first year, December 2000, the Purple Ribbon Bus was a contributing factor in the elimination of drinking and driving arrests on New Year's Eve. The following year the bus was even more popular, and only a few driving-while-intoxicated (DWI) offences were recorded, which may have been due to the significant increase in police road checks. This compares to an average of 20 DWI arrests on the previous New Year's Eve holidays

In this context, the agendas for a 'zero tolerance' policy to ensure public safety and the need to 'reduce harm' are balanced. In this case the substance of abuse is a legal one – alcohol. It is not the use of alcohol that is in breach of the law, but the combination of alcohol use and driving. Alcohol use is not prohibited and is thus tolerated as an acceptable social practice. The 'zero tolerance' therefore applies to breaching the law by drinking and driving with levels of alcohol in excess of 0.01mg in the blood. The police uphold this zero tolerance policy by prosecuting DWI offences, which carry serious legal consequences such as heavy fines, loss of the driving licence for a minimum of twelve months, and possible incarceration for repeated offences.

'Reducing the harm' is achieved by the implementation of the bus service, which is in support of the police effort. Without a reliable mass transit system many drivers have to use their discretion, at a time when they are impaired, and decide whether they are able to drive home. For many the option to hop on and off the bus is a novel one but it has provided a safe alternative to drinking and driving. The growing number of supporters across all socio-economic barriers suggests that we are in fact succeeding in changing attitudes towards drinking and driving.

The Cayman Islands, in particular Grand Cayman, can be described as a dual society with almost half of its population imported to meet demands for labour. Caymanians are traditionally religious in nature and view excessive drinking with some contempt, while many of the expatriate workers and their families come from places where drinking is a more accepted part of their culture. This can possibly explain why 'reducing harm' and 'zero tolerance' can coexist in this society. Those that feel drunk drivers should be punished for breaking the law are satisfied by the sanctions handed down by the court to those caught drinking and driving. And those who feel they can manage their alcohol intake and therefore choose to consume levels of alcohol that could place them in breach of the law can opt to reduce the chances of harming themselves and others by taking the bus.

Conclusion

Given the nature of the society, naturally the NDC was concerned that there might be some resistance to the concept of providing a free bus service catering for those who plan to consume alcohol during the holidays. Public acceptance of the project was therefore seen as further proof of the progress made in terms of changing attitudes towards drug use and abuse. All indications so far suggest greater understanding and support for policies and programmes that aim to reduce harm, even in the absence of a clear mandate for abstinence.

One has only to acknowledge the failure of our justice system to address the core issue of drug dependence to realize that the attendant problems are continuing to erode our society. Thus the promotion of a healthy society, one free of drug abuse and its ill-effects, has been accepted by a population that has not totally abandoned its need to punish those of its members that commit drug-related offences. The balancing act continues as new programmes emerge – such as alternative sentencing options that include non-custodial sentences, driver's education for DWI offenders, drug courts and youth-at-risk programmes. In many instances these new programmes are not focusing on abstinence as the only result, but seek to add more realistic outcomes such as changing behaviours that have been shown to be harmful to those that practise them and to others whose lives are affected.

CHAPTER 9

Ethical Dilemmas in Drug Research

Pitfalls of Gathering Sensitive Information in the Caribbean Context

JENNIFER HILLEBRAND

The Global Workshop on Drug Information Systems convened by the United Nations Office on Drugs and Crime in Vienna (3–5 December 2001) highlighted the need for ethical guidelines for collecting information on illicit drug use (UNODC, 2002). Drug information systems refer to networks within a country or region that gather all relevant information on illegal drug use, establishing the level of surveillance essential to the planning, implementation and evaluation of public health responses to the drug problem. UNODC has supported the development of such drug information networks through the Global Assessment Programme (GAP).

The impetus from the Global Workshop on Drug Information Systems and the current development of a global ethical framework for drug epidemiology by UNODC encourages one to attempt a critical assessment of current ethical practices and challenges in drug epidemiology and other fields related to illegal drug use in the Caribbean region.

The Caribbean comprises 28 countries and territories between North and South America. It is a multilingual, multi-ethnic and multicultural/religious region. Illicit drugs constitute a threat to the Caribbean. It is widely known that drugs are trafficked via the Caribbean as a result of its geographical location between producer and consumer countries. In addition to the region's own production of marijuana, illegal drugs have reached local markets, and drug-related problems such as abuse, dependence, drug-related psychiatric disorders, violence and crime have been emerging over the past decade. In response, public health strategies are emerging. These include research activities to assess the magnitude of the drug problem and drug-related risk behaviours, prevention programmes and treatment facilities. These responses create ethical challenges. Consequently the question of applied ethical practices enters the arena.

This chapter will outline the existence and application of ethics applied to drug research and data collection, drug treatment and policy in the

Caribbean to illustrate, with concrete examples, the ethical challenges and dilemmas encountered in the region. Finally, an attempt will be made to synthesize broad recommendations for ethical practices in the Caribbean and by this means encourage a debate on these important issues.

Ethics

It is clearly outside the scope of this chapter to outline in detail the development of ethical thinking; however, any attempt to addresses ethical issues needs to reflect briefly upon some of the major ethical principles in order to create a common understanding and basis for discussions.

The field of ethics, also called moral philosophy, involves systematizing, defending and recommending concepts of right and wrong behaviour. Numerous theories defining moral values have been developed, along with a wide spectrum of ethical applications. Philosophers today usually divide ethical theories into three general subject areas: metaethics, normative ethics, and applied ethics (Fieser 2001). Metaethics investigates where our ethical principles come from. For example, do moral values exist in a spirit-like realm or are they simply human conventions? Do they have an objective foundation, instilled by God, or are they grounded in social approval? (Fieser 2001).

Normative ethics attempts to arrive at moral standards that regulate right and wrong conduct. Many schools of thought and theories have been classified into different categories, depending on how moral standards are developed and defined. For the purpose of this discussion, several moral standards that usually form the basis of ethical codes in biomedical research and epidemiology call for special attention.

For example, deontological theorists base morality on specific foundational principles of obligation: thus they place the locus of right and wrong in autonomous adherence to moral laws or duties. Some of the these duties are believed to reflect moral convictions to which their adherents appeal in applied ethical discussions. Among these are *justice*, or acknowledging a person's right to due process; *beneficence*, or the duty to improve the conditions of others; and *non-maleficence*, or the duty not to injure others (Beauchamp and Childress 1994). Within the context of research practice, justice is generally understood to involve an obligation to share the benefits or burdens of research fairly throughout society. Non-maleficence refers to the researcher's responsibility to minimize risks of harm or discomfort to participants in research projects. For example, participation in an illegal drug use survey should not have any negative consequences for the participant.

Another deontological theory is that of the categorical imperative as developed by the philosopher Immanuel Kant. He integrated many principles under the 'categorical imperative', which can be interpreted as the duty to treat people with dignity and respect and never use them as instruments.

While deontological theories focus on duty, consequentialist theories state that moral conduct is determined solely by a cost–benefit analysis of an action's consequences. An action is morally right if the consequences of that action are more favourable than unfavourable to everyone concerned. This is commonly referred to as utilitarianism. For instance, the normative principle of social benefit acknowledges the extent to which an action produces beneficial consequences for society (Beauchamp and Childress 1994).

These and many other principles derived from normative ethics are applied to problems in societies we live in today. Applied ethics involves examining specific controversial issues such as euthanasia, abortion or capital punishment. By using the conceptual tools of metaethics and normative ethics, discussions in applied ethics try to resolve these moral dilemmas. In general, applied ethics comes into application if a particular issue is controversial in the sense that there are people both for and against the issue at hand, and it involves a moral dilemma.

In recent years applied ethical issues have been subdivided into expedient groups such as health care ethics and research ethics. Even though there is an increase in sub-specializations as they relate to ethical principles, the question remains whether these are necessary and helpful developments. Do all ethical codes rely on the same underlying moral standards or normative principles (such as justice, respect, beneficence)? What are the benefits of specifying for each area a set of ethical codes and guidelines?

Both questions have positive answers. Ethical guidelines, especially in the field of research, are often based on common normative principles and can be found in globally accepted declarations (such as the Declaration of Helsinki, 1964). But in addition, the discussion of these ethical principles in the sub-field of human action is necessary for awareness raising and assurance of the application of these core ethical principles.

In order to arrive at these specific codes of ethics or ethical agreements it is not sufficient to simply apply general normative principles similar to the use of a fixed formula. A common agreement upon ethical practices has to be built upon a dynamic process that actively involves awareness raising and debate among members of society that are working in the specific area of concern.

Applied ethics in the Caribbean

When examining the application of ethical codes in the Caribbean region it rapidly becomes clear that they are limited. The University of the West

Indies and the Caribbean Epidemiology Centre (CAREC) have ethics committees that oversee ethical conduct in biomedical research. CAREC does not have its own guidelines but follows the ethical guidelines for research involving human subjects adopted by the Pan American Health Organization and the World Health Organization. The guidelines apply broad ethical principles in advising on the ethical conduct to be followed in a study, and on how to obtain informed consent. They also provide some guidelines on how to review submitted study proposals through a set of criteria. Certain problems are attached to these guidelines, however. First, the extent to which they are applicable to drug use research and data collection in the drug field may not easily be ascertained by the research novice. Second, these guidelines are not necessarily in the public domain. They are not automatically promoted outside the margins of these institutions and therefore those who conduct research on drug use in the Caribbean are not directly attached to these institutions and their in-house ethical codes of practice. Those who have started to engage in drug epidemiological research activities are primarily national drug councils, but include private research companies (such as Teams in St Lucia); freelance consultants have also started to emerge over the past few years.

One of the major influences that explain a considerable increase in epidemiological research activities and data collection efforts in the Caribbean region is the Caribbean Drug Information Network (CARIDIN). CARIDIN was launched in 2001 under the management of the Drug Abuse Epidemiological and Surveillance System Project (DAESSP), implemented by CAREC and supported by UNODC/GAP and the Organization of American States (OAS). In many Caribbean countries, representatives of the national drug councils are currently developing drug information systems by implementing national school surveys and qualitative research studies, activities that were initiated under CARIDIN.

Despite these research activities, drug councils operate without any formal ethical oversight or research protocol that would define some of the core ethical principles that one needs to follow when collecting personal information about illegal behaviours. Although several international and regional ethical guidelines have been established, as mentioned earlier, no Caribbean ethical framework for research on drug use and related behaviours is actively promoted within relevant institutions such as national drug councils. This lack of coherence in ethical practices, and lack of integration among existing frameworks and strategies, places ethical responsibilities solely upon the individual. Within national drug councils, often, one person is nominated to conduct research activities – as in the case of the National Council on Substance Abuse (NCSA) in Barbados, where the research and information officer is responsible for all research exercises.

Consideration should be given to defining clear ethical guidelines that could be used within the drug councils and also by any private research company that plans to engage in drug-related research activities. Guidelines do not guarantee that ethical practices are applied, but they constitute a first step towards realization of such practices in the Caribbean.

Ethical dilemmas and challenges

The need for ethical oversight is best revealed by the ethical dilemmas and challenges that are currently encountered in the region.

Reporting of illegal activity

The first ethical dilemma refers to knowledge of a person's illegal drug use behaviour and the consequences that may result. Dealing with sensitive information is particularly difficult in small, confined societies that easily degenerate into a clutter of political interests, drug trafficking and corruption, as observed in St Kitts and Nevis in the 1990s. Charles Miller, also known as 'Little Nut', was for years the bane of this small state through his involvement in drug trafficking and crime. Despite his implication in murder and cocaine trafficking, he managed to evade conviction and deportation to the United States for years, presumably because he had exerted his financial influence in the country (CNN 4 March 2000)

Another area of concern can be found within the drug treatment setting. Seeking help and therefore potentially exposing oneself to others in a society that generally stigmatizes drug users may have serious personal repercussions. Efforts to protect the privacy of treatment seekers are therefore imperative. But up to the present time no culturally and contextually appropriate minimum standards of care have been developed in the region that would formally include standards on patients' rights and the guarantee of confidentiality.

Another example is the scenario in which illegal drug use should be reported within the school setting but isn't. While on the one hand there is a high prevalence of stigmatization of marijuana users, on the other hand, marijuana use and its production is accepted among the fragment of the population whose economic situation depends on its production and trafficking. This discrepancy paves the way for conflicts.

For example, in St Vincent and the Grenadines, a teacher in a secondary school discovers that a student is using marijuana but does not report the case because he is likely to face revenge by the perpetrator and his community. In St Vincent and the Grenadines, where marijuana is probably the largest export earner (INCSR 1994), production and also consumption is accepted, and those who oppose this acceptance may face overt disagreement. In this case two segments of the society claim to know the rights and wrongs of an illegal drug. Whose normative principles have priority? The principle of social benefit or the principle of harm? The teacher, the school principal and the team coach face the ethical dilemma of combating illegal drug use in their society despite the fact that the producers can argue that production and consumption are morally justified because they counterbalance the consequences of weak economies and high unemployment rates.

Free and informed consent

One of the most important ethical rules governing research on humans is that participants must give their informed consent before taking part in a study. As a minimum, free and informed consent refers to the process whereby the investigator accentuates the voluntary participation in the study and provides assurances that strict safeguards will be maintained to protect confidentiality. In addition, the nature of the study is explained in a way that is fully understood by the participant. Informed consent is commonly sought in writing. Thus the participant signs an informed consent form that should include all the required information. To what extent consent forms are used in drug-related research in the Caribbean remains vague because of the lack of ethical supervision and code of practices. To date, no guidelines are available for gaining the informed consent of substance abusers.

Free and informed consent is particularly important when studies involve under-age participants. In this case permission for participation usually has to be obtained from the legal guardian. Practices in the Caribbean vary. In some countries, for example, permission for participation from the legal guardian is made redundant when the ministry concerned has granted the implementation of the survey (as in the case of Dominica). In other cases, the 'silence is consent strategy' is applied, whereby the parents are informed and their permission is assumed if they do not respond to the information.

From an ethical point of view, both practices can be challenged – because one involves the overruling of the legal guardian, and thereby discarding parental autonomy and responsibility, while the other makes assumptions (that the letter of permission is understood, that information is actually received) that are not verified.

Anonymity and confidentiality

The collection of information from individuals should guarantee confidentiality and anonymity. Thus information about subjects in research studies may be unlinked information, which cannot be linked, associated or connected with the persons to whom it refers. However, even though this principle is taken into account, there are situations where it may be violated.

As mentioned earlier, when conducting research on drug use in the Caribbean one is confronted by a number of small societies with limited resources. This poses the risk of role conflicts. Police officers, teachers, counsellors, psychiatrists and probation officers may collect personal information on illegal drug use and may encounter situations where they know the interviewee in a professional capacity other than that of interviewer. Who will guarantee that the information collected is kept confidential? The interviewer may be tempted to convey information while enacting the duties attached to his/her profession. Clear guidelines as to how to proceed once this scenario becomes reality have to be considered. This especially applies to face-to-face interviews and focus group discussions with drug users.

Drug policy

Drug abuse and dependency affect lives thoughout society, either directly or indirectly. The cost to individuals and societies is immense and tackling the problem is as difficult for policy makers as for clinicians, counsellors and researchers. Although ethical issues permeate much of the work of all these groups, policy makers take the lead when deciding about priorities, the allocation of funds and the creation of laws, and thus indirectly or directly deciding about what is right and wrong when dealing with illegal drug use.

Drug-related policies are the product of a variety of influences. What is morally defensible or morally unacceptable often depends on the degree of influence of all aspects that impact policy making. Apart from the magnitude of the drug problem reflected by the demand for and supply and production of illicit drugs, drug policies may be based on factors such as political priorities, economic situations, personal philosophies and systems of belief – as well as international drug conventions. In the Caribbean, policies dealing with the legal status of marijuana are seen as particularly controversial because some argue that its illegality is predicated on foreign-imposed laws rather than on laws that were the result of a social process within the region.

A mixture of religious and cultural influences deriving from indigenous people in the Caribbean, African tribes, immigrants from East India, European Christianity and mainly British societal concepts and approaches have all contributed to the development of different social mores in the region. This background contributes to the multiplicity of viewpoints and controversy surrounding drug use in the region. As a consequence, some social mores violate the law – such as the sanctioned use of marijuana among a wide spectrum of the population (as in Jamaica). In ethical terms, two principles are clashing against each other –respect for social mores and the principle of lawfulness, meaning the duty to respect the law.

This conflict is not easily resolved. It requires a social dialogue between the different divisions of the population. In order to nourish the dialogue, more information is needed in order to demonstrate the social, economic and psychological impacts of drug use. Efforts need to be undertaken to gather neutral and objective information on the consequences of drug use and abuse within societies. This will enable policy makers to base their decisions on evidence that more clearly elucidates the harmfulness of illegal drug use. In this way, drug policies should be inoculated against personal doctrines, myths and incorrect assumptions.

Another controversy in Caribbean drug policy is based on the unevenly distributed resources devoted to supply and demand reduction initiatives. Although the Caribbean region is gradually shifting its drug policy from a focus solely on supply reduction to a more balanced approach that calls for more emphasis on demand reduction, the imbalance in allocation of resources is still very plain. In terms of money allocation, public sector spending in the Caribbean for interdiction and supply control has outweighed spending for demand reduction for most of the 1990s. Ideally, cost–benefit and cost-effectiveness analyses should be conducted to evaluate or justify responses within the two major drug policy directions – supply and demand reduction. These types of evaluation correspond to the principle of utilitarianism, which states that an action is morally right if the consequences of that action are more favourable than unfavourable to all concerned.

With regard to drug policy, more evaluations need to be conducted to examine whether efforts to reduce the supply of drugs or efforts to reduce the demand for drugs are more favourable to the society as a whole.

Conclusion

This chapter has outlined some of the ethical dilemmas societies in the Caribbean face when dealing with information on illegal drug use and related behaviours collected through national drug information networks, individual institutions, epidemiological surveys on drug use (such as national school surveys), and qualitative information gathering in focus group discussions and in-depth, face-to-face interviews.

The recommendations in response to the ethical dilemmas can be structured into a simple three-level hierarchy. At the top, there is a need for more awareness of the importance of applied ethics when dealing with illegal drug use. A regional body is best suited to lead this process, either working towards a regional set of minimal ethical guidelines for drug-related research and information gathering or promoting internationally accepted guidelines that apply in the Caribbean context. UNODC/GAP is currently developing a toolkit on ethical challenges in drug epidemiology that may also serve as a framework for the Caribbean. The toolkit objective is to provide a practical and accessible guide to collecting data on drug use, taking ethical practices into consideration.

In the middle of the hierarchy reside all individual institutions, treatment centres, schools, drug councils, private research companies and ministries. Through adaptation of their policies, standards of care and/or accreditations processes, they can adopt and enact ethical guidelines or include them in existing policy frameworks that will help to reduce ethical dilemmas, as outlined in this chapter. This level also includes national efforts to promote policy making based on evidence rather than assumption – an effort requiring the combined efforts of national drug councils, research institutions and ministries.

Finally, underlying the other levels is the fundamental ethical principle of honesty in all its applications. Essentially, its presence or absence determines whether any information on drug use is presented adequately, impartially and correctly.

REFERENCES AND SELECT BIBLIOGRAPHY

Beauchamp, T. and J. Childress (1994) *Principles of Biomedical Ethics*, fourth edition, New York: Oxford University Press.

Commonwealth of Australia (2001) *Human Research Ethics Handbook*, <http://www.health.gov.au/ nhmrc/hrecbook/misc/contents.htm>

Fieser, J. (2001) *Internet Encyclopedia of Philosophy* <www.iep.utm.edu>

PAHO/WHO (2002) *Ethical Guidelines for Research Involving Human Subjects*, Pan American Health Organization/World Health Organization.

UNODC (2002) 'Global Workshop on Drug Information Systems – Activities, Methods and Future Opportunities', unpublished, United Nations Office on Drugs and Crime, Vienna International Centre, Austria.

INCSR (1994) *International Narcotics Control Strategy Report* (INCSR), Washington, DC: US Department of Justice.

World Medical Organization (1996) 'Declaration of Helsinki', *British Medical Journal*, 313, 7070 (7 December):1448–9.

CNN (2000) 'Crime, Corruption, Drugs: St Kitts Ends Lively Election Campaign', Associated Press.

PART 4

Responses to Opportunity
Economics of Drugs

CHAPTER 10

Illicit Drug Markets in the Caribbean

Analysis of Information on Drug Flows Through the Region

MICHAEL PLATZER

WITH FLAVIO MIRELLA AND CARLOS RESA NESTARES

Market size

The illegal drugs market in the Caribbean generates an estimated income of US$3.3 billion. This represents 3.1 per cent of the registered gross domestic product in the region. Given the significance of the hidden economy in many countries of the Caribbean (it accounts for between 20 and 65 per cent of the total economy, depending on the country and estimation methods), this share could be markedly lower – under 2.5 per cent – when the overall economy (registered and unregistered GDP) is considered.

In the early 1990s, the size of the illegal drugs market was US$3.5 billion in 2000 constant prices. Although in current dollars the illegal drugs market has grown at 2 per cent annually during the past decade, it has recorded an annual decrease of 0.2 per cent in constant dollar value. This Caribbean decline, nevertheless, has not been uniform during the last decade; a reduction during the first part of the decade was followed by an expansion during the late 1990s, consolidated through the recovery of cocaine transshipment.

Cocaine is the most profitable illicit drug in the Caribbean. It accounts for 85 per cent of the drug market in the region. The amount of US$3 billion generated by cocaine in the region represents 2 per cent of the global cocaine market. This share is consistent with the notion that in global illicit drug markets most income is not generated in the production and trans-shipment countries but within the developed consuming countries.

Cocaine's share in the drug market of the region increased during the past decade from 72 per cent of the market in the early 1990s, at marijuana's expense. The marijuana market, which now only accounts for 13 per cent of the Caribbean's illicit drug market, was almost halved during the decade up to 2000. Heroin and amphetamine-type drugs each represent 1 per cent of the regional drug market. No transformation of coca leaves into cocaine takes place in the Caribbean. Security agencies of the region have shut down a dozen laboratories engaged in transforming raw cocaine into crack during the past decade. Against this low-profile background in production and transformation, transportation of cocaine in the area is rampant – 435 metric tonnes (MT) of cocaine crossed the Caribbean Sea and the mainland Caribbean in 2000, an increase of more than 100 MT in the cocaine flow through the region during the 1990s. According to the Caribbean Coordination Mechanism (CCM), 435 MT is the total amount of cocaine transiting the Caribbean area; only 62 per cent of that cocaine, or 270 MT, makes landfall somewhere in the region.

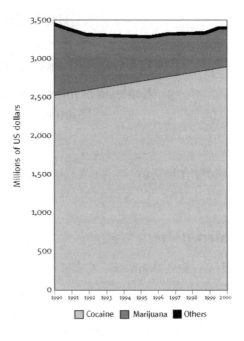

Figure 10.1 Drug income, 1990–2000 (in 2000 US$)

Marijuana is the only natural drug that is produced in the Caribbean. Total traffic of illegal derivatives of hemp in the Caribbean amounts to 375 MT. Locally cultivated marijuana totals 330 MT, which is grown in 485 hectares. Marijuana, therefore, covers 0.003 per cent of the cultivated area in the region. Caribbean marijuana represents hardly 4.2 per cent of the global production, an abrupt reduction from the region's share of 18 per cent in the 1980s. In 1980 Jamaica and Belize alone had an estimated area cultivated with marijuana that was five times the present Caribbean total – 2,650 hectares. Some sources, indeed, point to Jamaica as the top marijuana producer in the world between 1968 and 1981; in 2000, Jamaica did not make the top ten list. In 2000, Colombia produced 13 times more marijuana than the whole Caribbean region. Of the 330 MT of locally grown marijuana, hashish oil represents less than 15 MT. The rest of the marijuana flow in the region is attributable to the imports of Colombian marijuana to the region for internal consumption or for transshipment outside the Caribbean.

Neither poppy cultivation nor heroin production takes place in the Caribbean. Nevertheless, some 700 kilos of heroin circulates through the region. Most of it comes from Colombia en route to the burgeoning US market. The Caribbean is the transshipment area for 10 per cent of the total estimated production of heroin in Colombia, the source of 5.5 per cent of the American heroin market. The US is a minor market of opium derivatives in comparison to European or Asian markets. Heroin is the most profitable illegal drug in the region in relative terms – six times more profitable per kilo than cocaine and forty times more profitable than marijuana. Nevertheless, it barely represents US$50 million after a constant, moderate rise during the 1990s as a result of the renewed taste of Americans for heroin.

Although information has surfaced about the existence of amphetamine-type drug production laboratories in Puerto Rico and Hispaniola Island (Dominican Republic and Haiti), there is no concrete evidence regarding the manufacture of ecstasy tablets in the region. Apart from the rapidly growing local demand, now restricted to some islands, the ecstasy circuit of the Caribbean is driven by the supply of European production to the underdeveloped American market. Therefore, the region is used as a transshipment point for the importation of European ecstasy, primarily coming from the Netherlands and Spain, to the United States. However, the increased role of the Caribbean in this transatlantic trade is insignificant – less than 1 per cent of the American demand is met by ecstasy transiting the region. The Dutch-speaking Caribbean has taken a long lead in the positioning of the region as a transshipment route for ecstasy, which is partly a reflection of the powerful ecstasy industry in the Netherlands.

Illicit drugs and the foreign sector

Colombia is the origin of over 95 per cent of the cocaine imports within the region. Nevertheless, only 58 per cent of the cocaine that arrives annually in the Caribbean countries comes directly from Colombia. Venezuela is the source of an additional 29 per cent of these cocaine imports; Central America and Panama, 8 per cent; and Brazil, 5 per cent. More than 90 per cent of the cocaine that enters the Caribbean countries, or 240 MT, continues its passage in the direction of other consuming markets. Colombia and Central America are the main sources of cocaine for the Western and Central Caribbean. Venezuela and, to a lesser extent, Brazil are the origin of the cocaine flowing into the Eastern and mainland Caribbean (French Guiana, Guyana, Suriname).

The distribution of Caribbean cocaine exports has dramatically changed during the last decade. While two-thirds of the cocaine that enters the Caribbean countries is consumed in the United States and Canada, which remain the major market for the region's cocaine exports, Europe has increased its share of transshipped cocaine from 10 per cent in the early 1990s to 32 per cent, or 80 MT, in 2000. If the amount of cocaine that flows through the Caribbean Sea without touching any shore is taken into account, some 165 MT of cocaine pass through the region en route to Europe. This represents two-thirds of the European imports of cocaine. In the late 1990s, however, the growing participation of Brazil in the cocaine transatlantic flow has slightly eroded the dominant role that the Caribbean region has in the flow of cocaine between South America and Europe. While insignificantly reducing its participation in the cocaine trade to Europe, which has otherwise doubled during the last decade, the Caribbean has recovered its share of the transshipment market for cocaine en route to the United States. In 2000, the Caribbean corridor was the source of 47 per cent of the cocaine entering the United States, leaving Mexico behind as the main source of cocaine for the American market. Back in the early 1990s, the Caribbean was the transshipment area for less than 30 per cent of the cocaine going to the American market.

There are big differences in the cocaine export areas within the Caribbean. Generally speaking, the Western and Central Caribbean are inclined to service the American market and the Eastern and mainland Caribbean are more prone to direct their cocaine exports to Europe. Puerto Rico, Haiti, the Dominican Republic and the Bahamas re-export more than 90 per cent of the in-transit cocaine to the United States. The final destination of 80 per cent of the Jamaican and Belizean cocaine is also the United States. Reversing this pattern, the cocaine trade of the mainland Caribbean is directed towards Europe, the destination of 80 per cent of exports. Over half of the cocaine that transits the Eastern Caribbean ends up in Europe.

The Caribbean exports 100 MT of marijuana for extra-regional markets. Of these, 80 per cent is Jamaican marijuana and 15 per cent is Colombian hemp that is introduced into the region for re-export to North America. While large quantities of Jamaican marijuana dominate the participation of Caribbean marijuana in the world market, the exports have plummeted since the 1980s, when Jamaica and Belize were the second and the fourth largest exporters of marijuana, respectively, to the United States, then and now the single most important market in the world.

The flow of other illegal drugs is quantitatively marginal. Most of the 700 kilograms of heroin that transit the region are imported from Colombia, where opium poppy is grown and transformed into heroin. Less than 5 per cent of that amount is South Asian heroin that arrives from Europe. All but 5 per cent of the heroin is re-exported to the United States for consumption. The remaining 5 per cent corresponds to Colombian heroin that travels towards the European Union. In the case of ecstasy, the transatlantic flow goes westwards, from Europe to the United States; the Caribbean route is used to hinder detection of the drug. The ecstasy trade is segmented along linguistic lines. In one case, ecstasy travels from the Netherlands, considered the major single producer of the drug, to the Dutch Caribbean and then to the United States. A parallel, although more limited, trade line goes from producing areas in Spain to the Dominican Republic or Puerto Rico en route to the continental United States.

The participation of local illegal transshipment firms in the drug business is marginal. They are merely commissioned for transporting illegal drugs from one place to another and for storing them. The organization of the illegal trade within the Caribbean is largely done through subsidiaries of large, external groups with limited local connections. The exceptions to this model are the powerful Jamaican groups, usually with political leverage, that have been able to operate in retailing and distribution in the high-consumption, developed drug markets (US, Canada, UK). But the participation of these organizations in other markets is largely marginal, under 5 per cent. On the other hand, individuals of Dominican and Puerto Rican descent play an important role in drug retailing/distribution on the East Coast of the United States and, to a much lesser extent, in Europe, yet their connections to organizations engaged in drug trafficking in their respective homelands are limited. The traditional inability of the Caribbean drug groups to vertically integrate every step of the drug business, especially its most lucrative part – retailing/distribution in developed countries – imposes a serious obstacle to the creation of a globally oriented, Caribbean-based illicit trafficking organization in the short to medium term.

Product and national markets

Cocaine is the most profitable product among the illicit drugs in every country in the Caribbean region, but the distribution among the different sorts of drugs is not the same. In Jamaica, the local importance of marijuana reaches 37 per cent of the local market for illegal drugs, that is, three times the average of the region. The Eastern Caribbean and Belize also have drug markets in which marijuana plays a role that is greater than the Caribbean average. At the other extreme, on both sides of the border on Hispaniola Island, marijuana accounts for less than 5 per cent of the illicit drug market.

Import–export services, with its related operations, such as inter-mediation, transportation, protection and financing, are the largest income generators among the several parts of the illegal drug business. Import–export services account for two-thirds of the income drugs leave behind in the Caribbean – 70 per cent for cocaine and barely 50 per cent for marijuana. On the other hand, production and transformation of marijuana and crack cocaine barely represent 2 per cent. Intra-national retailing and wholesale drug distribution accounts for only 10 per cent of the drugs business in the Caribbean, or US$350 million. Of that figure, 55 per cent corresponds to marijuana, 40 per cent to coca derivatives and 3 per cent to heroin and amphetamine-type drugs. Of the total income, tourists in the Caribbean account for 8 per cent of the total retailing distribution market. The average Caribbean citizen spends US$11 on illicit drugs, an amount that is much lower than the US$300 spent by the average American adult or the US$200 spent by the ordinary British citizen. In comparison, a Caribbean adult spends 30 per cent more on marijuana than the American average adult, but just 10 per cent of the amount the American spends on cocaine.

By territories, the illicit drug market is relatively larger at the northern periphery of the region than in the central area. The fact that the last hurdle en route to the major consumer markets is the most lucrative region implies that the movement of drugs across the margins of the Caribbean is more profitable than intra-Caribbean distribution. For example, the drug trade in the Bahamas accounts for 9.5 per cent of the registered economy, or US$370 million. Meanwhile, in the mainland Caribbean (Central and South America), trade in illicit drugs is 6.5 per cent of GDP – in absolute terms, US$45 million for Belize and US$130 million for the South American (mainland) Caribbean. At the lower end, for Cuba, Puerto Rico and the Eastern Caribbean, the drugs trade represents less than 1.5 per cent of the registered economy. The only exception to this general pattern is Jamaica, where the cocaine flows of the late 1990s and marijuana production makes drug money account for 7.6 per cent of the registered economy

In absolute terms, however, the countries of the central area of the Caribbean are those that have the largest drug markets. In the Dominican Republic, the drug trade generates US$850 million, or 5.3 per cent of GDP. Puerto Rico has a drug market that exceeds US$650 million, or 1.4 per cent of the local economy, while in Jamaica, the drugs trade produces an income of US$560 million. Including Trinidad & Tobago and the Virgin Islands, the Eastern Caribbean represents a drugs market with a money flow of US$360 million. In comparative terms, the US consumers spent US$65.7 billion in illegal drugs in 2000, a figure that accounts for 0.7 per cent of the local GDP, while in the United Kingdom the drug trade generated an income of US$10 billion, also 0.7 per cent of the local economy.

Per capita income produced by the drug trade varies from country to country. For example, in the Bahamas, illegal drugs generate an average of over US$1,000 *per capita*. In Aruba and the Netherlands Antilles, drugs contribute US$500 per inhabitant, an amount that is almost double the drug *per capita* income of the Virgin Islands. Well over the average of the

Caribbean's *per capita* income generated by the drug trade are Jamaica, Belize and Puerto Rico, with US$160–200 of annual income *per capita*. The Caribbean average corresponds to the Dominican Republic, the countries in the Eastern Caribbean and the South American (mainland) Caribbean. At the opposite end of the spectrum, the drug trade yields a *per capita* income of US$8 in Cuba and US$18 in Haiti.

Quantitatively speaking, the jurisdiction that has the largest cocaine market is Puerto Rico, with an annual flow of 80 MT of cocaine. This figure indicates a moderate decrease in the cocaine flow entering the island since the mid-1990s, when 8–9 MT flowed per month. The Dominican Republic, Jamaica and the Eastern Caribbean, including Trinidad & Tobago and the Virgin Islands, show an annual cocaine flow of 60 MT. These three regions have registered an increase in their participation in the cocaine market during the late 1990s. Although this growth was bigger in Jamaica, the public exposure of the close relationship between cocaine traffickers and some security figures in 2000, with some large hauls in the Jamaica–Bahamas corridor, has meant a displacement in market concentration in the Caribbean. The Bahamas, where the cocaine market is closely associated with Jamaica's, presents the fifth largest corridor of cocaine in the Caribbean, with an annual traffic of over 40 MT. This figure is more than double the Bahamas' local flow of cocaine in the early 1990s, but lower than the volume of traffic during the cocaine golden years in the 1970s and 1980s. Haiti, the South American (mainland) Caribbean states and Belize are medium-size markets with 20–25 MT of cocaine imports each. Cuba and the Netherlands Antilles, meanwhile, record the lowest levels, with 15 MT. The highest *per capita* cocaine flow occurs in the Bahamas and the Virgin Islands, with over 100 grams *per capita* in annual transit. Belize, with 90 grams of cocaine per inhabitant, and the Netherlands Antilles, 60 grams, also record high levels of cocaine transit. All those countries share the common feature of largely uncontrolled coasts. The Dominican Republic, Haiti and Cuba, on the other hand, have *per capita* cocaine flows under 20 grams.

The busiest route for cocaine trafficking in the Caribbean since the late 1990s goes through the Western Caribbean from Colombia to the United States via Jamaica and the Bahamas. Under the control of the Jamaican trafficking organizations and the supervision of Colombian kingpins, almost 35 MT of cocaine travels annually on this route. Two cocaine routes converge in Puerto Rico – some 27 MT goes directly from South America to the US-associated state, while 30 MT reaches Puerto Rico via the Dominican Republic. The Dominican Republic is also busy as a transshipment point for cocaine going from South America straight to the United States – 18 MT. A similar amount of cocaine travels from the

Eastern Caribbean to Puerto Rico en route to the continental United States.

The cocaine routes to Europe are shaped by spheres of influence, colonial and linguistic ties. For Spanish-speaking countries, Spain is the destination of most cocaine exports to Europe, either for natives or for foreigners residing on the increasingly popular Mediterranean coast. Haiti and the French departments mainly direct their cocaine exports to France. Cocaine in transit through the Dutch territories and Suriname mainly reaches Europe via the Netherlands.

The United Kingdom is the major destination for cocaine transiting the Anglo-Caribbean states. These latter countries straddle the busiest route of cocaine with European destinations – 25 MT flow annually from the Eastern Caribbean to Europe, mainly the United Kingdom. The South American (mainland) Caribbean provides 17 MT of cocaine exports to Europe, mainly the Netherlands. The Dutch islands just off the Venezuelan coast and Cuba are the origin of over 10 MT of cocaine consumed in Europe.

The largest marijuana market in the Caribbean is Jamaica, which generates some US$210 million, almost half of the regional market and 2.8 per cent of the registered GDP. In 2000, exports of Jamaican marijuana generated US$160 million in revenues for the country, a figure that is much lower than the estimated US$1 billion that entered Jamaica for marijuana exports during the 1980s. Excluding the foreign re-export sector, the local consumption of marijuana generates a larger income for traffickers in Puerto Rico (almost US$80 million) than in Jamaica.

Other important marijuana markets, in relative terms, are in the South Eastern Caribbean, Belize and the Eastern Caribbean. St Vincent & the Grenadines, the largest exporter in the Eastern Caribbean since the 1990s, is the origin of 55 per cent of the marijuana consumed in that area. For that country, marijuana exports provide some US$10 million, an income that represents 18 per cent of the St Vincent & the Grenadines' legal exports and 3 per cent of local GDP. It also generates an average income of US$85 for every Vincentian.

Jamaica produces 180 MT of marijuana annually over a cultivated area of 265 hectares. This represents 55 per cent of the total Caribbean marijuana production. The Eastern Caribbean, including Trinidad & Tobago and the Virgin Islands, produces 45 MT of marijuana. St Vincent & the Grenadines has surpassed Trinidad & Tobago as the first producer in the area, with an estimated total production of 25 MT of marijuana on an approximate surface area totalling 20 hectares. That is the highest ratio of marijuana cultivation per total arable area in the region, 0.24 per cent, well over the Bahamas, with 0.12 per cent, or Jamaica, 0.06 per cent.

Market organization

There is no region-wide organization in the Caribbean drug market, not even one for any particular drug. And there are no signs to indicate the emergence of a regional organization that may aspire to a monopoly of the regional drug market. The Colombian traffickers, who traditionally exerted a great influence over the cocaine market through their ability to control the supply of cocaine available in the region, and who have the capacity to favour some organizations over others, seem to feel comfortable under this framework of limited competition. Instead, there are several unconnected markets and organizations operating in segmented markets. National groups continue to be powerful because they have better access to a valuable national resource – corruption. Mexican nationals dominate the cocaine market in Belize; Jamaican groups strictly control the Jamaica–Bahamas corridor for cocaine. Dominican organizations, in close collaboration with Colombian subsidiaries, have a prominent role in the cocaine trafficking in the area around Puerto Rico, as well as Hispaniola Island and the northern islands of the Eastern Caribbean. Venezuelan, Brazilian and European groups, in collaboration with local traffickers and launderers, are prominent in the cocaine trade in the southern islands of the Eastern Caribbean and the South American (mainland) Caribbean. For marijuana, the trade is even more fragmented, with Jamaican traffickers exerting a great influence derived from their control of production. Communications between the dominant groups in each area are almost non-existent. Language seems to be a strong facilitator of the drug trade for every drug available in the Caribbean.

Beyond this ethnic division, the organization of the drug trade in the Caribbean tends to be more like a free market than a monopoly or even an oligopoly. Business opportunities are widely available for any agent expecting to participate in the market. Arrests and disruption of existing networks made by local and international security agencies guarantee a continuous place for newcomers. But the weakness and lack of resources that are plaguing police forces in the Caribbean also inhibits the creation of national monopolies. Competition between drug organizations has generated a limited amount of violence, to a large extent concentrated in Puerto Rico and Jamaica. Nevertheless, the easy and open entry to the drug market in the Caribbean does not mean it is costless. First, in a market that is inherently illegal the acquisition and access to relevant information for the entrepreneurs is expensive. Second, participation in the drug market has required increased investments, including the funding of corruption, that have imposed high entry costs for new traffickers.

The increasingly higher entry costs in the drug market have imposed a pattern of organization of the market that is common to the Caribbean jurisdictions. Against the notion of a career in the illicit business that starts as a street dealer and finishes as a national drug lord engaged in transnational trade, a pattern has emerged in which drug businessmen tend to combine illegal and legal activities. In 2000, an Antigua-based businessman was arrested in the United Kingdom with 500 kilos of cocaine; a Dominican entrepreneur with interests in many legal sectors was later arrested and accused of introducing 30 MT of cocaine into Puerto Rico. In 1999, two Spanish businessmen with interests in Cuba were charged with using the island for cocaine smuggling. To minimize risks, operations in legal activities provide a cover for the movement of goods and money, but also the connections to the political and business elites that facilitate drug transit. Drug trade represents one of the most lucrative methods in the Caribbean for diversifying a previously successful business career in legal activities. Therefore, the social origin of drug businessmen is no longer confined to the popular strata that largely monopolized the drug business in an earlier period, but now includes the ruling elite.

Competition in the drug business in the Caribbean is based on prices and costs rather than quality. For cocaine, geographical location – being between producing and consuming countries – is the main competitive advantage. The extent of the cocaine trade within the Caribbean is based on the ability of local traffickers, or a subsidiary of foreign traffickers, to minimize the risks of state interference and guarantee a constant flow of drugs. Weak states where corruption is easy, the availability of physical and financial infrastructures, and economic and human networks connecting the region with drug-consuming countries all make transshipment of drugs a not-so-difficult business in the Caribbean. Costs of cocaine transshipment in the Caribbean are substantially lower than in Mexico, the main competitor, where corruption has made transshipment a costly business. This cost differential, to a great extent, is the cause of the comeback of Caribbean cocaine trafficking in the late 1990s. In a more mature market, like marijuana, quality is at least as important as prices and costs. The average quality of local marijuana has developed more slowly than in other areas of the world, especially in the consuming markets. The marijuana cultivation and transformation process in the Caribbean still uses mostly traditional methods that have been replaced elsewhere to produce high-quality marijuana, particularly indoors. That is the underlying reason for the constant decrease in Caribbean participation in the world market. The taste for high-quality marijuana in the consuming markets of North America and Europe has not been met by a Caribbean supply. Even in the local markets, Colombian marijuana has been gradually displacing locally grown hemp.

The most popular transportation means in the Caribbean for cocaine, at least in weight terms, is by ship: 82 per cent of the cocaine that travels through the Caribbean circulates by maritime transportation means (42 per cent in speedboats, 11 per cent in fishing and recreational ships and 46 per cent in sea containers). Because they provide a way to conceal cocaine, during the late 1980s containers experienced a remarkable growth at the expense of speedboats, whose relative importance has declined. Only 3 per cent of the cocaine flowing around in the Caribbean is transported through terrestrial means, an option that is mainly localized on the Dominican–Haitian border. Air transportation accounts for only 15 per cent of the cocaine circulating through the Caribbean. Couriers, who make up a large proportion of those detained on drug trafficking charges in the Caribbean, only transport 3 per cent of the cocaine in the region.

There are big differences in the use of transportation modalities, depending on origin and destination. Maritime means are prevalent for both export and importation, but are more often used for taking cocaine out of the Caribbean than for introducing it into the region or for intra-Caribbean exchanges. Speedboats take aboard almost 50 per cent of the cocaine that arrives in the region, while containers represent over one quarter. A mere 17 per cent of the cocaine entering the region comes through air transport and human couriers only account for 2 per cent of the total cocaine available in the Caribbean. If fast boats dominate the scene for cocaine entering the Caribbean, the sea containers are the most important way to take the cocaine out of the region: 70 per cent of the cocaine leaving the Caribbean is concealed in ship-bound containers. Only 7 per cent of the total amount of the cocaine that goes from the Caribbean to consumer countries in the developed world travels with human couriers. For routes whose final destination is Europe, these percentages are higher in both cases. Pleasure boats have a larger-than-average role when it comes to the United States. In the intra-Caribbean movement of cocaine, go-fast boats account for 62 per cent of the traffic.

Between 100,000 and 125,000 individuals are directly involved in the production and commercialization of illegal drugs in the Caribbean. This represents less than 1 per cent of the total labour force in the region. Indirect employment generated by the drug trade may quintuple that figure. Marijuana, which accounts for two of the more labour-intensive segments of the drug production process – cultivation and retailing distribution – generates almost 60 per cent of the total employment in the drug business. The cocaine business in the Caribbean, which is heavily dependent on the capital-intensive transportation, creates barely 45,000 jobs. Drug retail distribution is responsible for 65 per cent of the employment created in the region, while production involves another 20 per cent of the jobs. Under the accepted notion of the substitutability of legal and illegal income, drug income in the Caribbean seems to be largely a complement to legal activities. More than 70 per cent of the people who obtain an income from drugs also earn an income from legal activities. The number of individuals whose income depends exclusively on drugs is under 35,000. These are concentrated in the middle levels of the drug business because both high earners (businessmen), and low earners (producers and retail distributors) usually combine their drug income with other kinds of legal incomes. In this sense, drug income distribution is driven by inequality – the highest 10 per cent of earners accumulate more than 85 per cent of the income. In other words, some 12,000 drug businessmen, including some public sector entrepreneurs, receive an annual income that exceeds US$200,000. At the other end of the spectrum, 70 per cent of drug employees receive less than US$2,900, the region's *per capita* income.

Table 10.1 Busiest routes in the Caribbean with US as final destination

	2000		Trend
	MT	%	
South America–Jamaica–Bahamas–Continental USA	34	21	▲
South America–Puerto Rico–Continental USA	27	16	▼
South America–Dominican Republic–Puerto Rico–Continental USA	19	11	▲
South America–Dominican Republic–Continental USA	18	11	▲
South America–Eastern Caribbean–Puerto Rico–Continental USA	18	11	▼
South America–Haiti–Dominican Republic–Puerto Rico–Continental USA	13	8	▼

Domestic demand

Against the usual notion that producing and transit countries tend to emerge, sooner rather than later, as consuming markets, drug use in the Caribbean remains surprisingly low in spite of three decades of heavy drug trafficking. While statistical under-reporting and fragmentation of the region in drug matters make the figure a tentative one, annual drug-use prevalence in the Caribbean may be given as 3.7 per cent of the adult population. This proportion is slightly lower than the global average, 4.2 per cent, and well below the prevalence found in the major markets – 8.2 per cent in North America and 10 per cent in the European Union. The lifetime prevalence is under 10 per cent. Between 950,000 and 1 million Caribbean residents consume illicit drugs annually – a mere 0.7 per cent of

Table 10.2 Busiest routes in the Caribbean with Europe as final destination

	2000 MT	2000 %	Trend
South America–South Eastern Caribbean–Europe (Netherlands, France)	18	23	▲
South America–Eastern Caribbean–Europe (UK, France, Netherlands)	15	19	▲
South America–Netherlands Antilles and Aruba–Europe (Netherlands)	10	13	▲
South America–Cuba–Europe (Spain)	10	13	▲
South America–Trinidad & Tobago–Europe (UK)	9	11	▲
South America–Dominican Republic–Europe (Spain, Netherlands)	5	6	▼

the global supply of drug consumers. About 75 per cent of those are heavy users – that is, they consume drugs at least twice per week. Only 150,000 individuals are users of more than one drug.

This general percentage is unequally distributed across the region as a response to very diverse cultural and historical dynamics. The country with the highest annual prevalence of drug consumption is Jamaica, at 12.8 per cent, with the Eastern Caribbean at 10.5 per cent. The Virgin Islands, the Bahamas and Puerto Rico, as well as the Netherlands Antilles and Aruba, also show annual drug prevalence over 7 per cent. By contrast, in Cuba, the Dominican Republic and Haiti, incidentally the most populated countries in the region, less than 3 per cent of the adult population used illicit drugs during the past twelve months. According to the limited available statistics and the perception of demand reduction experts, drug consumption is on the rise in almost every country in the Caribbean.

Marijuana is the drug of choice of the Caribbean. Nearly 700,000 adults use it annually – an annual prevalence rate of 2.5 per cent, against a global annual prevalence rate of 3.4 per cent. The Caribbean accounts for a mere 0.5 per cent of the marijuana users around the world. Unlike other parts of the world, where hashish oil is more prevalent, in the Caribbean marijuana is normally smoked with little transformation or, occasionally, consumed as a tea. Marijuana use, nevertheless, is extremely diverse in the Caribbean. Jamaica and the Eastern Caribbean record use prevalence over 10 per cent. In Jamaica, one survey reported a lifetime prevalence of 34 per cent. The English-speaking Caribbean has a marijuana annual prevalence rate of 8.8 per cent, well over the regional average. By contrast, less than 2 per cent of the adult population in Cuba, Haiti and the Dominican Republic used marijuana in the previous twelve months. In total, Caribbean residents consume about 185 MT of marijuana, while tourism adds 7 per cent of that amount to the domestic demand.

Cocaine use in the Caribbean is relatively higher than the world average but lower than the Western Hemisphere/developed countries' use prevalence. In fact, cocaine is the only illicit drug whose consumption in the region is higher than the global average. The most refined estimate of annual use prevalence is 0.6 per cent of the adult population, a figure that is double the global average of 0.3 but far below the 2.2 per cent recorded in the United States. Some 180,000 Caribbean residents used cocaine in 2000, of whom 65 per cent were heavy users. Nearly two-thirds of the cocaine users in the region consume crack cocaine, a highly addictive derivative of the coca leaves with powerful physical effects for the users. The new, younger users increasingly prefer sniffing cocaine powder. Three-quarters of the region's cocaine users live in Puerto Rico and Jamaica. With current local use patterns, 3.9 MT of cocaine are consumed in the Caribbean, a mere 1.5 per cent of the annual flow of cocaine through the region. The highest ratios of locally consumed in-transit cocaine are in the Bahamas and mainland Caribbean. Only 4 per cent of the total amount of local cocaine use is attributable to tourists.

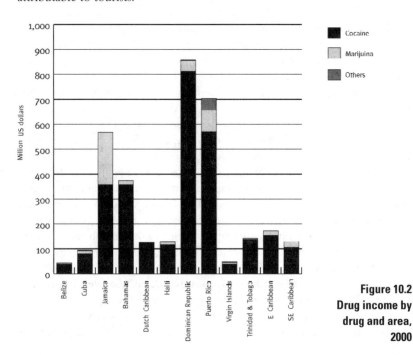

Figure 10.2 Drug income by drug and area, 2000

Social characteristics of cocaine consumers are highly polarized according to the type of cocaine derivative used. The average user of crack cocaine (whose invention is attributed to a Bahamian dealer in 1982, two years before the first case appeared in the United States) lives in poor urban or semi-urban areas and shows high levels of substance abuse or addiction, mainly induced by the lack of psychological and economic alternatives to drug consumption. The use of powder cocaine is concentrated among the higher social classes who can afford to pay the usually high price of the drug.

The use of opium derivatives is very low in the Caribbean, with the exception of Puerto Rico and the Dutch Caribbean. Only 70,000 people used heroin during the past year – an annual prevalence of 0.2 per cent. In Puerto Rico the introduction of heroin is attributed to veterans of the Vietnam War. Its use, far from being eliminated, expanded to poor urban or semi-urban areas. In the Dutch Caribbean heroin use is derived from migrants returning from the Netherlands. In some jurisdictions its use is simply unknown. There are certain components of the Caribbean cultures that seem to be resistant to the expansion of heroin use. Especially relevant for this pattern is the case of the Dominican Republic, where individuals and groups of Dominican descent control a significant part of the retailing/distribution of heroin on the East Coast of the United States – one-third of this burgeoning market according to some analysts – while heroin use in the Dominican Republic is virtually absent. And this very low local consumption takes place in an environment where poverty and frustration in urban neighbourhoods may be expected to be conducive to heroin use. It appears that Dominican dealers were driven by nationalist ideas that keep them away from the local market, and it can be concluded that certain features of Dominican society, especially related to leisure activities, prevent an increase of heroin use in spite of the great potential for it.

Amphetamine-type use in the Caribbean is also very low, with an annual use prevalence of less than 0.2 per cent – or 55,000 people in absolute terms. Although ecstasy use has experienced a rapid increase in the region during the past two years, its consumption is relatively new in comparison to the United States and Western Europe, and much less prevalent. In these sophisticated societies, the annual prevalence rate of ecstasy is well over 0.5 per cent of the adult population. But the gap between the Caribbean and those developed regions may be closing quickly. Similar perceptions about the rise in ecstasy use may be found all over the region. Unlike users of crack cocaine, ecstasy users are more likely to be concentrated among socially integrated young people who consume ecstasy as a weekend pastime associated with the dance scene while remaining active in their daily lives. This model of consumption makes the region potentially vulnerable to the same kind of massive use of ecstasy among teenagers that was seen in Europe first and in the United States afterwards. Nevertheless, the unit prices in the Caribbean, US$30 for one tablet – compared to 20–25 dollars per tablet in the United States and Europe, as well as divergent consumption patterns in leisure time, seem thus far to have prevented a more massive use of ecstasy in the region.

Public regulation

In the Caribbean region, public activity to confront illegal drugs is biased towards the supply control side, aimed at diminishing the amount of illicit drugs available in the region, rather than on demand reduction. Despite the limitation of the available statistics and the difficulty in differentiating between drug control and policing activities in general, it is estimated that in the Caribbean between 0.2 and 0.7 per cent of the public sector budget is dedicated to interdiction and supply control, depending on the country. On average, this amount is ten times higher than the money invested in demand reduction. In general terms, there is a positive relationship between the money allocated to drug issues and the level of development of the country. However, the effectiveness of the supply side operations seems to be limited in terms of reducing the use and availability of illegal drugs in the local markets. Between 70 and 90 per cent of the drug seizures were destined for consumption in foreign markets. Accordingly, the amount of drugs withdrawn from the local market is under 15 per cent, a figure that has almost no effect on the local price of drugs. This figure is far below the 60 per cent of seizures that has been proven by some studies to be the effective lower limit in terms of having an impact on the price of illegal drugs.

In 2000, the countries and territories that comprise the Caribbean region seized 19 MT of cocaine from traffickers. This represents 4.4 per cent of the estimated amount of cocaine that enters the region and an interception rate of 7.7 per cent if the estimated amount of cocaine that arrives in a Caribbean country is taken into account. The seizures in the Caribbean totalled 5.3 per cent of global cocaine seizures. The year 2000 showed the lowest levels of effectiveness in terms of cocaine seized over the previous decade. Only Cuba and Hispaniola Island improved their records of cocaine seizures in 2000. Total cocaine seizures fell by 33 per cent over the previous year. Cocaine seizures were reduced to an annual interception rate of 6.5 per cent from its peak in 1994.

While drug interception data are not a reliable reflection of drug flows, since they can be affected by both police efficiency and the total amount of drugs in circulation, they can reveal some major developments in the cocaine market in recent years. With this in mind, the Western Caribbean corridor that goes from Colombia to the United States via Jamaica and the

Bahamas had 3 per cent of the total cocaine seizures in 1994 as compared to 49 per cent in 2000. Puerto Rico and Hispaniola Island, which in 1995 had 78 per cent of the cocaine seizures in the region, reduced their contribution to 40 per cent in 2000. The contribution of the Eastern Caribbean to the Caribbean cocaine seizures declined even more dramatically from 32 per cent in 1994 to a mere 7 per cent in 2000.

The division of cocaine seizures according to linguistic groupings shows an even clearer evolution over the past decade, reflecting to a large extent different models of police cooperation and the changing dynamics of the cocaine flows. The English-speaking Caribbean, which accounts for 16 per cent of the total population, recorded an accelerated participation in the amount of cocaine seized in the region, rising from 15 per cent in 1994 to 40 per cent in 2000. Meanwhile, the Spanish-speaking Caribbean, with well over 60 per cent of the population, reduced its contribution to cocaine seizures from 74 per cent in 1995 to 52 per cent in 2000. The French-speaking Caribbean did not present a consistent trend, but its participation in the seizures has always been under-represented population-wise, a feature that can be attributed to very low interception efficiency in Haiti. The Dutch-speaking Caribbean has never reached 6 per cent of the total cocaine seizures, in spite of the increasing role played by Suriname, Aruba and the Netherlands Antilles in the international cocaine trade. A more marked trend appears when the Caribbean jurisdictions are divided between dependent territories and independent countries. The independent nations, which have 86 per cent of the Caribbean population, are responsible for only 38 per cent of the regional cocaine seizures averaged over the 1994–2000 period. Nevertheless, their participation in the Caribbean cocaine seizures has doubled during that period from a mere 25 per cent in 1994 to 55 per cent in 2000.

By countries, the highest interception rates registered in 2000 are those of Cuba, with 23 per cent, followed by Puerto Rico with 13 per cent. However, both jurisdictions are favoured by their location and/or special status: in the case of Cuba, the majority of their seizures are made through the so-called *recalos*. Traffickers coming under pressure from law enforcement vessels in the Jamaica–Bahamas corridor dump their drugs overboard to eliminate evidence. This washes up along the Cuban shore and is seized by the Cuban authorities. Puerto Rico, meanwhile, is the base of the well-equipped American drug enforcement agencies that are active throughout the Caribbean. The interception rates of Jamaica and the Bahamas also exceed the regional average. For the rest of the Caribbean, interception rates are around 2 per cent. Belize showed the lowest interception rate for cocaine in 2000 – a mere 0.1 per cent.

Marijuana seizures have recorded an almost continuous decline in kilogram terms during the last decade, a general trend that was broken in

2000, when total seizures of 91 MT increased by a third from a decade-low of 68 MT recorded during the previous year. The marijuana interception rate reached 20 per cent, which is partly explained by the ease of detection given by the non-mobility of the plants in connection with the eradication efforts and the large bulk volumes involved in marijuana transportation in comparison to the low detection probabilities involved in cocaine transshipment. Marijuana interception rates have risen three-fold during the decade, despite the falling levels of production and exportation. Jamaica has been credited with 44 per cent of the marijuana seized in the region during the 1994–2000 period. Eradication of crops is a much easier task than detection while being transshipped. The marijuana interception rates in the Bahamas, the Eastern Caribbean and Puerto Rico are about 15 per cent. The mainland Caribbean and Hispaniola Island present low marijuana interception rates of less than 5 per cent, with a sudden peak in 2000 of 62 per cent.

The geographical and language segmentations of marijuana seizures almost reverse the cocaine interception scene. The Central Caribbean route and the Spanish-speaking countries have gained ground at the expense of the English-speaking countries and the Western corridor centred in Jamaica. The Western Caribbean accounted for 90 per cent of marijuana seizures in 1995, but its share fell to 58 per cent in 1999. Marijuana interception in mainland Caribbean countries plummeted from 20 per cent of total seizures in 1994 and 1996 to 0.3 per cent. (The English-speaking Caribbean, which had almost monopolized marijuana seizures in 1995 with over 95 per cent of total captures, dropped its contribution to 72 per cent in 1999.) Meanwhile, Spanish-speaking countries increased their share of marijuana seizures during the same period from 4 to 27 per cent. Marijuana seizures in the French- and Dutch-speaking jurisdictions are almost non-existent. Cuba and Jamaica show the highest marijuana interception rates in the Caribbean, with 39 and 30 per cent respectively. In the case of Cuba, a large part of the seizures correspond to effortless *recalos*; for Jamaica, eradication is a much easier task than detection while being transshipped.

Police cooperation within the region remains at very low levels, a reflection partly of legal constraints but particularly of corporate police behaviour. Only European countries with territorial interests in the region and the United States have permanent ongoing cooperation. Language differences impose an insuperable barrier to close cooperation. Perception of corruption, internal operational inertia and cultural stereotypes also play a role in preventing increased cooperation. The Caribbean Spanish-speaking countries are unable to cooperate to their benefit with coca-producing countries or their English-speaking neighbours in the Caribbean. Cuba's isolation also affects potential cooperation between the largest country of the Caribbean and its closest neighbours.

In this context, the only information-sharing process that works takes places between almost all Caribbean jurisdictions and the United States, the regional hub for law enforcement cooperation and, on occasion, the general supervisor and facilitator of drug enforcement activities in the region. Under these conditions and in the light of much needed cooperation against largely transnational crime, the drug flows for internal consumption or trafficking to Europe remain relatively under-supervised in contrast to the pressure imposed on drug networks that export illicit drugs to the United States.

Justice systems in the Caribbean with respect to drug trafficking and consumption present strong differences, but the severity of the laws and prison sentences for drug use are common features. In Cuba, capital punishment is within the repertoire of sentences available in the legal codes to deter drug trafficking. As a result, more than 25 per cent of the inmates in the region are imprisoned on drug use or trafficking charges in every country. Incarceration rates in the region are among the highest in the world. In the Caribbean 85,000 people, or 0.3 per cent of the adult population, are in prison. Five countries of the region – the Cayman Islands, the Bahamas, Bermuda, Suriname and the Netherlands Antilles – are in the top ten of the world incarceration rate list, with rates of well over 450 people per 100,000 residents. Every jurisdiction in the Caribbean, with the exception of Haiti, has higher incarceration rates than the most punitive-minded country in the European Union. This readiness to send people to prison for minor drug crimes contrasts sharply with the reluctance to sentence big drug entrepreneurs accordingly.

Treatment and rehabilitation of drug addicts in the Caribbean are greatly constrained by the lack of public resources invested in the area of demand reduction, the limited and ill-coordinated participation of NGOs, the existence of especially punitive penal systems to deal with drug use and abuse, and a prison system that sharply subordinates the reintegration of individuals into society to the fulfilment of its punitive role. Conditions in Caribbean prisons emphatically contradict rehabilitation principles. The average occupancy rate – the ratio between the real occupancy rate and the official capacity – in Caribbean prisons is 160 per cent. In Grenada, the Dominican Republic, St Lucia, Belize and Haiti, the number of inmates is double the official prison capacity.

Beyond official policies, the public sector has another opportunity to influence the drug market – through corruption, which facilitates drug production, circulation and distribution. In 2000, illegal drugs generated an income of US$320 million for the public sector employees in the Caribbean – 0.3 per cent of the region's GDP or 9.4 per cent of the income produced by illegal drugs. This percentage almost perfectly assimilates to the average official fiscal pressure in the region. Nevertheless, the public sector employees'

Table 10.3 Cocaine seizures in the Caribbean region, 1996–2000 (in kilos)

JURISDICTIONS	1996	1997	1998	1999	2000
NORTH SECTOR					
Bahamas	115	2,565	3,347	1,860	2,779
Turks and Caicos Islands (UK)	393	1	2,075	1	303
WEST SECTOR					
Belize	470	2,691	1,221	38	13
CENTRAL-WEST SECTOR					
Cayman Islands (UK)	2,219	1,054	1,213	1,401	1,812
Cuba	7,905	1,444	956	2,444	3,144
Jamaica	254	414	1,143	2,455	1,655
CENTRAL-LEFT SECTOR					
Haiti	956	2,100	1,272	380	n/a
Dominican Republic	1341	1,225	2,337	1,071	1,306
CENTRAL-RIGHT SECTOR					
Puerto Rico (US)	11072	15,153	10,344	9,977	n/a
US Virgin Islands (US)	n/a	n/a	n/a	n/a	0.1
CENTRAL-RIGHT SECTOR					
Aruba (NL)	203	408	794	464	346
Netherlands Antilles (NL)	710	1,302	639	18	n/a
EAST SECTOR					
British Virgin Islands (UK)	1765	838	75	10	534
Anguilla (UK)	289	0	0	0	n/a
St Kitts–Nevis	0	150	1	1	0.052
Antigua–Barbuda	6	126	1	25	24
Montserrat (UK	0	1	0	0	n/a
Guadeloupe (FR)	1224	21	44	593	292
Dominica	3	101	29	83	10
Martinique (FR)	17	37	46	36	14
St Lucia	20	8	58	121	110
Barbados	36	88	35	141	179
St Vincent & the Grenadines	2	1	13	15	50
Grenada	9	213	3	42	101
Trinidad & Tobago	180	31	79	137	303
SOUTH-EAST SECTOR					
Guyana	91	66	3,222	38	163
Suriname	1,413	117	283	180	213
French Guiana	45	167	175	446	25
NORTH-EAST SECTOR					
Bermuda (UK)	23	4	11	392	13

Source: Caribbean Coordination Mechanism (CCM) and Police Forces

Table 10.4 Marijuana seizures in the Caribbean region, 1996–2000 (in kilos)

JURISDICTIONS	1996	1997	1998	1999	2000
NORTH SECTOR					
Bahamas	2,606	3,763	2,598	3,500	4,134
Turks and Caicos Islands (UK)	17	22	8	10	2
WEST SECTOR					
Belize	202	263	1,557	392	249
CENTRAL-WEST SECTOR					
Cayman Islands (UK)	3,188	3,423	4,063	5,100	6,621
Cuba	5,369	6,023	4,610	5,559	8,801
Jamaica	31,587	24,729	35,911	22,740	55,869
CENTRAL-LEFT SECTOR					
Haiti	n/a	9,000	9,255	31	
Dominican Republic	246	788	650	184	2,934
CENTRAL-RIGHT SECTOR					
Puerto Rico (US)	8635	1,337	1,285	12,605	n/a
US Virgin Islands (US)	n/a	n/a	n/a	n/a	27
CENTRAL-RIGHT SECTOR					
Aruba (NL)	77	13	n/a	141	12
Netherlands Antilles (NL)	650	n/a	541	112	n/a
EAST SECTOR					
British Virgin Islands(UK)	119	85	84	26	103
Anguilla (UK)	1	1	0	8	n/a
St Kitts–Nevis	5	67	31	16	120
Antigua–Barbuda	1,485	628	105	94	66
Montserrat (UK)	1	3	0	2,677	n/a
Guadeloupe (FR)	667	1,057	688	515	1,016
Dominica	136	405	361	192	467
Martinique (FR)	166	355	136	199	749
St Lucia	326	622	352	352	1,803
Barbados	3,083	1,092	96	745	6,500
St Vincent & the Grenadines	1,227	527	1,321	7,188	1,708
Grenada	191	123	127	218	194
Trinidad & Tobago	1,408	3,120	1,850	1,558	1,546
SOUTH-EAST SECTOR					
Guyana	52,377	20,179	8,860	3,954	123
Suriname	17	65	105	177	107
French Guiana	99	40	51	134	59
NORTH-EAST SECTOR					
Bermuda (UK)	107	92	83	n/a	n/a

Source: Caribbean Coordination Mechanism (CCM) and Police Forces

participation in the drug business varies according to products, phases of the productive process, and geographical areas. Cocaine is concentrated in the most capital-intensive part of the drug business and accordingly needs a greater injection of corrupt money in order to guarantee a safe transit. Cocaine thus leaves a trail of US$290 million in Caribbean civil servants' pockets, or 10 per cent of the total income generated by cocaine in the region. Public participation in the marijuana business is much lower and the payment to civil servants is only 4.5 per cent of the total income. Accordingly, 92 per cent of the drug income pocketed by civil servants comes from the cocaine business, with marijuana contributing a mere 6.5 per cent. In terms of the steps involved in marketing drugs, trans-border transportation is the most vulnerable activity and so more investment in corruption of customs and law enforcement personnel is needed – 12 per cent of the total income is earned in this phase. On the other hand, retailing/distribution only gives 4.4 per cent of the value-added to civil servants.

The agreement between drug entrepreneurs and public services always involves a negotiation process, with results that very much depend on the particular bargaining power of the agents. Accordingly, the outcome may be the subordination of the public servants to the economic power of the drug traffickers (a result associated with powerless states); an egalitarian relationship between independent actors (the Colombian model); or a kind of agreement in which the public sector regulates the market to maximize the profits of the public servants (the traditional Mexican model). With a couple of exceptions – found within the biggest state structures of the region, which have the ability and the power to govern the drug market in their respective countries – the most usual corruptive association in the Caribbean is shaped by a combination of the first and second models, in which the traffickers have the same bargaining power, at least, as their public counterparts to construct a long-standing relationship.

In weak and poor states with a small economic base, scarce endogenous resources and limited means to exert legitimate authority, an external or internal agent with enormous economic power – a drug businessman, for example – can exert pressure so massive and unrelenting as eventually to jeopardize the survival of the government or, at least, its legitimacy. The most flagrant case of this kind of unequal relationship between drug traffickers and public officials took place in St Kitts–Nevis, where Charles 'Little Nut' Miller was able to challenge the state authority through intimidation or violence for years until the public authorities were able to extradite this notorious drug businessman. A regional military operation was needed to restore state authority over the power of the trafficker.

There are at least two sets of factors that seem to influence the participation of the public sector in the drug business in the Caribbean –

economic and political freedom. Although both concepts are difficult to measure in practice, and incorporate moral biases by definition, both seem to be negatively related with larger-scale participation of public servants in the illegal drug market. Taking the Freedom Index developed by the organization Freedom House, in which political rights and civil liberties are measured on a one-to-ten scale, with one representing the highest degree of freedom and ten the lowest, the participation of the public servants in the drug sector grows 2 per cent for each percentage point of political freedom, with a degree of public sector participation of 7.5 per cent for the highest level of political freedom. Low levels of political freedom are associated with authoritarian or totalitarian regimes in which the state is involved in particular issues with the consent or the non-consent of the individuals or, alternatively, with a weak state apparatus to guarantee human rights and political liberties for the individual living within its territory. Although both kinds of non-liberal regime (authoritarian or police state) are associated with high degrees of public sector participation in the drug business, their relation to drug markets is completely different. Under an authoritarian regime, the involvement of public servants in the drug market is an absolute require-ment if the industry aspires to survive, because the presence of the public sector is everywhere. In a failed state, the degree of uncertainty for doing business, whether legal or illegal, is so great that businessmen need to bribe a lot of public agents in order to protect property rights in the medium run. The lack of control over public sector activities (law enforcement) that is associated with the weakness in the protection of civil liberties and political rights is universally conducive to corruption, including drug-related corruption. In the Caribbean context, low levels of political freedom may be facilitated by inequitable income distribution, small population size, or the lack of democratic traditions.

Similar conclusions can be drawn if the participation of public servants in the drug business in the Caribbean is correlated with the level of economic freedom as measured by the Heritage Foundation on a one-to-ten scale, with one representing the highest degree of freedom and ten the lowest. In this case, each point of economic un-freedom increases in 3 percentage points the participation of public servants in drug business, with 0 per cent in those jurisdictions with the highest levels of economic freedom. The same degree of intervention in the legal markets is usually associated with the interference of public servants in the drug business. Economic freedom does not mean a mere reduction of the public sector participation in the economy; instead, it means a public sector that has the ability to guarantee economic rights to every individual or firm, whatever the state contribution to the economy is. The correlation between the public sector's participation in drug business and an interception rate is statistically insignificant. A possible explanation is that, in some instances of corruption, the agreement between protected drug traffickers and public servants usually involves the arrest of independent drug entrepreneurs and planned seizures in order to exhibit an apparent efficiency in the official drug fight. In the same way, when all other variables are controlled, there is no correlation between corruption and legal tradition – Common Law or Civil Law.

The actual drug policies being implemented have not been immune to illegitimate, selfish manipulation by ruling elites within the Caribbean countries to maintain the existing internal power distribution. First, drug use has been used to stigmatize the poor people in the region. Instead of focusing drug policy on rehabilitation to help drug users, some politicians, in close collaboration with mass media and many in the civil society, have tended to criminalize and demonize every aspect of cultural or political expression associated with poverty, especially when emanating from young people, as a form of drug-influenced criminal behaviour. Since drugs are illegal, people who coexist with drugs are also considered 'illegal', if not 'evil'. The demonizers express this biased linkage between poverty and drugs even if drug use is also frequent among the power elites. By articulating opinions that are driven by a dichotomy between good and evil, in which evil is identified with drugs, they have tended to marginalize drug use among poor people, to stigmatize these consumers and, in general terms, to torpedo the ultimate aim of the drug policy – reducing the number of drug users. Instead, these views, which uncritically associate poverty with drugs, are functional because they are used by the ruling elite to justify disempowering the poor and to condemn all social protest. In an official explanation that has not been unusual in the region, high-ranking state officials accused the rioters that rallied against the power blackouts in the

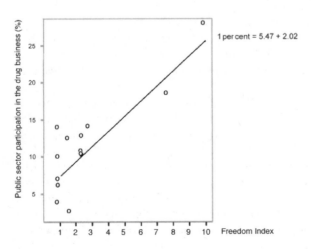

1 per cent = 5.47 + 2.02

Figure 10.3 Public sector participation in the drug business

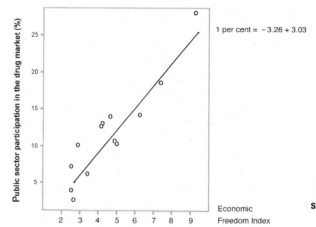

1 per cent = − 3.26 + 3.03

Figure 10.4 Public sector participation in the drug market

Dominican Republic in 2001 of being financed by drug-trafficking interests and acting under the influence of drugs. Widespread accusations about drug involvement in politics that appear around the region have been used, in some cases, with the intention of illegitimately altering public policy or the existing power distribution without checking the accuracy of the charges involved. These practices of defamation have been used as a weapon, not only in internal politics but also to influence relationships among Caribbean states and between regional jurisdictions and extra-regional countries.

Some public policies implemented by Caribbean governments in their legitimate pursuit of their people's economic well-being have been counterproductive for the general effectiveness of the drug control efforts. This contradiction between an effective drug policy and other public policies has manifested itself in at least two instances − free-trade areas and offshore financial centres. Free-trade areas have been established by many Caribbean governments since the 1970s with the purpose of attracting foreign investment and offering better opportunities for local industry. By 2000, a large proportion of import and export industries in many Caribbean countries had been brought together in these areas. For example, 80 per cent of the Dominican Republic's exports move through the free-trade zones. In an effort to minimize the obstacle to economic activities in these special development zones, some governments have tended to confuse tax-free with control-free jurisdictions. As an unintended consequence of this lack of customs controls, free-trade areas have often been the subject of discussion among law enforcement agencies for their vulnerability to be used as transshipment points in the drug trade. An estimated 40–50 per cent of the cocaine that circulates through the Caribbean in ship containers goes through these virtually uncontrolled free-trade areas. In some countries, where the controls over the entry and exit flow of goods are almost non-existent, this proportion reaches 70 per cent.

The Caribbean offshore banking system and its assumed connection to money laundering has been at the centre of the debate on anti-money-laundering practices even before the Financial Action Task Force (FATF) issued its list of uncooperative jurisdictions. Four Caribbean offshore centres were placed on the list at the beginning. At the core of this discussion have been the apparent conflicting interests of the national governments, striving to diversify their economies under the increased pressures of globalization, often asserted in a strongly nationalistic manner, and the equally legitimate concern of the developed countries to restrict the flow of illicit money through their economies. With the presentation of the debate as a nationalist fight between rich and poor countries, the opportunity for a real cost–benefit analysis for Caribbean countries has been lost. In this sense, the profits of offshore financial centres for the Caribbean populations have been rather small.

The Caribbean countries offering offshore banking services represent only 3.8 per cent of the total regional population. With the exception of the Cayman Islands, Bermuda, the Bahamas and Anguilla, offshore banking generates less than 10 per cent of the GDP of the local employment and an even lower proportion of the public sector revenues. In fact, the good jobs provided in the offshore financial centres are almost universally monopolized by foreigners. Moreover, the possibilities of developing a successful offshore centre have diminished during the 1990s as onshore and offshore banking services have tended to converge and many offshore centres have emerged outside this region, including some in the developed countries. Against this background of diminished profits, almost every offshore financial centre in the region has been involved in penal cases of fraud or money laundering, as well as having to defend itself against FATF accusations and establish a regulatory system. Although less than 1 per cent of the funds flowing into the Caribbean offshore centres correspond to drug money, these penal cases have dangerously weakened a very fragile but highly marketable asset in an increasingly globalized economy, especially in the banking sector – reputation. Given that for the general public it is rather difficult to differentiate between Caribbean countries or offshore centres, this declining reputation, which has reached an all-time low as the international mass media focuses on the high-profile cases and the blacklists, has universally affected the possibilities of economic development of all Caribbean countries, even if there are strong differences in money-laundering regulations among regional offshore centres. Additionally, corruption and its negative influence on local politics have usually been associated with offshore financial centres.

Offshore banking has not been the only institution under local regulation that has attracted international criminal organizations, including drug traffickers, to the region. Criminals, given the general lack of control of economic citizenship programmes, have found illegitimate uses for another public policy that was established with the aim of increasing local public revenues. The facilities given under these programmes to change names and identities have proven especially attractive to international criminals. Although the number of criminals buying these passports has not exceeded 200 for the entire Caribbean, these legal instrumentalities have had at least two unintended consequences: one, becoming a source of conflict with those developed countries where these criminals are sought; and, two, increasing the regional pool of criminals who will eventually try to apply their economic power to exert a corruptive influence on the countries that have provided them with refuge.

In recent years, the debate on the legal status of the currently illicit drug marijuana has been rife in the Caribbean, especially in the English-speaking countries. In 2001, a government-backed National Commission on Ganja in Jamaica recommended that the executive and legislative branches amend the laws so as to decriminalize marijuana for private, personal use in small quantities by adults and consumption for religious purposes. In substance this recommendation has already been implemented in some European Union countries during the last decade. The petition for partial or complete legalization or decriminalization has been based on religious, moral, political and economic grounds. Support for these proposals remains a minority position in the Caribbean according to the limited surveys available. However, the official government positions about drugs in favour of keeping them illegal have not remained neutral in spreading drug fears among the general public. From this perspective, the official discourse should look for more rational and pragmatic arguments to support the illegal nature of drugs than simply stressing their intrinsic evil.

Accordingly, the region may find a more scientific, and less visceral, way of addressing the question of the legal/illegal nature of drugs by analysing both the pros and cons of the available public policies to apply to drugs. An essential trail to be explored would be the quantification of the probable increase in drug use that may be expected under legalization, and whether society can economically and socially afford the consequences of this expansion in drug addiction. Some recent economic studies have shown that demand for drugs is more price-sensitive than was previously believed in the light of the addictive nature of the demand. Substitutability among legal and illegal drugs has not received enough attention; neither has the concept of marijuana as a 'buffer' or gateway drug been sufficiently examined. It has also to be demonstrated whether the damage associated with the illegal nature of drugs, such as organized crime or corruption, would be significantly reduced under a licit trade or whether decriminalization would be counterproductive in crime terms. Corruption associated with the previous illegal drug trade might not necessarily be eliminated under a new legal status, because bribery is far from being an unknown business even for licit firms in the Caribbean.

Political consequences

Differences in law, economic circumstances, and social traditions among countries in the Caribbean are substantial. However, there are some features that are common – the major one being an almost universal state weakness. In spite of the progress achieved in previous decades by states to acquire resources and legitimization, some deficiencies remain unaltered. Under these circumstances, drug use and trade implies an additional challenge to the governance of the individual political systems. It erodes the notion of national sovereignty; it hinders the construction of national and regional identities; it interferes in the process of consolidation of a political culture; it confuses the distinction between legal and illegal; it promotes an anomalous functioning of the legislative, executive and judicial branches; and it is a source of expensive international conflicts. Most of these effects are derived from the illegal nature of drugs rather than an intrinsic effect of the drugs, although it is difficult to separate these components.

National sovereignty is the basic foundation of political structures and the international relations system, and continues to play an important role in spite of the progress of economic and social globalization. Drug trafficking poses a great challenge to any state's claim to completely control its borders, and the entry of goods and people into the country. If the only law that drug entrepreneurs recognize is the law of supply and demand, there is no reason to think that frontiers pose a threat to their operations. Some 1,200 MT of illegal drugs cross a Caribbean border annually – 50 kilograms of drugs per kilometre of border, but still less than 0.1 per cent of the licit traffic of goods in the Caribbean. States can present an insignificant rate of success in implementing their own laws against the importation of drugs – only 7 per cent of the total trans-border flow. This percentage is four times higher for human couriers and is less for ship containers. The low interception ratio erodes each state's claim to control its own territory, while at the same time powerful drug-trafficking cartels contribute to the establishment of illegitimate networks that are able to introduce other unwanted goods and people.

The erosion of the sovereignty notion among local populations in the Caribbean has also been affected by unilateral actions implemented by extra-regional countries that see the weakness of the local governments. Although in some cases these undesired interferences have been exploited by unscrupulous local politicians to exhibit nationalistic postures aimed at gaining an electoral base or hiding their own limitations, these actions have given much support to the notion that drug policy is not the result of local consensus on the issue but a foreign imposition. Drug policy is thus considered as epitomizing the lack of autonomy of local politics.

Linked to the widespread view of the drug policy as an imposition from outside is the idea that the origin of Caribbean drug problems is European and American demand. If one follows this argument, there is no need to devote scarce local public resources to resolve other people's problems. Without denying the reality of supply and demand, one has to point out that this perspective ignores the benefits of some international relationships that are, by their nature, complex and mutually profitable. Unfortunately, simplistic approaches do not favour the formulation of indigenous national drug policies; too often they amount to a mask of hypocrisy, and private thoughts do not match public performance.

The most evident effect that the drug trade has on Caribbean politics is corruption and state involvement in illegal activities. The corruption pressures have affected all state branches in the Caribbean, whatever the size of the country or the power of the state. In 1989 a popular Cuban division general was tried and executed for organizing a drug-trafficking ring with fellow military officials. In 1985, the Prime Minister of the Turks and Caicos Islands was imprisoned for introducing cocaine into the United States. Direct involvement of high officials in drug trafficking more often gives way to cooperative models in which drug entrepreneurs provide management while politicians protect the business, to mutual benefit. The existence of presidential regimes or parliaments that are widely subordinated to the executive branch in most Caribbean jurisdictions weakens the opportunities of the legislative branches to be involved in drug-related corruption schemes. Cases of influencing the normal functioning of the justice system through bribery or intimidation for the benefit of the drug entrepreneurs are not unusual. One leader of a Jamaican trafficking group was charged with murder fourteen times, but always acquitted because witnesses disappeared or were murdered. Juries have also been influenced by corruption or intimidation.

Although drugs generate an income of US$320 million annually for civil servants in the Caribbean, they were already being corrupted before drugs arrived in the region. The Caribbean countries that appear in the Corruption Perception Index elaborated by Transparency International obtain very low marks. In 2001 the Dominican Republic received a 3.1 rating on a scale that ranges between 10 (very clean) and 0 (very corrupt), while Trinidad & Tobago obtained 5.3. In 1999, Jamaica's rating was 3.8. Drug-generated corruption in most countries flourishes in a business environment in which corruption is the rule rather than the exception. Its main effect is that drugs increase the size of the corruption market in the region and can help to institutionalize corruptive relationships. Drugs also introduce corruption in the law enforcement area, which is especially sensitive to public perception of delegitimization, and reinforces the obstacles to the emergence of a real rule of law.

Drug consumption and trade also have strong implications for political culture, the set of attitudes that inform the political activity and participation of the citizens. The quantitatively limited but more manifest consequence is that it affects political thinking and the participation in politics among drug abusers (opiate of the masses). This effect, nevertheless, should not be overstated in the Caribbean – only 0.2 per cent of the adult population may be categorized as compulsive abusers. Of those, between 65 to 75 per cent correspond to lower-class strata whose participation in politics is limited everywhere. The majority of the users consume drugs in a recreational way that has no significant consequences in the formation of political activity, at least in the short run.

Illicit drug production and commerce also affect the Caribbean political culture by blurring the line that separates legal and illegal acts on which the rule of law is based. First, drug-induced corruption leads many citizens to think that money rather than ideas and commitment determine politics and government, thus generating a great deal of distrust between politicians and their electorate. Second, drug trafficking creates deviant rules for upward social mobility in which legality is seen not as a common framework for social cohesion but as an obstacle to individual advancement. For about 125,000 people, or 0.8 of the labour force, who extract a direct income from their involvement in drugs in the region, there is a radical con-tradiction between the rule of law and their way of living. But the concentration of the income extracted from the drug trade creates tens of thousands of people who accumulate an incredible wealth and, with their flashy way of life, may become a role model for young people. With the Caribbean unemployment rate of over 17 per cent of the labour force, high-income strata increasingly concentrated, and very limited upward mobility, drug dealing has become the only chance of escaping poverty for many people in poor areas where access to basic resources is scarce. Apart from the general idea that money provides prestige for those who have it, some traffickers grant social assistance in the poor neighbourhoods that the public sector cannot provide. Jamaican drug lords have become heroes in their communities and, when security agencies try to arrest them, the population protects them. Therefore, for many there is a real contradiction between what is lawful and real opportunity, between a political system that many perceive as unfair and the chance of obtaining prestige and money through drug business.

The deficit of civic trust in existing institutions, organizational cleavages created by drug dealers and the sympathy that drug traffickers generate among some people produce an individualization of social and political relationships that is extremely dangerous for the governance of complex societies. Although strong leadership has been an almost universal feature of Caribbean politics during the past half-century, drug trafficking produces alternative loyalties that are not institutionally based but are individualistic in nature. Even when drug-related loyalties are not established for the purpose of challenging the state, their foundation on inter-personal trust is in direct confrontation with the notions of merit and the rule of law. Political parties and loyalty are based almost exclusively on patron–client relations. When notorious Jamaican politicians attend the funerals of notorious drug traffickers, a situation that has not been unusual during the past two decades, the social legitimization of drug trafficking and its alternative deviant culture is being honoured.

Drug trafficking interferes with relationships between countries within the Caribbean. Some areas and jurisdictions are stigmatized and, in some cases, punished on the basis of allegedly intense drug trafficking. Even if some situations are real, some conflicts have been intentionally fired up by politicians who opt for externalizing the problem and so avoiding accountability for the problems in their own countries. For instance, St Vincent & the Grenadines is blamed by its Eastern Caribbean neighbours for being the source of the marijuana problem in their countries. In the Dominican Republic, allegations against Haiti and the Haitian migrants for being the source of the local drug problem has been used for the implementation of some other policies against Haiti. Dominican immigrants are, in turn, censured as drug traffickers in Puerto Rico. And deportees are almost universally blamed in the Caribbean for their role in increasing and providing sophistication to local crime. Illegal drugs, therefore, affect the relationships between states and Caribbean peoples and also damage the reputations of migrant communities.

Drug entrepreneurs, beyond trying to influence the state's judicial system, have an interest in creating their own justice system in order to enforce contracts and eventually achieve a monopoly over the criminal activity that makes profit maximization and risk minimization possible. Without the constraints of state justice, violence is a common recourse in this private justice system. Under these extra-legal conditions, drug-related murders are not unusual in the Caribbean. Drug trafficking is said to be the cause of 80 per cent of the over 800 violent deaths that take place annually in Puerto Rico. In Jamaica, 40 per cent of murders are attributed to territorial turf wars between drug gangs. Jamaican traffickers were accused of 5,000 violent deaths in the United States during the 1985–92 period. The drug dealers' recurrent use of violence is conducive to more private violence by non-drug-tainted individuals (potential murderers and robbers) who lose confidence in the state's judicial system and can plainly see how avoiding state punishment can be not only possible but usual.

Illicit drug production and trade, through the enforcement of this internal justice code, has contributed to increasing the level of violence in Caribbean societies. But it also makes private violence in general more lethal by increasing the number of firearms available in the region. An illicit market, in which drugs and firearms as well as stolen goods are exchanged, is functioning in the Eastern Caribbean.

In Suriname, a kilogram of cocaine costs the price of an AK-47 rifle. In general, about 60–80 per cent of the weapons illegally held in the Caribbean come from the United States, where most of them are legally acquired and then exported to the region. Thus drug trafficking not only increases the demand for weaponry but also stimulates availability in the Caribbean by providing petty crime and private violence with a lethal capacity not previously known.

Drug-induced proliferation of firearms has expanded governance problems in the Caribbean societies. This problem has particularly altered the functioning of national security agencies. First, the establishment of impunity sanctuaries in poor neighbourhoods in Puerto Rico, the Dominican Republic, Jamaica and some other countries has almost removed state presence and control in these areas. Second, better-equipped criminals have provoked an even more violent reaction in security agencies. Lacking other investigatory and legal powers, the latter have turned to massive violence as an allegedly effective method to control poor neighbourhoods. In some cases, these actions have the sympathy of a population that is fed up with criminal violence. In the Dominican Republic and Jamaica, annual killings by police agents are in three-digit figures.

Both countries lead the Western Hemisphere in state crime. Third, widespread private violence, combined with human and equipment shortages, has driven police agencies to categorize many killings, especially those considered politically irrelevant, as drug-related score-settling that does not merit further investigation.

The planning and implementation of public policies has been made more difficult and confused by illegal drugs. On the one hand, the collection and compilation of information has become a more difficult task because a large part of the economic and socially beneficial activities are illegal and implicitly hidden to official statistics. On the other hand, the implementation of public policies is unclear when relevant data about the recipients of those policies are largely unknown. In some cases, public policies may involuntarily become a piece of the drug traffickers' strategy to keep the social environment under their control.

Therefore, rather than being the recipient or major base of political violence, the Caribbean has more often been used as a place for the acquisition of weaponry and money laundering by organizations acting by violent means in some other parts of the world.

The lax state controls in the Caribbean have been used by terrorist organizations. In 1989, ten tons of firearms in transit to the Colombian Revolutionary Armed Forces (FARC) were seized in Jamaica. This group has also exploited Surname's interior areas to carry out arms-for-drugs deals. Many elements of the Caribbean's political, economic and social structure that have been preyed upon by criminal elements in the past, such as the offshore financial sector, the economic citizenship programme or the weakness of the state, are also attractive to terrorist groups.

Drug users and traders, although made illegal by a public decision, ordinarily do not have an anti-establishment political programme. The overwhelming majority of drug entrepreneurs and users try to maximize their utility within the existing political environment and have no interest in subverting it. In the Caribbean, the weaknesses of the existing states, which provide widespread opportunities for coexistence and mutual profit, are also a disincentive to confrontation.

Economic effects

Drug trade and production is a source of income for the Caribbean region. But it also has a price. First, while the costs are borne by the entire society, the number of beneficiaries of the drug income is very limited – 125,000 people in the region. Second, as has been noted above, this has been an income with enormous costs for the social fabric of the Caribbean societies. Using a methodology previously applied for the United States, the direct costs in terms of violence and health cost would reach US$300–325 million, that is, 0.3 per cent of GDP. This figure ranges from the 1.1 per cent of GDP in Jamaica and 0.8 per cent in Puerto Rico to less than 0.1 in Cuba. Comparatively, illicit drugs cost the American economy US$98 billion – 1.1 per cent of the GDP. Indirect costs, nevertheless, are hardly measurable, especially when considering the opportunity costs of using the available resources for drug use and trade.

The most visible effect of illicit drugs is the productivity losses that drug abuse produces and the violence associated with drug dealing. The fact that young people are the main victims of drug abuse and drug-related violence

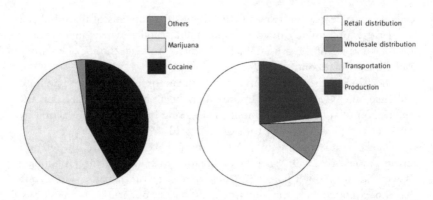

Figure 10.5   Drug employment by drug type and production processes, 2000

increases this productivity loss effect, while the fact that drug abuse and violence is concentrated on low-skilled young people would tend to dismiss the strength of the effect. In any of the gross estimations used for this analysis, drug-induced productivity losses are marginal, ranging from 0.1 to 0.4 per cent of total GDP.

Drug use and trade favour the already large concentration of total income in the Caribbean. On the trafficking side, the benefits concentrate in a few hands – about 12,000 people obtain 75 per cent of the total drug income. The social origin of these individuals is often the ruling elites rather than the poor, making this no contribution to open upward social mobility. On the drug abuse side, the consumption promotes an income transfer from the usually poor users to the better-off dealers. This situation ultimately contributes to the creation of above-ground and black markets, and to a society-wide increase in the prices of some goods and services, thus decreasing the relative income of the poor people.

Drug-induced violence tends to be a disincentive for foreign and local investment. Violence increases the fixed and variable costs of locally established firms, which have to pay a premium for security and higher taxes to strengthen the state law enforcement agencies. But the main effect of violence is introducing a higher degree of uncertainty in doing business. Although it is difficult to measure the real effect of this intangible on the Caribbean economies, there is ample evidence in the media regarding specific cases in which foreign and local firms have said that violence was a major cost for them. Additionally, drug investments are chiefly made with the aim of money laundering and not for productive and long-term return reasons. Therefore, the participation of companies that are fronts for money laundering often allow these firms to sell their goods or services under the cost price, which means that legal businesses are pushed out of the market, unable to compete in these unfair competitive circumstances.

Drug trafficking also exacts a price from the main industry of the region – tourism. First, except for the marginal drug tourism, the image of the Caribbean in the international mass media as a haven for drug trafficking constitutes bad publicity for the region as a whole. That image has a negative effect on the highly volatile preferences of the tourists, especially sensitive to public security concerns. Second, the violence indirectly generated by illegal drugs inhibits the spreading of the positive effects of tourism to local merchants by encouraging 'all-inclusive tourism' in which only the foreign firms and the local workers directly employed in these resorts benefit from tourism, and not the adjacent services and industries. In the construction sector, often used for money-laundering purposes, a limited but positive effect for the construction firms appears to be evident. But this laundering does not seem to result in a general increase in the price of real estate in the region.

The most important consequence of the illicit drug trade in the Caribbean comes from the disincentive to business entrepreneurship. Facing high returns for investment in the drug trade, the opportunity costs of legal entrepreneurship, with more limited, long-run profits, are disadvantaged. From this perspective, the opportunity costs of human capital investment are very high for young people, especially those who are living in a poor neighbourhood where the wealth effects of drug trafficking are clearly visible. As a consequence, in many poor areas of the region, children and young people who have the dream of escaping poverty do not see education and entrepreneurship as a major avenue for an upwardly mobile career (those elements being the main catalysts for endogenous development of Caribbean societies), but as a mere loss of time that would be more profitably spent in drug business in the short run.

CHAPTER 11

The Ganja Industry and Alternative Development in St Vincent and the Grenadines

AXEL KLEIN

Among Caribbean countries, St Vincent and the Grenadines boasts the most significant cannabis industry. Though smaller in size than the Jamaican export cultivation, the Vincentian industry plays the most significant role in relation to the overall size of the economy. In contrast to its neighbours, Barbados, St Lucia and Grenada, St Vincent's tourist sector is poorly developed. With the demise of the banana export, ganja planting remains one of the few openings for the young. Initiated in the 1970s by young farmers who are now in their middle age, cannabis production is the only field of rural activities recruiting the young back onto the land. Young farmers do not earn high returns over the production cycle, but can earn large amounts of cash when the harvest is sold.

As considerable quantities of Vincentian marijuana are exported to other parts of the Caribbean, the government is under significant pressure from regional neighbours and the US to step up eradication. The new Prime Minister, however, has put his sympathy for the plight of the farmers on the record. To negotiate the pressures of external partners and the demands of the domestic ganja lobby will depend on political finesse and the launch of a successful drug demand reduction programme at home.

During the seventeenth and eighteenth centuries, the mountainous terrain, covered by dense vegetation, discouraged the sprawling sugar plantations found in other parts of the West Indies. Along long stretches of St Vincent's coastline the adage normally applied to Dominica, as the only country that Columbus would recognize, still rings true. Geography, history and economics, therefore, have contributed to setting the scene for a distinctive social phenomenon: the ganja industry.

A small island with a population of 120,000, St Vincent has developed a reputation as the Eastern Caribbean's foremost producer of marijuana, known locally as ganja (EC 1996; Griffith and Munroe 1995).[1] At the fourth joint meeting of the Inter-Governmental Taskforce on Drugs and Ministers

Responsible for National Security,[2] St Vincent was identified in the intelligence analysis of drug threats as the main source of cannabis in the region. Figures on the acreage of cannabis eradication published in the Multilateral Evaluation Mechanism (MEM) of the Inter-American Drug Abuse Control Commission (CICAD 2000) are illustrative: St Vincent (171 acres of 263 identified); Dominica (nil); St Lucia (nil); Barbados (39 plants); Antigua (1 acre); Grenada (no mechanism in place for estimating area under cultivation). These figures are reinforced by the estimated quantities of cannabis trafficked in 1999 (Table 11.1).

Table 11.1 Estimated volumes of trafficked cannabis, Eastern Caribbean, 1999 (kgs)

Antigua–Barbuda	75
Barbados	333
Dominica	105
Grenada	217
St Kitts–Nevis	16
St Lucia	267
St Vincent	7,188

Source: UNODCCP, *Global Illicit Drug Trends* 2001.

A prime destination for the illegal Vincentian produce is the island of St Lucia, a mere 15 miles to the north. More lucrative for traffickers still, though more dangerous, is the market of Martinique, one of the French Départements de Outre Mar, one night's boat ride away, with direct air access to Paris and thus Europe. Further to the east lies Barbados, with a burgeoning domestic market fuelled by a vibrant tourism industry.

The changing role played by regional states makes for an interesting complexity. When they first began to acknowledge the drugs problem in the mid- to late 1980s, the Eastern Caribbean countries cast themselves in the role of victims, sucked into the web of international drug trafficking by Latin American production and North American/European demand. They maintain this role when negotiating with international partners, as this statement by the former Vincentian Prime Minister Sir James Mitchell goes to illustrate:

> I want to be able to blame the US for what is happening because they say we are not doing enough. If any drugs are passing through our country and going to the US then the US agencies have the authority by sky and sea to deal with it. The ball is in their court and not mine. (*Financial Times*, 25 October 1996)

These sentiments have been and are echoed at conferences and summits across the region.

When it comes to ganja, however, roles are different. Policy makers privately express their dismay at the failure of the Vincentian government to curtail production. Such reproaches are yet to be complemented by a significant acceptance of responsibility for the regional demand that is fuelling such production. Nor has it ever been thus. Indeed, Vincentian ganja cultivators claim that prior to the establishment of marijuana production on the island, ganja was imported from Colombia and Trinidad.[3] In Trinidad, in turn, people reminisce about the quality of home-grown marijuana.[4] Today, goes the lament, they are being supplied with Colombian cocaine and inferior Vincentian pressed marijuana.

Regardless of its relatively recent origin, the Vincentian ganja industry today is of an order of magnitude without parallel in the Caribbean. Though it is safe to assume that all countries in the region have some domestic production,[5] and that Jamaica may arguably export a greater volume, the importance of the ganja industry to the economy of St Vincent remains unique. To qualify the position of Jamaican marijuana producers it should be said (1) that they play a less significant role in relation to the much more diversified overall economy; and (2) that the role of marijuana as an underground activity has been largely eclipsed by the trafficking in cocaine.

Our definition of St Vincent as a producer country therefore rests on three critical attributes:

• a significant proportion of the GDP is accounted for by the production and trade in marijuana;
• an important percentage of the workforce is engaged in the marijuana trade;
• a high ratio of households are dependent on marijuana income.

National drug control policies

The government of St Vincent has joined its neighbours in signing up to the various initiatives sponsored by the US, the UN and the EU to combat drugs. It is a signatory to the Barbados Plan of Action (BPA) of 1996, and the US–Caribbean summit of 1997 with its resulting accord, the Partnership for Prosperity and Security in the Caribbean, which clearly states as an objective the 'intensification of efforts to eradicate the cultivation of cannabis'.

In December 1999 US special forces launched Operation Weedeater,[6] a week-long air and land assault combining Marine helicopters, DEA agents, Vincentian police and troops from the Regional Security System (RSS)[7] on the hide-outs of ganja farmers on the slopes of Mount Soufrière.[8] In the process of burning several million plants, seven tons of cured marijuana and 250 drying huts, one farmer was killed and 13 arrested.[9] The government had stood by its international treaty obligations, at the risk of alienating key domestic constituencies. Within weeks a vociferous movement calling itself the Association for the Advancement of People (ADAPT) was demonstrating outside the Prime Minister's office, stating the demands of poor farmers for a decent living and petitioning for legal reform.

Smouldering public dissatisfaction was reignited in April 2000, when the government announced substantial hikes in the salaries and pensions of parliamentarians. Led by the opposition MP Ralph Gonsalves, protesters blocked the roads into Kingstown, bringing government and commerce to a halt. An agreement was finally brokered under the auspices of regional politicians in Grenada, including bringing the next round of elections forward. In the spring of 2001 the Labour Party under Ralph Gonsalves sailed into office under the wind of a strong call for revisiting the existing ganja legislation.

The course open to the new government is not an enviable one. It has to navigate through regional and US pressure to move against the producers, without sparking off local protests. It is embarking on this course without the guidance of a functioning drug council, no information base, and limited capacity. Nowhere else in the region are the implications of the war on drugs as profound as in this country where the production of illicit crops has become the mainstay for a significant part of the population. Unfortunately, the perceived difficulty in accessing ganja farmers and traffickers has inhibited research into the industry. The findings presented below are designed to provide pointers as to where policy makers can engage with what to all intents and purposes is a marginal community, as well as to direct further research exercises.

Ganja farming

A ten-minutes drive out of Kingstown is the town of —— [10] where Mungo lives with his family. Every other day he collects members of his team to walk up the steep mountainside. On this day, encumbered by the curious gaze and shaky legs of a researcher, the normal 60-minute hike to work takes three hours. In the course of the journey to his farm we could count a good 20 fields under cultivation, as well as several abandoned ones now grazed over by herds of goats. Everywhere in this lush, tropical garden, the licit and illicit economies merge seamlessly. Deceptively, the thick vegetation suggests a wilderness to the urban eye, when in fact the abundance of tree crops, including mango, breadfruit and passion fruit, testify to a long history of cultivation.

At every bend the bush gives way to plots of remarkable similarity. Containing between 100 and 300 plants, each plot is worked by a team of 3–5 men, who will share in the proceeds if and when the crops are finally sold. Women will only come at harvest time, or exceptionally to do the weeding. In the main this is men's work, 'cleaning' the bush, hoeing terraces into the hillside, and digging holes for the small ganja bushes that are transplanted from seedbeds.

At the centre of each farmstead is a multipurpose shack which serves as a shelter for the team and visitors, a store for the farm tools and finally as a drying shed for the harvest. It is built from cedar wood and covered with tarpaulin over a dirt floor. Most farmers prefer to have someone sleep on site at all times, but this becomes mandatory before harvest time, when the plants are ripe and liable to be stolen. Interspersed among the cannabis plants lining the hillside are a 'high leaf' tobacco crop, planted primarily for domestic consumption. In addition, as on any other farm throughout the world, food crops are grown in a kitchen garden close to the shelter. In this instance, Mungo has planted yam, sweet potatoes, callalloo, tanya and peppers in the adjacent plots.

The farms are self-sufficient in nearly all respects, producing most of their food crops, fuel and implements. To most farmers, ganja is the sole cash crop and their only source of income. While the rotting mangoes at the base of David's farm look like an embarrassment of riches, the difficulty of the inaccessible terrain, together with the prevalence of a mango weevil that causes a ban on the importation of certain mango varieties into other islands, especially Barbados, reduce the commercial value of the crop to less than the harvest cost. While some would prefer a less stressful work regime and alternative legal crops, there is a resigned recognition of the difficulty of marketing these, or competing with imported produce (often from the US) on price.

At a different location, in Duvallee village (Windsor Forest) one farmer concedes that the money from ganja is good, but this is offset by 'police harassment, thieving and trickery'. He wants the government to help with the planting of ackee trees, of which there is a shortage in these parts, but sighs at the difficulty of bringing any produce to market. These laments over the demise of licit agriculture are echoed by other villagers, the oldest of whom is 80 years old, and has lived in the village since he arrived on his mother's back. The men agree that the banana was 'the number one crop' and wish that it were 1988 again. While stoically acknowledging the economic necessity of ganja cultivation, they preferred the regularity of a guaranteed income, the security and social status that banana farming had given them.

We find, then, suggestions of an intergenerational differentiation in outlook and attitude to farming. Most of the men heading the work teams, who are the bosses, if not owners, are in their mid-thirties to forties. They learned farming from their fathers, and picked up ganja as a habit in their youth when marijuana first became available. At that time the island was a net importer of ganja from St Lucia and Colombia. The first people to experiment with growing it locally were large landowners, who could absorb the risk. In the late 1970s a new generation of specialized ganja farmers emerged. These men had to discover for themselves the art of marijuana cultivation through trial and error. They entered the marginal lands, hitherto neglected for commercial farming.

Mungo began smoking in 1973, when he was still working with his father. In 1979 he struck out for himself, bringing in his first harvest of cannabis. He has not looked back since, and now counts as one of the most experienced, though not necessarily the most successful, ganja farmers. Having worked in these mountains for over 30 years, Mungo knows every trail and footpath. This is his country and his training was in the art of farming and land management. The only time a hint of doubt seems to come to him is when I question him about his father's attitude to marijuana. No, his father did not smoke, and like many of the older men did not approve of its cultivation. Yet what else is there to do, he asks.

The men who run the ganja-planting enterprises, the current 'bosses', therefore, are essentially farmers who have ventured into a new cash crop. They combine the conservatism of traditional farmers with an entre- preneurial spirit. This is best borne out by one of Mungo's friends, known as 'the scientist'. A graduate of the University of the West Indies, he experiments with seeds, growing cycles and fertilizers. With some pride, he points to a stand of imported skunk weed,[11] which he has just transplanted from its seedbed.

It becomes evident, then, that the performance of farmers varies. In one field, Mungo shows me the difference between 'man plants and woman plants'. On his own field, he destroys the former, to breed the valuable and highly potent sinsemilla. In contrast to the reputation of ganja as a hardy weed, Mungo and his assistants maintain that it is a very sensitive plant that has to be treated delicately, 'just like a woman'. The analogy is continued with reference to the moon. As with the planting of all crops in the West Indies, ganja farmers are observant of the lunar cycle, with transplanting taking place during the last quarter to assure a successful harvest.

If all this sounds like rustic harmony, the nervous, even hostile stares I get from some farmers provide a quick reminder of the tenuous legal situation. Even Mungo leads me down by a different path from the one that brought us up, ensuring that he has covered the tracks in my memory. His own fields have been raided twice and he has several stints in prison under his belt, one of the reasons why his current plot lies far from the road just below the mountain top. Now in his late forties, his ambition is to leave the mountain, leave the island and move to the US where he has family. In the meantime he is careful to keep the seeds from his last crop in reserve. Seeds as well as the stash of weed for his own use are hidden under a tree away from the field, insurance for another harvest in the event of eradication, theft or destruction by mother nature.

Insecurity is the hallmark of ganja cultivation at every step of the cycle. A man may lose the carefully tended crop to thieves or eradication. En route to market he may be ambushed by rivals, arrested by the police or cheated by the buyers. Even after the sale has been concluded successfully there are difficulties in banking his income, which leaves him with a large hoard of cash, an attractive target to thieves or enterprising law enforcement agents. Banana cultivation, by contrast, provided a regular weekly bankable income, guaranteed throughout the year.

The question arises why so many young men are still drawn to the hills. Mungo's work team is replicated in structure and configuration all over the hillside. One man, senior in years and experience, organizes a crew who are in their late teens and early twenties. They have little or no schooling and few skills. 'Earthman', who is guarding the neighbouring farm and comes over for a spliff and company, is a case in point. He left school at Grade 2 and later worked as a labourer in a metal factory in the industrial complex for a few years before being recruited to the work gang planting ganja on the mountain. The boss is a family friend from the same neighbourhood who has known him since birth.[12]

Earthman is typical of a new generation of Vincentians, who are half inside and half outside the formal education system, yet have no farming background. They grow up in the informal sector around the main settlements. They learn the tricks of the trade and the knowledge of the land from their bosses – the difference being that, while their bosses (people like Mungo) grew up as farmers and turned to ganja because it was the most lucrative cash crop, Earthman and his contemporaries are learning ganja cultivation first and farming second, in the pursuit of self-sufficiency during the lean months. As the second generation of ganja cultivators, they have been acculturated into the life on the land via an illicit and potentially dangerous activity. Ironically, farming for them is becoming synonymous with a life outside the law, as part of an independent and defiant community of brethren. Due to the low level of collective organization among the ganja farmers, and the competition intrinsic to a clandestine trade, a hardy individualism has emerged, tempered by camaraderie and the values of Rastafarianism.

There are implications here for the long-term land management of the region. But for more immediate purposes, this disconnection from farming 'proper' facilitates the cross-over of workers in the drug economy from cultivation to trafficking, and from ganja to other substances. Already outside the law, and under pressure from the state, the shift from cannabis to cocaine is for some people only a small adjustment. Mungo and his team, however, make a critical distinction. They say that the ganja crop is 'uplifting', economically, spiritually and morally. Growing a crop which is desired by the community, which raises people's spiritual consciousness and makes them happy, is a noble pursuit – especially in face of the persecution visited upon them by Babylon, a term that denotes the industrial world of North America and Europe.

This fits in squarely with a Rastafarian-inspired outlook, propagated across St Vincent and other Eastern Caribbean islands by the Nyabinghi order. The level of religious organization is difficult to establish from a brief survey. It seems, however, that few of these nominal Rastas engage in collective worship or ritual. Religious beliefs are most strongly expressed through adherence to a moral code, the wearing of dreadlocks, and the copious consumption of ganja. For the growers of an illicit crop, however, Rastafarianism plays several important functions. First, it creates a moral community of shared belief and outlook: this is important in an arena where authority is tenuous. In the absence of laws of contract, where claims to ownership are unenforceable, the system can only be maintained by secrecy and trust.

Second, it insulates the growers against the assault from the outside. However much ex-Prime Minister James Mitchell may have insisted that the eradication exercise was carried out by Vincentian troops, to the ganja farmers it was the product of US aggression, the wrath of Babylon. In this sense, Vincentian ganja farmers have far more ideological commitment than the apologetic Afghan poppy growers flouting the laws of Islam (UNODC 2003), or the economically driven coca producers of Colombia (Vargas 1999).

Third, a strong belief in the righteousness of the work helps sustain the work groups over the lean period before the harvest, and allows them to cope with the sudden loss from eradication or fraud.

Before and after the harvest

Each field yields two to three crops each year. One or two short crops are grown for 2–3 months, followed by the long crop, which is harvested in November, for the Christmas market. The production cycle is determined by consumer demand, which in turn coincides with the festive cycle. The fact that growers adjust to Christmas, Carnival and Emancipation Day festivities is an interesting commentary on the consumption patterns. It suggests that ganja smokers are in control of their consumption, and do not require a continuous supply, as theories of dependency and addiction would suggest.

The growth of the plants is aided by the use of various forms of fertilizer and herbicide. Methods vary between planters, according to means, experience and ideology. Leo is an organic farmer, who uses the residue of the previous harvest mixed with dung from a chicken farm in a nearby valley. Mungo, on the other hand, uses calcium which is purchased at EC$42 a bag. Inputs are used sparingly, partly because of the outlay, but more importantly, I suspect, because of the difficulty in bringing them up the mountain.

As the plants mature, the mountains come alive with activity. Men sleep on the farm to protect the maturing plants and while bringing in the harvest. At this stage friends and neighbours cooperate by forming work gangs of up to 30 men. These will move from field to field, collecting the leaves over a period of four to five days. Once they have been picked they are dried for a couple of days, and then pressed in a bucket. David's field is typical, with an estimated yield of 200 pounds. These are small fields, however, several informants point out. On the leeward side, the main growing area, individual harvests of over 2,000 pounds are not uncommon.

At this stage things become tenser. While Mungo maintains that the cultivation of ganja is 'uplifting' – he means morally – he concedes that greed and commercialism are present. Having suffered raids and attacks in the past, most farmers are armed nowadays, though the weaponry remains well concealed. Once the boss has made the 'connection', the ganja is packed in 50-pound bags and headloaded to the beach. As most farmers refuse to allow buyers to come near their fields, since 'you cannot trust any shadow', it is difficult to speak of farm gate prices. On the first leg of the journey to market, transport costs and risks are carried by the producers. They expose themselves to interception by the security forces, which patrol the roads and coastline, as well as to criminal activities. Once stacked into bags and carried to the beach, ganja's uplifting qualities provide precious little protection to the farmers in search of a sale. The purchaser arrives by boat at an agreed place, but has to run the gauntlet of coastguard cutters and rival speed boats; punctuality, already a rare commodity in the tropics, is rarely achieved.

In the meantime the farmers are left vulnerable on the beach. The landing place may be used by more than one group at a time, especially since boat owners are liable to have several deals going on with different farmers in order to fill their vessel. With different groups of armed men descending on a beach at night, tension runs high. Old scores and rivalries may be settled, though most farmers insist that there is little violence among them. When the boat fails to arrive, however, they have the choice of sitting it out during the day, increasing the chance of arrest, or hiding the ganja on the beach. On one such occasion Mungo was secretly observed, and his entire harvest had been stolen when he returned for it on the following night.

When the boat finally does arrive, the haggling begins. Though the price has been agreed in advance, prices and payment schedules are sometimes re-negotiated. In June 2001, for example, the price per pound had been set at EC$300 (US$110), but when the boat arrived the captain could only pay EC$200 (US$74). At this stage the relationship between farmer and purchaser is crucial, as payment is usually staggered over a period of time. One form of operation has the boatman forward a deposit before the harvest is brought in, with a further payment upon receipt of the processed ganja, and the remainder paid after the produce has been sold on. Yet few such relation-ships are permanent, and new buyers are continually entering the fray. While local buyers are preferred, the farmers maintain that increasingly boats from St Lucia, Dominica and Barbados are buying up the harvest. This makes for difficult bargaining, as they have less control over these foreign traders, and are in no position to collect debts.

Still, most agree that the money when it does arrive is good. When the entire harvest is paid for in one transaction, a group of four or five farmers who have together brought in 200 pounds of marijuana may find themselves in receipt of EC$40,000 (US$14,800), in a country where the GDP *per capita* is estimated at US$2,600. 'When it comes, the money is plenty.' And if it doesn't, for any number of reasons, they return to their plots, and start again. The land will feed them, their families will stay with them, and the promise of the next harvest provides a surety for credit. It is this cycle of productivity with minimal inputs that goes to explain the comparative absence of violence among ganja farmers. It sets a striking contrast to the groups getting involved in the cocaine trade, where everything is won or lost on a single deal.

Obtaining the money may be cause of celebration, but is not the end of the problems. Legislation to counter money laundering, introduced in the fight against organized crime, requires farmers to state where they have obtained their income. For men with no employment and no documented source of income, this is a formidable obstacle. Money is therefore spent quickly, lent out on easy terms to relatives, or simply hidden. The latter is particularly irksome, as it attracts crime, where, once again, the farmers and their families have no recourse to the law. As a result, farmers oscillate between feast and famine. Cash income may indeed be great, but is followed by long periods of drought. Farmers are therefore dependent on a web of shared obligations and goodwill, which is lubricated by the one commodity they possess in abundance: ganja.

The traffickers

Among the coastal communities, where men have for generations alternated farming with fishing, a process of diversification into trading has occurred.

One such man is Waves, a portly man in his mid-30s, who describes himself as an old pirate. He owns a wooden boat, ten foot long and powered by two 60-horsepower outboard engines, with which he sails to Dominica, St Lucia, the French islands and Barbados.

Contacts with two marine communities lead us to propose a new profile of the typical Caribbean trafficker: in his late twenties to early forties, he is semi-literate, working with one or two helpers on an opportunistic basis and living with his mother. These men are often unwilling to conform to the mores of the farming community, and value adventure over tranquillity. None wears locks, and the substance of conspicuous consumption is rum, not ganja. Without the family values of their farming brethren, the proceeds of the trade are channelled into motor-cars, not houses. But though the men gathering around the boatyard in the afternoon have been in the business for years, lasting wealth has eluded them. Business is volatile and risky. The coastguard is always on the lookout, forcing traffickers to dump their load in the sea. When they arrive in neighbouring islands they may find the police waiting on shore, or a gang of men surrounding the boat and hijacking the load; or their connection may start 'stealing your mind', lowering or not paying the agreed price. These are the risks of trading outside the law, with a knock-on effect of distrust, suspicion and violence right to the farm.

Ideally, Waves gets the money upfront, or, when working with old connections, in instalments. Like the farmers, he faces the problems of banking the proceeds and regularizing his cash flow. A number of traffickers have devised a strategy to circumvent money laundering control measures: they import cocaine, and sell it as and when cash is needed. With a guaranteed market among St Vincent's growing population of crack users, cocaine is as good as cash, but easier and safer to stash. In addition, trading ganja for cocaine can facilitate the working relationship with business partners abroad.

Another convenience is that cocaine when retailed is paid for in Eastern Caribbean dollars, whereas ganja is sold for US dollars, Barbadian dollars or French francs. To change foreign currency, the traders, as well as the farmers to whom the money is passed on, have to change in shops where no questions are asked, and the rate is lower than that offered by the banks. After buying for EC$200–300 per pound, and selling for EC$500–600 per pound, there is little profit left at the end of the operation when insurance, cover for previous losses, outgoings and the shares paid to assistants are factored in.

Duvallee village

With a pound of quality marijuana selling for less than US$100 on the beach of embarkation, and scarcely twice that much on the other side, it is becoming clear that ganja farming persists mainly because of lack of other opportunities. Duvallee village is a community of some 30 households on the northern side of Soufrière. It can be reached only via a series of bush paths, or by sea. Approaching the village over the water, the ganja fields and shacks become visible along the ridge of the volcano. The village itself is screened by dense foliage, visible only because of the boats bobbing in the surf.

Duvallee village is a community untouched by state services. For medical help or supplies, or to enjoy the benefit of electricity, people travel by boat to Petit Bordel. They farm and fish, but engage in no trade. None of the boats belonging to the village, it is pointed out to me, carry ganja, though people come here from other towns, and even Barbados, St Lucia and Dominica to buy up the harvest. In good years there is a veritable auction, with bidders vying for the high-quality marijuana.

But the farmers talk about bananas and ackee trees. 'I grow this marijuana, but I am tired of the helicopters and the thieving.' Others, like Mr Brown, who came to this place as a newborn and is now 85 years old, do not grow marijuana at all. To him, and other subsistence farmers, the raids with their indiscriminate burning and spraying are a biblical visitation. With the changes in village culture accompanying the switch to ganja cropping, he feels increasingly out of place in his own community. According to his nephew, who grows ganja and food crops, holding on to the established cropping patterns is becoming increasingly difficult. But it is evident from the shacks of the cannabis growers that engaging in ganja cultivation is not a high road to riches either.

Social implications of ganja farming

In contrast to the widespread Caribbean phenomenon of matrifocal households, the ganja farmers appear as solid champions of family values. There is a definite need for a rigorous analysis of family patterns, yet the impressionistic evidence suggests that ganja farmers are better family men than more professional and urbanized population groups. Benefits include the education of uncounted Vincentian children, whose school fees are being paid out of marijuana proceeds, and the housing of thousands of families. The construction of commodious family houses is a striking feature of the active ganja-growing communities. As is usual among most West Indian communities, housing construction is staggered, with sections of the house built at different times, depending on the size and sale of a new harvest.

Stable families, high school attendance and a penchant for investing proceeds in bricks and mortar may be characteristics not normally associated with drug producers. Indeed, they defy the widely held assumption that drugs equate with crime. What the data from St Vincent suggest is that ganja can be produced like any other cash crop, with benefits for families, communities, and poverty alleviation. It is not the crop which generates violence and crime but the legal status of the commodity. In the case of the ganja industry, violence is associated with two instances: law enforcement interventions, and at the point of sale, where fraud or robbery may occur. It may be argued, however, that both these forms of violence are the product of legislation, which impels direct violent intervention in the first instance, and, in the second, achieves the same result by removing the protection of the law.

This is not to say that wholesale involvement in the ganja industry is free from negative consequences. The most striking of these is the incessant smoking of marijuana by the men involved in the cultivation. Up the mountain, down to the village, each visit would be commemorated by the ritualistic preparation of the leaf, the rolling of the joint, and the solitary smoking, each participant having his own spliff. Only when working the fields did Mungo and his two assistants remain temporarily 'drug-free'. As soon as the tools were downed, the weed was collected from the farm stash, each man plucking and cutting the leaves, crunching them into rolling paper ('Bamboo' brand, imported from Trinidad), and rolling them into the size of a small cigar. Many would mix dried, home grown tobacco leaf into the mixture, for taste and against the cough: a rare instance of carcino-diminishing tobacco use. There was little passing of spliffs outside the farm, though the farm bosses would sample each other's produce. Smoking would commence in the morning and continue through the day until nightfall. While children were not allowed to smoke until 14 or 15, there was little effort to prevent the secondary inhalation of smoke. In fact, there is no awareness of the harmfulness of smoke and yet the Ministry of Health epidemiologist reported that 40 per cent of communicable diseases in the nation is acute respiratory infection. Much is made of the fact that the herb is natural, and therefore not a drug[13] – and therefore cannot be harmful.

Discussion

The above sketch of the Vincentian ganja industry raises a number of issues over the future of illicit crops in the region. The response by Vincentian farmers to demand signals from the market is similar to that of Afghan opium farmers described by Mansfield (UNDCP 1998). While the Afghan farmers faced moral opprobrium and state persecution, the ganja industry is morally inscribed in the tenets of the prevalent Rastafarian religion. Far from offering apologies, the informants claimed that ganja growing was 'uplifting'. It enjoys widespread support across the nation as well as the region, with a groundswell of public opinion favouring decriminalization or outright legalization. There is every possibility of a convergence of the call to 'legalize it' with demands for national assertion in the face of US pressure.

It is important, at the same time, not to exaggerate ideological arguments. There were a good number of farmers who desisted from cannabis cultivation, while others wistfully spoke of banana as the number one crop. Ganja, in short, provides a market, can be grown on land that is currently unclaimed, and needs little by way of inputs. In a country with a narrow opportunity structure this provides a rare opening. In the context of the Eastern Caribbean, we then have an interesting study of contrasts between different development models.

Most neighbouring countries have developed extensive tourism sectors. Antigua, Barbados, St Lucia and even Grenada are generating significant proportions of GDP through tourism. On the back of the attendant improvements to infrastructure, light industries have emerged, though their longevity has come into doubt following the conclusion of the North American Free Trade Agreement (NAFTA). More promising is the growth of data processing or informatics.

The divergent development of different countries is paralleled by the markedly different career paths of men and women. With the service sector and light industry accounting for an increasing proportion of the economy, the role of women in the labour force is gaining ever greater significance. As gender-specific recruitment patterns are reinforced by divergent educational scores, a growing proportion of young men are becoming locked out of the licit urban economy (Freeman 2000). At the same time farming opportunities in 'conventional' crops are declining as regional producers are losing their preferential access to European export markets. And even domestic markets are under serious pressure from international competitors.

One of the consequences has been the growth of large informal sectors. In Jamaica, the attempt by elites to mobilize the urban informal sector for party political ends has ended up in so-called garrison politics and contributed to the crises of the state. With large sectors of Kingston now to all intents and purposes outside the state, the service-providing role of the government has been taken over by new community leaders, called dons (Whetton et al.). In its attempts to contain the threat of these crime-based 'big men', the security services have traded the defence of the law for the maintenance of order (Harriott 2000). Their conduct in large parts of inner Kingston is thus compared to that of an occupying army, at war with the inhabitants. The question of law enforcement raises wider concerns about state legitimacy and the future of democratic politics.

At the moment, however, the Vincentian ganja producers, while on the wrong side of the law, and on the margins of society, do not seem poised on the verge of open rebellion. They speak with bitterness about helicopter raids, the police checkpoints, and the coastguard cutters interfering with their livelihood. They resent not being able to swap their foreign exchange for EC dollars at the going rate, and the difficulties faced in opening a bank account. In the main, however, they are farmers eking out a living on the land in a long line of peasant producers who, in the Caribbean, 'have grown in the crevices of their societies'. Mintz argues that peasantries established themselves 'outside the geographical spaces where the plantation system could not work, because of soil or slope or aridity or distance from sea' (Mintz 1985: 131). The geographical circumstances of the ganja farmers are identical to those of these peasant producers. The role of the plantation system has now been taken over by the post-colonial state. While maintaining a fair degree of independence, and a basic self-sufficiency, the peasantry is linked to the state in a series of symbiotic exchange relationships. While the ganja farmers depend for most of their non-alimentary needs on the market, the state and the formal economy, in turn, are buoyed by the ganja-financed demand for goods and services.

In St Vincent these outlaw farmers have, of course, a powerful historical precedent. During the seventeenth and eighteenth centuries, the difficult terrain of the island's interior provided a protective screen for one of the most famous maroon societies of the Caribbean. For over a century, the 'Black Caribs' resisted planter colonialism and slavery. It took the British army and settlers two sustained military campaigns, known as Carib Wars, in 1773 and 1795–6, to overcome this society descended from African runaways and Amerindian Caribs. In 1797 their lands were expropriated and the defeated population of a few thousand banished to Roatan Island and thence to Honduras and other countries in Central America, where their descendants live on as the Garifuna people (Craton 1997: 237; Nanton 1983: 223).

The post-colonial state is faced with a dilemma, of being unable to diversify the economy and provide opportunities outside the farming sector, while at the same time the main crop, the banana, is being rendered uncompetitive by changes in the tariff structure of the main markets in Europe. As farmers plant alternative crops, powerful international development partners are leaning heavily on St Vincent[14] to abide by its international treaty obligations to eradicate the offensive ganja production. If these obligations are not complied with, sanctions may be applied – which will hurt the country, and its governing elite even more.

The case of St Vincent raises some difficult questions about the legitimacy of international conventions and treaties in determining domestic and economic policy. The commitment to eradicate marijuana, for example, subscribed to in the BPA, the 1997 Partnership for Prosperity and Security concluded between the US and 15 Caribbean states, and the 1998 UN convention, was made without consulting domestic opinion. It would be erroneous, however, to ascribe the conclusion of these international agreements entirely to pressure from powerful partner countries. From the mid-1980s concern over the illegal drug economy has been spreading throughout the region. The Caribbean governments, assembling at their meetings in Barbados and Santo Domingo, were there of their own accord. It was not, however, the fear of ganja farmers that motivated them, but concern over the power of international cocaine-trafficking cartels and their disproportionate financial muscle in relation to mini-states. Since then, despite the effective action that has been taken on both a national and a regional basis, the threat continues to exist. Police powers have been raised, extensive training provided to all services, equipment transferred to all countries, and information shared between services in the region – but these measures have done little to stem the flow of cocaine and cocaine cash through the region.

Furthermore, despite the continued flow of cocaine, most of the bilateral objectives of the US have been achieved by the conclusion of shiprider agreements, Mutual Legal Assistance Treaties and extradition treaties with every country. Early recognition of the seeming success of these measures was provided by the UNDCP statistics of cocaine flows in 2000, registering a year-on-year drop for the first time. While the US State Department disputes the figures, US law enforcement officers privately share the view that the region is losing its significance as a transit route to North America – not because of the efficacy of regional interception, but because of the redirecting of heroin and cocaine through Central America and Mexico since the conclusion of NAFTA, and the rerouting of drug consignments through the same conduits. Since Europe receives the bulk of its cocaine imports from South America, it has yet to be seen if the quantity of cocaine transiting the Caribbean and bound for Europe has dropped.

In the meantime the government of St Vincent has to contain the demands of the ganja lobby at home while fending off the allegations from regional and international partners. It can follow in the slipstream of Jamaica's Ganja Commission, and hope that regional attitudes towards its number one export crop will abate. With the tone being set by the most powerful player in the hemisphere, however, this is an area of policy making largely beyond national control.

Alternatives

There are different options that can be pursued. First of all, St Vincent has to participate in the lobbying of the multilateral agencies, principally the UNDCP and CICAD, to look at alternatives to existing penal regimes. Current legislation provides for the application of custodial sentences to people convicted of drug-related crimes. According to community activist and radio commentator Bongo Shaka Dadreo, 'putting people in this old pirate prison is a terrible crime'. With heavy overcrowding, conditions are abysmal, producing embittered, hardened criminals.

Second, the government needs to take measures to understand the nature of the local drug scene, to generate knowledge, and to extend the drug treatment and education services. It can build on the experience of Marion House, an NGO working with crack users. A rigorous demand reduction policy is necessary to vaccinate St Vincent against the impact of crack cocaine, which has had a devastating effect on parts of Jamaica and Trinidad. Much of the fault lies with current education campaigns, which make no distinction between different substances. The blanket warnings that all drugs are deadly are lost on young people who have grown up with rum and ganja, and therefore treat crack as just another substance to be rolled up in a spliff. Reinvigorating the National Substance Abuse Council will serve another purpose, offering a first line of defence against future allegations by regional and overseas partners that St Vincent is not doing enough in the fight against drugs.

Third, as the major cannabis producer in the region, St Vincent must begin to work on alternative development programmes. Experience from coca-growing regions in the Andes shows that eradication unaccompanied by development interventions aimed at providing farmers with an alternative income will simply displace cultivation to new regions. Furthermore, in the present political climate of St Vincent, further eradication may be read as a breach of the social contract, and trigger violent protests and a call for a change in government.

The international treaties governing drug control at regional level (BPA, Santo Domingo, Partnership for Prosperity) make little or no mention of alternative development. The region, after all, was seen as a transit route, not a producer, and the drug of concern was cocaine, not cannabis. While a commitment to eradicate marijuana crops was included, there were no provisions for finding new incomes for ganja growers. One of the reasons for this oversight lies in the conceptualization of the drug threat at that time, and the prevailing image of those engaged in it. The agreements were based on fear of international cartels, with limitless resources and sophisticated networks. The image was one of criminals posing a threat to society. What was never considered was that the cannabis sector comprised an army of rural and urban poor, responding to opportunities in the informal sector. Their criminality is not incurred in the ruthless pursuit of profit, but is a function of their social marginalization and economic dislocation.

Cutting down the supply of illicit drugs, therefore, will require a complex set of interventions to provide alternative modes of income. But who is to drive such a programme? The UNDCP, which was set up as the axis of drug control strategy, has yet to draw up a plan of alternatives for Caribbean cannabis producers, yet it plays a key role in advocating and implementing alternative development programmes in nearby Colombia. What this suggests is that St Vincent cannot rely on external impulses, but needs to develop its own strategy if future eradications are to be avoided, and to preclude the threat of sanctions.

It is evident to the hill farmers that there is not an alternative crop at present. Indeed, the most attractive existing alternative, the banana, is now being phased out of Vincentian production, ousted by changes in the international market structure. A clear product swap, substituting, say, mangoes for marijuana, is therefore not feasible. Indeed, alternative development as a strategy owes much to the realization that straightforward crop substitution, as practised during the 1970s, does not work. An integrated rural development approach is therefore the one that promises the greatest hope of success. There are no direct parallels in the region, though both Jamaica and the Bahamas have implemented community drug abuse action council (CODAC) programmes. They have succeeded in both providing alternative modes of employment and diverting people from drug trafficking, if not from drug production. One of the first lessons applicable, however, is that such programmes require long-term commitment, and need to recognize that results cannot be achieved overnight. This long-term view is also required in St Vincent, where farmers can simply move more deeply into the bush. It also needs to be based on participation and consultation. Without the willing participation of the target population, little can be achieved.

A first step in the CODAC model is to undertake an audit of community resources. Hiking up to the hill farms, it becomes obvious that one of the prime assets of these farmers is the land and the rich vegetation that covers it. They are drawn to the steep wooded slopes of the mountains precisely because of their inaccessibility. Yet their very activity – cleaning the bush – destroys the forest cover, which attracted them in the first place. Yet another challenge to be addressed is environmental degradation caused by watershed loss. What happens to the land after the farmers have finished? 'Pasture', is the swift reply. Small herds of environmentally dangerous goats can be seen grazing on the exposed patches of former cannabis farms, now overgrown with grass.

According to community organizer Junior Cottle, some of the farmers are replanting trees after they have finished, but their efforts are poorly organized and underfunded. The members of ADAPT are therefore discussing ways in which they can formalize this system and raise the scale of the replanting operation. One of the most promising proposals foresees the systematic provision of saplings by the government nursery to registered members of the scheme. Farmers would then be paid at the daily labourer rate to take the saplings up the mountain and plant on the abandoned patches. The benefits of the scheme are two-fold: ganja farmers participating in the scheme would have an alternative income, and the forest cover of the mountainside would be replanted. One of the great hopes for economic diversification in the future, especially into ecotourism, could therefore be safeguarded. In the meantime, the government would at least begin to engage with the people currently working outside the official system. And with a degree of cooperation between the two sides, there is the opportunity for reaching consensus on contracting production and accompanying export reduction in the future.

In anticipation of the protests that such a project is likely to provoke, we should consider the consequences of inactivity. A repetition of Operation Weedeater is then merely a matter of time and foreign pressure. In the meanwhile the patches of 'pasture' on the wooded slopes will expand into larger stretches, until much of the mountains are as denuded of forest as Haiti. On a small island without a tourism sector or an informatics industry to speak of, this will not bode well for social stability.

NOTES

1   St Vincent has yet to experience the mass tourism that characterizes such islands as Barbados, Antigua and St Lucia.

2   Held on 13–14 June 2000 in Antigua.

3   Interview with Bongo Shaka Dradeo, radio journalist, 1 August 2001.

4   Interview with Darius Figueiras, researcher in Trinidad & Tobago, 9 July 2001.

5   Production was large enough to trigger eradication activities in Trinidad & Tobago, Guyana, Belize, Dominica and St Lucia.

6   US-sponsored eradication exercises in the region began in 1974, with Operation Buccaneer in Jamaica.

7   A military alliance set up in 1982 by Antigua–Barbuda, Barbados, Dominica, St Lucia and St Vincent & the Grenadines. St Kitts–Nevis and Grenada joined in 1984 and 1985 respectively.

8   Claims that the actual eradication was carried out by men from the region, with the US providing 'mere' logistical back-up, fail to account for the active participation on the ground by DEA officers.

9   *San Jose Mercury News*, 15 February 2000.

10   All names are suppressed or disguised to preserve the anonymity of the informants.

11   Skunk is a hybrid variety of cannabis with a high level of tetrahydrocannabinol (THC). It is usually grown indoors, either under grow lights or in greenhouse conditions using 'hydroponic' techniques (i.e. growing plants in nutrient-rich liquids rather than in soil).

12   Co-residence and neighbourhood are important recruitment grounds in St Vincent, an interesting contrast to cash cropping in West Africa, where labour and land titles move through lineages.

13   The following biblical passages are quoted in justification: Genesis 1:12, 3:18; Exodus

10:12; Psalms 104:14.

14 St Vincent has signed up to the 1988 UN Convention but not the previous ones, claiming that this is not necessary since the UK, the colonial power at the time, did so. Both the UNDCP and CICAD have urged the government of St Vincent to sign up to the 1961 and 1971 conventions.

REFERENCES AND SELECT BIBLIOGRAPHY

Ankomah, Augustine and J. Whetton (1999) *Illicit Drugs and the Poor in Transit Countries: Case Studies from the Caribbean and Southern Africa*, Swansea: Centre for Development Studies.

Austin, D. J. (1979) 'History and Symbols in Ideology: a Jamaican Example', *Man*, 14: 497–514.

Beardsworth, R. (2000) 'Multilateral Narcotics Interdiction Measures in the Caribbean', in I. L. Griffith (ed.), *The Political Economy of Drugs in the Caribbean*, Basingstoke: Macmillan.

CICAD (2000) 'St Vincent and the Grenadines', Multilateral Evaluation Mechanisms Report, Inter-American Drug Abuse Control Commission.

Clissold, G. (1998) *Divergent International Perspectives on the Caribbean: the Interaction between the Ongoing Caribbean, US and European Adaptations to the New Global Economy*, Publication of the Caribbean Project, Washington: Georgetown University.

Craton, M. (1997) 'Forms of Resistance to Slavery', in Franklin Knight (ed.), *General History of the Caribbean*, Volume II: *The Slave Societies of the Caribbean*, London: Macmillan/ UNESCO, pp. 105–37.

EC (1996) *The Caribbean and the Drugs Problem*, Report of the Experts Group, European Commission.

Eltis, D. (1997) 'The Slave Economies of the Caribbean: Structure, Performance, Evolution and Significance', in Franklin Knight, (ed.), *General History of the Caribbean*, Volume II: *The Slave Societies of the Caribbean*, London: Macmillan/UNESCO, pp. 222–70.

Figueira, D. (1997) *Cocaine and the Economy of Crime in Trinidad and Tobago*, Trinidad and Tobago: Daurius Figueira.

Fineman, M. (1999) 'Economy Hooked on Marijuana', *San Jose Mercury News*, 6 February.

Freeman, Carla, (2000). *High Tech and High Heels in the Global Economy: Women, Work, and Pink Collar Identities in the Caribbean*, Durham NC: Duke University Press.

Griffith, I. L. (1993) *The Quest for Security in the Caribbean: Problems and Promises in Subordinate States*, New York: M. E. Sharpe.

—— (1996) 'Caribbean Security on the Eve of the 21st Century', McNair Paper 54, Institute for National Strategic Studies, National Defense University, Washington, DC.

Griffith, I. L. and T. Munroe (1995) 'Drugs and Democracy in the Caribbean', *Journal of Commonwealth and Comparative Politics*, 33: 358–75.

Harriott, A. (2000) *Police and Crime Control in Jamaica: Problems of Reforming Ex-colonial Constabularies*, Kingston: University of West Indies Press.

Mintz, S. W. (1985) 'From Plantations to Peasantries in the Caribbean', in S. W. Mintz and Sally Price, *Caribbean Contours*, Baltimore: Johns Hopkins University Press, pp. 127–54.

Nanton, P. (1983) 'The Changing Pattern of State Control in St Vincent and the Grenadines', in Fitzroy Ambursley and Robin Cohen (eds.), *Crises in the Caribbean*, London: Heinemann, pp. 223–46.

Ramsaran, R. (1995) 'Challenges to Caribbean Economic Development in the 1990s', in Anthony T. Bryan (ed.), *The Caribbean: New Dynamics in Trade and Political Economy*, Coral Gables, Florida: North–South Centre Press.

UNDCP (1998) *Strategic Study 2: The Dynamics of the Farmgate Opium Trade and the Coping Strategies of Opium Traders*, Islamabad: United Nations Drug Control Programme.

—— (2000a) 'Strategic Study 5: an Analysis of the Process of Expansion of Opium Poppy to

New Districts in Afghanistan', Second Report, November 1999, Islamabad: United Nations Drug Control Programme, p. 28.

—— (2000b) *Strategic Study 6: the Role of Women in Opium Poppy Cultivation in Afghanistan*, Islamabad: United Nations Drug Control Programme.

—— (2001) 'The Community Fights Back', unpublished draft report, Barbados: United Nations Drug Control Programme.

UNODCCP (United Nations Office for Drug Control and Crime Prevention (2001) *Global Illicit Drug Trends, 2001*, Vienna: UNODCCP.

—— (2003) *Strategic Studies, No. 9*, Vienna: United Nations Office on Drugs and Crime, May.

Vargas, Ricardo (1999). *Fumigacion y Conflicto. Politicas Antidrogas y Deslegitimacion del Estado en Colombia*, Bogota: Tercer Mundo.

Wilson, P. J. (1973) *Crab Antics: the Social Anthropology of English-Speaking Negro Societies of the Caribbean*, New Haven: Yale University Press.

INDEX

245